Piri-Muridi Relationship:
A Study of the Nizamuddin Dargah

Piri-Muridi Relationship:
A Study of the Nizamuddin Dargah

DESIDERIO PINTO

MANOHAR
2006

First published 1995
Reprinted 2006

© Desiderio Pinto, 1995

ISBN 81-7304-111-3

Published by
Ajay Kumar Jain for
Manohar Publishers & Distributors
4753/23, Ansari Road, Daryaganj
New Delhi 110 002

Typeset by
A J Software Publishing Co. Pvt. Ltd.
New Delhi 110 005

Printed at
Lordson Publishers Pvt. Ltd
Delhi 110 007

Distributed in South Asia by
FOUNDATION
B●●KS
4381/4, Ansari Road
Daryaganj, New Delhi 110 002
and its branches at Mumbai, Hyderabad,
Bangalore, Chennai, Kolkata

PREFACE

The *piri-muridi* relationship is central to Sufism or religious life in Islam. Unlike other Muslim modes of initiaton into religious life, this institution admits peoples of other faiths also. However, very little research has focussed on this relationship, which is of interest in several ways.

The present monograph tries to fill this gap. It analyses the *piri-muridi* relationship as it exists in India in its various dimensions and makes an indepth study of the Nizamuddin Dargah. It will interest all those who wish to understand Sufism and Islam as it is lived in India.

I am deeply grateful to friends and colleagues in India and abroad who have inspired and helped me during the preparation of this volume, specially my many respondents in the Nizamuddin Dargah, and Dr. M. Talib and Dr. N. Nanda.

We all regret the sudden demise of Dr. N. Nanda while this monograph was in press. He will be sorely missed as a competent, inspiring and ever-helpful friend.

My very special thanks go to Professor C.W. Troll, S. J., Richard Pereira, S. J., and last but not least to all the members of the Jesuit community of St. Xavier's School, Delhi who were with me right through the four years I was privileged to spend in their company. Finally, I wish to thank the Provincial of India of the Society of Jesus for encouragement and financial support towards the project that resulted in this volume.

Desiderio Pinto

CONTENTS

INTRODUCTION

About four years ago, while trying to understand the phenomenon of Muslim saint veneration, I once came across a Hindu gentleman and his companion sitting at the shrine of Nizamuddin Aulia. This gentleman, who owns a shop in Karol Bagh, Delhi, told me that he was not really interested in the saint. He visited the tomb from time to time, however, in order to please a venerable old man with a flowing beard. The old man, he explained, was a *pir*, who sometimes sat in one of the small rooms situated along the boundary wall of the *dargah*. This *pir*, he added, gave him advice, helped him to get out of every kind of difficulty related to his business and personal life, and gave him a serenity and peace that he did not merit as a sinner.

This, in effect was my introduction to a phenomenon that I was later to discover as *piri-muridi*. The man's explanation turned my attention to the men (*pirs*) sitting in those small rooms scattered around the *dargah*, men with long hair, long flowing beards and caps, whose right hands were invariably covered with rings fitted with stones of different shapes and colours. They were usually busy attending to guests and visitors. Some of these visitors, I noticed, came at regular intervals (some once a month, others once a week, and so on). They would enter the room respectfully, kiss the hand covered with rings, and rub the stones into their eyes. Then, some would lay their foreheads on the feet of the squatting *pir*. And very rarely, someone would also kiss his feet. This done, they would sit back respectfully, listen to what the *pir* had to say, answer questions, tell him about their problems and joys, and sometimes take *tawizes* (amulets) from the *pir*, learn a prayer formula, and give him some money. When the time came to leave, the *pir* would make a prayer for them. That finished, they would again kiss his ring covered hand and/or lay their foreheads on his feet, and on the rare occasion walk out backwards.

Some of these regular visitors told me that the *pirs* are spiritual

directors. They themselves are *murids*. *Murid*, they explained, means
the one who desires, or novice. They wanted to experience the
content of their faith and, thus, attain union with God. And they
believed that the special relationship with their *pir*, *piri-muridi*, would
enable them to achieve this end.

THE ORIGIN OF *PIRI-MURIDI*: THREE ACCOUNTS

The origin of *piri-muridi*, like that of Sufism itself, is lost in history.
It is possible, however, to posit that the practice of *piri-muridi* began
some time between the earliest known stage of asceticism, and the
time when Sufi doctrine (i.e. the theory of stations and states together
with the Sufi world view and the methods on the path) began to take
mature form in the fourth and fifth centuries A.H. The Sufis I have
met place the origins of *piri-muridi* variously at the beginning of time,
the time of Mohammed, or soon after the sacking of Baghdad by the
Mongols.

Very often it is said,

Mohammed's relationship with Ali, his son–in–law was the
beginning of the *piri-muridi* relationship. Mohammed gave the
secret doctrine to Ali. This secret doctrine concerns the inner
meaning of the Quran and the ways of attaining that knowledge.
Ali gave the secret knowledge to the heads of the various Sufi
orders, who in turn passed it on to their spiritual successors, and
so on, so that *piri-muridi* in its original form lives on today. The
differences between the various orders are secondary.

Some others say that *piri-muridi* began at the time of the Mongol
destruction of Baghdad. This destruction, they say,

resulted in a general loss of faith among the Muslim survivors.
After all, they had been defeated by a non–Muslim people.
Hence, they needed to be reassured in their faith so that they
could continue to follow Islam. And the only reassurance that
could bring about this result was an experiential knowledge of

the faith. Those who had such knowledge and knew how to communicate it began to collect groups of people and teach them. This practice, in effect instituted the *piri-muridi* relationship which carries on till today. However, since the knowledge passed on was experiential and came from the experiences of the *pirs*, there arose different types of experiential knowledge of the same one Islamic faith. These different methods with their variations in experience were preserved and passed on by the spiritual successors of the first teachers. And these different methods with their different lines of transmission gave birth to the different Sufi orders in Islam.

A few Sufis explain the origins of *piri-muridi* in yet another way:

The length of time for the existence of the world has been predetermined by God. But then, at the same time, God has also predetermined that the continued existence of the world depends on whether the people living in it, or at least one person living in it, practises Islam. Consequently, if they are all heedless or forget God and what He has commanded, the world will come to an end. Now the people of this world are such that they stubbornly insist on walking on the path of blame. Hence, the world has always been in danger of being destroyed before its time. God in His mercy, has prevented this destruction, first at the beginning of the world by sending down the first prophet who was also the first *pir*. This prophet prevented the imminent destruction of the world by teaching people to live by the Quran. When he died people went back to heedlessness and, thus, again endangered the continued existence of the world. This was again prevented by the sending down of the second prophet, the second *pir*. And so it went on till the coming of the last prophet and *pir*, Mohammed. But even after Mohammed's death people went back to the path of the blameworthy. Hence, God in His mercy sent down the *pirs*, who bring people back on to the right path and, thus, ensure the continued existence of the world. *Pirs* ensure the existence of the world after their death by training successor *pirs* through the *piri-muridi* relationship.

The presence of these three stories, which are sometimes narrated by one and the same person at different times, reveals ignorance about the origin of *piri-muridi*. But at the same time, the stories demonstrate that the origin is important because, first, it gives the practice legitimacy, i.e. it is instituted either directly by God, or the Prophet, or in order to save the Muslim community. Second, the stories point to some important aspect of its purpose: to lead people on to the right path, to teach men how to live Islam, to save the world from final destruction, and to give Muslims an experiential knowledge of their faith.

PIRI-MURIDI IN WORKS OF SUFISM

Piri-muridi has been variously depicted as a teacher-student, a parent-child,[1] and a prophet-people relationship.[2] In other words, the *pir* is expected to interact with the *murid* in the roles of teacher, father and mother, and prophet. And the *murid* is expected to interact with the *pir* in the roles of student, son or daughter, and a person who is in need of correction and conversion. The *piri-muridi* relationship, which includes all these roles, is established with the initiation ceremony, called *bai'a*. In the course of this rite, the *pir* holds the hand of the *murid*, if male, and if female, one end of a scarf, the other end of which is held by the female *murid*. This act symbolizes the *pir's* acceptance of the *murid's* self-surrender to him, and the *pir's* willingness to train and help him on the spiritual path. On the part of the *murid*, it involves complete obedience and respect. Then the *pir* may give the *murid* a *kirqah* (a woolen frock), or a four-edged cap and coat, or a *chaddar*, and advice like, do not rob, beg, insult, etc. and follow the *sharia*. The ceremony may end with a cup of sweet syrup from which the *pir* drinks first, and the *murid* next.[3] The *piri-muridi* relationship may also be established without the initiation rite. The mutual recognition of mutual acceptance and trust on the part of the *pir* and *murid*, and the *pir's* recognition of the *murid's* earnest desire to surrender is deemed enough to establish the *piri-muridi* relationship in such cases.[4] Once the relationship is established, the *pir* in his role as teacher will watch the *murid* and, thus, assess his character and talents, instruct him in the practice of *dhikr* (remembrance of God), interpret his dreams and visions, even read his thoughts, and teach him how to behave in each mental state.[5] As father and mother, or parent, the *pir* gives birth to a new heart in the *murid*, and as father, he controls and leads the *murid* on the right path.[6] As prophet, the *pir* will teach the *murid* to compare his own faults with God's perfection, his own weakness with God's power, his own injustice with God's justice, etc.[7] The *murid*, as student, seeks knowledge from the *pir*, considers visits to the *pir* a religious duty,[8] and follows the rules for *murids*.[9] As son or daughter, the *murid* will obey every command, try to make the *pir* happy, try to make himself as docile to the *pir* as possible, even to the extent of emulating a corpse in the hands of an undertaker,[10] and serve the *pir* with his life and possessions.[11] As a person in need of correction and conversion he will examine himself with respect to the goodness of God.

The above shows nothing out of the ordinary, though it seems to be going to an extreme in order to make the *murid* open to the good influence of the *pir*. There is a paragraph in Khan Sahib Khan's book, *The Secret of Ana'l-Haqq*, however, that shows another aspect of the *piri-muridi* relationship:

> The *Murid* must observe the *jamal* of *Pir*. The *Pir's jamal* must be reflected in the mirror of the *murid's* heart. In the mirror of the *Pir's jamal*, the *murid* observes the *jamal* of God, the heart of the *murid* is the mirror of the *Pir's* face... "Whoever hath seen me, hath seen God", says a *Hadith* of the Prophet (Peace be on him). "The reality of *Eman* (faith) is the observance of me," says another *Hadith*...[12]

Jamal means beauty and manifestations of divine attributes.[13] Perhaps, another quotation from John A. Subhan's book, *Sufism, Saints and Shrines*,[14] will help to explain the above quotation.

> The *pir* is believed to be able to 'transmit' spiritual power to his *murid*. This he does by the exercise *tawajjuh* 'concentration'.

When a *pir* desires to exercise *tawajjuh*, on one of his disciples, he seats himself near him and proceeds, in imagination, to picture his own heart as in close proximity to that of his *murid*, at the same time concentrating his mind upon the idea that his power is now being transmitted from his own heart to that of the other. At the same time the *murid* is required to concentrate his mind on the idea that he is receiving the power from his *pir*. This rite is generally performed at the time when the *pir*, after the performance of *dhikr*, is in an abnormal state of mind.

Tawajjuh is regarded as the one great means of producing a spiritual change in the life of another....

....The hypnotic process (implied in the practice of *tawajjuh*) by which the *pir* helps his *murid* to reach the stage of 'annihilation' is described by J. P. Brown in the following words: "The *murid* must, mystically, always bear his *murshid* in mind, and become mentally absorbed in him, through a constant meditation and contemplation of him. The teacher must be his shield against all evil thoughts. The spirit of the teacher follows him in all efforts, and accompanies him wherever he may be, quite as a guardian spirit. To such a degree is this carried that he sees the master in all men and in all things, just as a willing subject is under the influence of the magnetizer. This condition is called 'self-annihilation' into the *murshid* or *shaykh*. The latter finds, in his own visionary dreams, the degree at which the *murid* has reached, and whether or not his soul or spirit has become bound to his own.

At this state of the disciple, the *shaykh* passes him over to the spiritual influence of the *pir*, or original founder of the particular *tariqa* or 'path' to which they belong, long since deceased, and he sees the latter only by the spiritual aid of the former. This is called 'self-annihilation' into the *pir*. He now becomes so much a part of the *pir* as to possess all his spiritual powers, and may perform even all his supernatural acts.

The third grade also leads him, through the spiritual aid of the *shaykh*, up to the Prophet himself, whom he now sees in all things. This state is called, like the preceding, 'self-annihilation' into the Prophet.

The fourth degree leads him even to God. He becomes a part of Divinity, and sees Him in all things.

...the final stage of the journey, 'absorption in the Deity,' is not attained until the aspirant has annihilated himself in his *pir*.

To summarize: Within the *piri-muridi* relationship, the *murid* is utterly dependent on the *pir* for any spiritual attainment. The purpose of *piri-muridi* seems to be the annihilation of the *murid* in the *pir* in order to finally attain union with God. Annihilation in the *pir* leads to union with God via two other stages, annihilation in the founder of the order, and annihilation in the prophet, Mohammed.[15] And both these annihilations depend on the mediation of the living *pir*.

STUDIES ON *PIRI-MURIDI*

Bikram N. Nanda and Mohammed Talib's article, "Soul of the Soulless: An Analysis of the *Pir-Murid* Relationship in Sufi Discourse",[16] displays the *piri-muridi* relationship along the lines of the above quotations. In this article, the *murid* respondents describe the relationship in many ways. It is a divine relationship which is sacred and private and, hence, cannot be revealed without distorting the relationship and outraging modesty.[17] It is an experience of Truth that is above the capacity of reason and normal understanding and, hence, beyond description and discussion.[18] It is a relationship of divine love that can at least be described if not understood,[19] and a relationship of *adab* which may be more simply rendered as a master-slave relationship.[20] Finally, the *pir* may be a model sufferer for the suffering *murid*.[21]

Divine love is described as immortal, as that which grows in the *murid*, and that which restores him to his divine destiny. Divine destiny seems to be the dissolving of the self in the divinity of God.[22] Within the *piri-muridi* relationship, divine love becomes the endless longing of the *murid* for the *pir*, which grows in intensity.[23] And the dissolving of the self in divinity becomes the dissolving of the self in the *pir*.[24] The growth of this divine love (longing for the *pir*) has been divided into three stages. At the initial stage the *murid*, as lover, loses all sense of himself, and becomes aware of only his *pir*, his beloved. The second stage in this divine love relationship is characterized by overwhelming discomfort and anxiety, and the final stage is the union between the *murid* and the *pir*, and in such a way that only the divine love remains.[25] Imagining the *pir* is the *murid's* technique for increasing divine love (the longing of the *murid* for the *pir*). Imagination increases divine love by, first, bringing the *pir* within the body of the *murid*, and second, by making the *pir* who is now in the *murid's* body, the central force, as it were, of the *murid's* body. The *pir* as the centre of the *murid* becomes the ruling principle of his life, in the sense that everything that the *murid* does, says and thinks is at the command of the *pir*.[26] Consequently, there comes a time when there is no difference between the *pir* and the *murid*. Further, the *murid* is able to exercise the power of the *pir* over other people,[27] perhaps, as effectively as the *pir* himself. Whatever be the stage of the imaginal union[28] between the *pir* and the *murid*, a peculiar communication system is set up between them, so that the *murid* knows when the *pir* is angry with him even though the *pir* is several miles away.[29] The *pir*, on his part, also knows when the *murid* needs help.[30] Then, the *pir* may appear to the *murid* in imaginal form and, thus, give him the courage to act appropriately while making his acts effective.[31] Or the *pir* in his imaginal form may instruct the *murid* in a formula of prayer that will be effective, i.e. give the *murid* a way out of the serious problem in which he finds himself.[32] And this communication system carries on even after the death of the *pir*.[33]

In the master–slave relationship, the *murid* is obedient to the *pir*, seeks to honour, obey and serve the *pir* even when it is not demanded or necessary,[34] and even when the current circumstances make the service look ridiculous.[35] In this way the *murid* forgets his own august social status in the presence of his *pir*.[36] Further, the *murid* does not question the *pir's* decisions or demands, and takes whatever the *pir* gives.[37] The *pir*, as master, showers the *murid* with spiritual and material blessing, solves his problems,[38] and even gives him problems and suffering in order to prevent the possible unintended dysfunctions of continual blessing.[39] Finally, the master-slave relationship which defines the distance between the *pir* and *murid* in terms of fixed statuses is believed to be closely related to the divine love relationship that unites them into a single reality. But, the way in which these two opposites are intimately related is supposed to be beyond the scope of logic and normal understanding.[40] Where suffering is concerned, the *pir* is a model sufferer who shows that suffering is necessary for union with the divine.[41]

The article shows the *murids* synthesizing two contraries, and then saying that the synthesis arrived at is above normal understanding. On the one hand we have union with the *pir* as the goal of the *murid*.[42] On the other hand we have union with God as the goal.[43] The synthesis seems to be, union with the *pir* is in actual fact union with God.[44] As long as the *pir* is only a man and, thus, as in common Islamic understanding completely different from God, union with the *pir* cannot be construed as union with God. Obviously, the *murids* believe the *pir* to be God in some way. But then, the *murids* also believe that the *pir* is a man like themselves in the description of the *pir's* suffering: The *pir* suffers because he is a man in very much the same way as the *murids* are men. And he too, like the *murids* themselves, is working towards his own union with God.[45] Important here is how the *murids* can conceive of the *pir* as God, and yet not God at one and the same time. It is enough at this stage of the argument to accept the *murid's* implicit contradictory definition of his *pir* as God, and yet not God. He is God within the *piri-muridi* relationship, and not God outside the *piri-muridi* relationship or in his own personal life.[46] Consequently, it may be useful to posit: The *murid* expects the *pir* to act as God, or in the role of God, within the *piri-muridi* relationship, while knowing with all certainty that the *pir*, far from being God in himself, is actually a man like himself. Does the *pir*, on his part, accept the role of God within the *piri-muridi* relationship and expect the *murid* to behave towards himself in terms of this God role? This is something that will have to be discovered at a later stage in the argument.

Mohammed Ajmal throws more light on the *piri-muridi* relationship in his article, "A Note on *Adab* in the Murshid–*Murid* Relationship".[47] He says that the *piri-muridi* relationship is practised within a
context,[48] a world view that preaches the true nature of things, most
specially man's dependence on God. This is a religious doctrine.[49]
Piri-muridi is the method that gives this doctrine an almost existential
character so that the *murid* can begin to consciously live out his
dependence on God.[50] In more simplified terms, *piri-muridi* seems to
be the method for learning how to live out one's dependence on
God.[51] This living out of one's dependence on God may be termed
as awareness of one's dependence.[52] Further, this awareness of
dependence, expressed in acts of self-surrender opens the *murid* to
receive the self-manifestation of God, and consequently leads to
union with God.[53] Within the *piri-muridi* relationship, the *murid* is
forced to be completely dependent on his *pir*. This dependence
opens the *murid* to the reception of the self-manifestation of God as
represented in the *pir*.[54] This type of relationship is possible because
of the symbols involved in the *piri-muridi* relationship: the role of the
pir, the role of the *murid* as expected and symbolized in *bai'a*, the *adab*
or rules for the behaviour of the *murid* in the presence of the *pir*, the
purificatory exercises, the *dhikr* (remembrance of God), and the
meditation.[55] In *bai'a* the *murid* surrenders himself entirely to the *pir*
and restricts himself to that one *pir*.[56] By following the rules of *adab*
the *murid* shows complete obedience and displays the attitude of
respect and awe before the *pir*.[57] In general, he acts in such a way that
he is completely dependent on the will of the *pir*; he acts as the slave
of the *pir*. In the purificatory exercises he works to destroy his own
sense of independence.[58] In *dhikr* he opens himself to receive from
God, and in the meditation he becomes acutely aware that he is
nothing in himself: he receives everything from God and what he is,
is just a reflection of what he really receives from Him.[59] The *pir*
represents and transmits God,[60] i.e. he manifests God by using the rite
of *bai'a*, the *adab*, the purificatory exercises and disciplines, the *dhikr*,
and the meditation to produce states of Glory and Peace in the
murid.[61] The intensity of these states depends on the ability of the
murid to receive them, as judged by the *pir* with his intuitive

knowledge of the *murid's* character and temperament.[62] And it is this experience of Glory and Peace that makes the religious doctrine take on an almost existential character.[63] The state of Glory is an experience of the self-manifestation of God. The presence of this state is indicated by agitation, turmoil, inability to use one's senses, etc.[64] The state of Peace, which is indicated in stability and a return to one's senses, is an experience of the *murid's* awareness of his dependence on the *pir*. This state comes to the *murid* in the imaginal form of the *pir*.[65] Both states are given by the *pir*, who receives them as coming directly from God.[66] Consequently, he is the medium by which God becomes present to the *murid*. Here the *pir* is heir to the prophet inasmuch as he experiences both the states of Glory and Peace.[67] At the same time he is the manifestation of God to the *murid*. Consequently, here again, the *pir* is God, and yet not God. Thus, both the above articles make God the central focus of the *piri-muridi* relationship. Ajmal's article explains how the *pir* is God. He is God in the sense that he represents and transmits Him to the *murid* in the form of states of Glory and Peace. These states are induced through *bai'a, adab*, the purificatory exercises, the *dhikr*, the meditations, and the imaginal form of the *pir*. The states make the *murid* aware of his dependence on the *pir*, and consequently, on God.

Irina Tweedie, in her diary *Daughter of Fire*,[68] gives us, mainly an account of the experiences resulting from her relationship with her *pir*,[69] together with the *pir's* terse explanations of those experiences. Hence, this book may help to understand further the states of Glory and Peace, mentioned in Ajmal's article. Using Ajmal's classification (Glory and Peace), we may classify Irina's experiences into experiences of Glory and Peace. In her account, the manifestations of the state of Glory (agitation, turmoil, and the loss of the senses) are rendered as, her heart missing beats or beating too strongly, two hearts beating within her, loss of memory, inability to think, moving about in a drunken state, sleeplessness, fright, anger, constant weeping, etc. And the manifestations of the state of Peace (stability and the return to one's senses) are rendered as sleep, heightened ability to concentrate, happiness, serenity, the appearance of the image of her *pir* before her, etc. Neither of the two states lasted too long: Glory gave way to Peace, which in turn gave way to Glory and so on in never ending cycles. These states, she firmly believed, were induced by her *pir* through his strange powers, and his insults, slights and kindnesses. At the beginning she was frightened of the *pir* because of this awesome power to produce states within her. And she thought of him as God in some way, even though she knew very well that he was merely human. The experiences of these states, together with the hints and explicit orders of her *pir* moved her to make free decisions that resulted in increasingly higher degrees of surrender to the *pir*. And as the self-surrender to him increased, dependence on him expanded. The reliance was emotional, mental and also economic. At first, she had to surrender her will and trust that the *pir* had the ability and the desire to lead her to her explicitly stated goal of realizing God. Then, she had to confess her sins to him, give up all her wealth, and finally her beliefs. All these decisions of self-surrender, the experiences of Glory and the acute awareness of dependence involved great suffering. But the suffering bore fruit, in the sense that she began to love the *pir*, and see his image within her and all the things she beheld. A little later she began to conceive of God as different from the *pir*. The *pir* is not God. He only points the way to God. But then, at the same time, she also realized that the more aware she was of her dependence on the *pir*, and the more she sacrificed for him, the closer she came to God. This was also the time when the painful experiences began to take on a new meaning: They became the process of gifting love to her, the path of love.

This account, like the two previous articles, demonstrates that God is central to the *piri-muridi* relationship. At the beginning, God is closely associated with the *pir*, even though the *murid* knows that the *pir* is a human being. He is associated with God because of his special power of inducing the states of Glory and Peace that lead to an awareness of one's dependence. Later, God is clearly differentiated from the *pir*. Even so, the *murid's* relationship with God is closely related with one's relationship with the *pir*.

Other than the two articles, the diary of daily experiences, and the passing references in general works on Sufism, quoted above, there seems to be no work on the *piri-muridi* relationship in the

English language. Some scholars of Islam and sociology have told me that there is no monograph devoted to the *piri-muridi* relationship. A few scholars of Islamic history, and a few *pirs* have expressed the contrary opinion. But further questioning revealed that all they meant were standard works on Sufism (which have been dealt with in the preceding pages), *adab* literature (or the rule for novices which far from explaining the relationship presuppose some understanding of it), and *malfuzat* literature. The *malfuzat* are records of the sayings and stories that *pirs* narrated to groups of *murids* and outsiders, and a record of the miracles of other *pirs*. They only serve to demonstrate how the *pir* uses hints and suggestions and stories in order to teach the *murids*. They do not explain the *piri-muridi* relationship.[70] Other *pirs* have pointed out that literature on the *piri-muridi* relationship does not and cannot exist because it can be understood only through a life of self-surrender to a *pir*. Whatever be the differences in opinion, it is clear from what has been discussed so far that the *piri-muridi* relationship rests on the *murid's* desire for union with God, the *murid's* belief in the *pir's* ability to mediate God to him, his own willingness to surrender himself to God in the person of the *pir*, and the *pir's* acceptance of him. But before we can progress further in this study, we shall have to inquire into how God, a non-empirical reality, can be treated in sociology.

GOD AND RELIGION AS TREATED IN SOCIOLOGY

Bryan Turner in his book, *Weber and Islam*,[71] outlines a method and a theoretical perspective that would enable sociological description and explanation of the *piri-muridi* relationship. His exposition may be divided into three parts: 1) Should belief in gods and other supernatural beings be considered a core variable in the definition of religion? 2) If this is so, how is this core variable to be theoretically understood in the sociology of religion? 3) And, how is interaction in terms of superhuman beings to be described and explained sociologically?

Turner begins by trying to discover whether the sociological definition of religion should include the belief in superhuman actors.

Weber gives no definition of religion.[72] But as Turner points out, his definition of religion can be inferred from various aspects of his sociological studies. In them, religious belief is a system of meaning, a theodicy (vindication of divine providence in view of the existence of evil) that has a justifying and legitimizing nature in dealing with the disparities between expectations and actual experience in order to make life meaningful. Then, his explanation of what constitutes a social actor leaves out, by intention, superhuman actors, sociological investigation into the ways in which men cope with the interactional dilemmas arising out of their commitment to supernatural actors, and any analysis of the social orientation to sacred objects and places. And he believed that the aim of the sociology of religion is not to explore religion in terms of what it is, but to compare the conditions and effects of different theodicies on the different cultures. Thus, Weber is very similar to Durkheim. Weber, however, as we shall see later, contradicted this stand.

Durkheim, unlike Weber, defined religion as

... a unified system of beliefs and practices relative to sacred things, that is to say, things set apart and forbidden—beliefs and practices which unite into one single moral community called a Church, all those who adhere to them.[73]

This definition omitted any reference to God and other superhuman beings because Durkheim wanted to include belief systems like Buddhism, which he believed had no beliefs and myths referring to supernatural beings. Further, he believed that the sociology of religion, rather than discover what religion is in itself, should explain the relationship between systems of belief as supported by religious practice, and social collectivities, i.e. the sociology of religion is meant to discover the social effects or functions of religious beliefs and practices. Turner says that Durkheim while giving this definition was aware of and argued against Taylor's statement that a minimum definition of religion should include a basic reference to belief in sacred beings.[74] More recently, this minimum definition of religion has found advocates among modern anthropological theorists; researchers who find the distinction of sacred and profane less than helpful in understanding the concrete field situations they are faced with; researchers who find that beliefs in superhuman beings in Buddhism cannot be dismissed as lightly as Durkheim did; and authors like Robin Horton and Melford Spiro, and unwittingly Weber himself.

Robin Horton argued for the positive value of including Taylor's definition of religion for sociological research because the way in which human beings interact with superhuman beings is similar to the way social interaction takes place between human beings. Further, the inclusion of belief in superhuman beings in the definition would, he believed, help to compare the interaction with sacred objects and the interaction between human beings. Melford Spiro[75] explicitly defended Taylor's definition by saying that the belief in superhuman beings and their power to assist or harm men is a core variable that ought to be included in any definition of religion. This inclusion would not make the definition lose its cross-cultural applicability—as Durkheim who confused the cross-cultural applicability of concepts with the criterion of universality believed—since mythological belief systems that do not refer to God can be considered as interesting cases in their own right and contrasted with systems where God is an important factor. Then, Weber unwittingly supported Taylor's definition by not following his own definition of what constitutes a social actor. He forgot his exclusion of superhuman beings from the category of social actor, and his exclusion, by intention, of the ways in which sociology could investigate the interactional dilemmas coming from the human actors' commitment to the superhuman one in his explanation of the rise of the Protestant ethic. The rise of the Protestant ethic is, in his explanation, the direct consequence of the dilemma arising out of the social relationship between the Calvinist and his God, who as a social actor is all-powerful, predestining to salvation or damnation, unmovable and unpredictable.[76] The result of interaction with such a God is psychological anxiety about personal salvation. And this problem is resolved by trying to live, as an instrument who is predestined to salvation, the Protestant ethic which includes the inner-worldly calling with its dedication to hard work and an ascetical lifestyle, and the commitment to believe that one is predestined to salvation. In this analysis Weber completely followed the principles of his *verstehen* sociology. Given Weber's example together with the light it brings to bear on that particular situation, the limitations of Durkheim's definition as pointed out by theorists and researchers, the demands of the principles of *verstehen* sociology that have become basic to sociology[77] (this will be explained in greater detail later), and what Spiro and Horton have to say about Taylor's basic definition, Turner reasons that an inclusion of the belief in superhuman beings would be more beneficial for sociological research and understanding than a definition that excludes belief in superhuman beings. This brings us to the second theme in Turner's chapter—how do we treat God and other superhuman actors as social actors in sociology?

Turner begins by analysing Weber's *verstehen* sociology, which focuses on the subjective meaning of social action as determined by the definition or the viewpoint of the social actor, not the sociologist.[78] Social action for Weber, is didactic or relational, in that it consists in the actor orienting his behaviour or action to the behaviour of other social actors. This orienting to the behaviour of other social actors involves interpreting and defining the activity of the others by the use of terms, concepts and theories. Hence, overt physical activity alone is not enough to understand the actor's meaning of the action, e.g. prostration could have a number of meanings: submission, obedience, inferiority, or just exhaustion. And, consequently, it is very important to have the actor give the meaning of his action. Further, since what counts as the other social actor (the one to whom action is oriented) in the mind of the social actor is an integral part of the interpretation and definition of social action, it is as important to have the social actor decide what constitutes a social actor. Weber seems to agree with this only when human actors are involved: Both individuals, personally known or unknown, and a plurality of human beings who cannot be possibly known personally by the actor and who may or may not be physically present, are considered as social actors. Nevertheless, solitary human beings, non-humans like animals, inanimate objects, and superhuman beings are firmly excluded from the social actor category. Superhuman actors are excluded even though the actors themselves commit themselves to the belief that they are social actors, e.g. God answers prayer. This position, Turner points out, contradicts Weber's *verstehen* sociology that makes the actor's definition of the situation in the fullest sense, the starting point for sociological explanation. It also contradicts, one may add, Weber's treatment of the intercourse between the Calvinist and his all-powerful, predestining, unmovable and unpredictable God, as seen above. Hence, *verstehen* sociology, despite Weber's contradictions, offer a theoretical and methodological basis for explaining the God-man relationship.

Finally, Spiro says that it is inappropriate at the beginning of a research project to get involved in questions concerning whether superhuman beings really exist, or what counts as a superhuman being, because these problems will resolve themselves in the course of examining the concepts and theories employed by the actors themselves to distinguish between true and false gods, real and unreal divine-human encounters. In other words, it is more important to take seriously the actor's definition of the situation and, thus, undertake to discover and explain culturally patterned interaction with culturally postulated superhuman beings. This brings us to the third part of Turner's exposition: how can interaction with non empirical superhuman beings be explained sociologically?

As seen above, Weber presents us with contradictions: in *The Protestant Ethic and the Spirit of Capitalism* God is a social actor, but in the definition of what constitutes a social actor, God is not one. Further, the dilemmas arising from the orientation to God, and the attitudes to sacred objects are not subject matters for the sociology of religion as far as Weber is concerned, but it is the subject for sociological explanation in his treatment of the Protestant ethic. Besides the problems Weber's contradictions place us in, Weber never really gave us an explicit method for dealing with God as a social actor: His method for dealing with God as a social actor in *The Protestant ethic* is implicit in his *verstehen* sociology and is somehow mixed up with his definition of social actors. Hence, the need for external help in order to determine what in Weber's definition of social actors would serve as the basis of such a methodology.

Robin Horton says that there is a basis for comparing the God-man relationship and interaction between human beings. In human interaction, the alter is, in principle at least, immediately available to ego. Hence, ego can easily interpret the signs, symbols, and gestures presented by alter. Interaction with alter is, consequently, flexible, immediate, and open. On the other hand, in ego's interaction with superhuman beings (who are rarely present directly or physically) ego cannot immediately interpret the divine alter's moods, meanings, and intentions. He has to depend on delayed signs which are complex and unpredictable (e.g. ill health, poor harvests, a safe delivery, etc., which may take days, weeks or months to come) in order to gauge the divine alter's moods, meanings and intentions. Consequently, interaction with divine alters is commonly stereotyped. It is also inflexible, and differential because gods are the status superiors of human beings. This difference between the God-man and man–man relationships, however, Horton says, does not imply that there is an absolute and essential difference between the God-man and man–man interactions. On the contrary, both the man–man and the God-man interactions share common interaction strategies (like manipulation, coercion, cooperation, submission, etc.) that enable one to consider religious objects and actions as an extension of the field of human social relationships. Consequently, the assumptions and theories employed to analyse man–man relations can be employed to analyse the God-man relationship.

The situation, as outlined by Horton is, according to Turner, precisely Weber's social interaction with a plurality of human actors who are not personally known to the actor and physically absent. But, since Weber gave no detailed and sustained description of how *verstehen* sociology is to deal with such action (interaction with a plurality of personally unknown and physically absent social actors) we have to turn to Alfred Schutz, who developed this aspect of Weber's theory.

Schutz says that we understand the lived experiences of others by using objective and subjective meaning. Objective meaning refers to signs, symbols and actions that have a meaning in the public realm, independent of the intention of its producers. Subjective meaning, however, has no such independent and public meaning and, hence, can be understood only by directly attending to, or being physically present with the other as he lives out his experience. Hence, the greater the distance between the actor and the observer, the greater the use of a series of typifications that approximate to objective rather than subjective meaning in order to understand the subjective experience of the actor. On the other hand, our own experience of the social reality is not homogeneous, but takes place at different levels. The most important levels are those of direct and indirect social experience. Direct social experience takes place in face to face relationships, i.e. with consociates and fellows who are physically present. Indirect social experience is oriented to a whole range of others (e.g. contemporaries, predecessors, successors) who may or may not be physically present. As social experience moves from direct to indirect social experience it becomes increasingly necessary to use ideal types in order to conceptualize the increasing anonymity of others. In this movement, one can have a whole continuum of degrees of anonymity: We may begin with character types where individuals are expected to behave in certain ways because they are like that, move on to habitual types (e.g. office bearers like clerks, ticket collectors, policemen, etc.), social collectivities (e.g. states, the economy, the working class, etc.), language, and cultural objects and artifacts (e.g. tools and utensils). The believers' interaction with postulated distant and powerful superhuman actors, which takes place in terms of stereotypes and comes under Weber's interaction with a plurality of social actors, is precisely the problem of indirect social experience as explained by Schutz.

But as Bryan points out, sociologists may remain sceptical about the value of Schutz's account of indirect social relationships, and also about the Taylor-Spiro approach to the relationship between human and culturally postulated superhuman beings. They can and may claim that a sociology of the God-man relationship is based on a utilitarian view of atomistic relations where men act in a private world of their own gods; and that the God-man relationship allows an outdated idealism to creep in by the back door of sociological theory. Hence, it is important to show that the God–man relationship is of genuine sociological interest in its own right, that the relationship as experienced requires a fundamental social and public framework, and that the God–man encounter can be explained with materialistic assumptions.

Turner goes about doing this in the following way: He says that there is an everyday distinction in social situations. They are either experienced as predictable, easy and fluent, or as problematic, tricky and awkward. The first kind is experienced in interaction among friends and equals, where ego characteristically draws on the past knowledge and experience of the styles, biographies and social positions of the social alters in order to perform successfully in the present, i.e. detailed social portraits are built up by ego and alter over time which allow them to interact on the basis of trust and confidence. The second type of experience, on the other hand, is among strangers who may be people from other cultures, status superiors or superhuman actors. These people occupy entirely different social spaces from ego. Hence, ego finds it difficult to draw on trust, spontaneity, and common assumptions in order to interact with them. Consequently, he uses strategies to cope with the situation. These strategies are Schutz's typifications, typologies and caricatures which, besides being shared with others, outline certain stylized expectations for appropriate behaviour. These typifications are not different from the stereotypes that Horton demonstrates, and are characteristic of the interactions with superhuman beings. And these typifications, Turner says, are found in theologies. Theologies, as collections of such typifications, outline for the believer what sort of God is encountered in religious experience, what sort of relationship one can expect with such a God, and the appropriate styles for interacting with Him. These theological typologies are also demonstrated by Weber in his dichotomy of ascetical and mystical orientations. They point to alternative modes of action with God. And Weber gives us an example of the ascetical typification by working out the one presented in Calvinism. The Calvinist is equipped with the typification of God as distant and all-powerful, unresponsive to petition, arbitrarily predestining men to fixed fates, and willing that all men work to bring about the kingdom. Man's only adequate response is to be an instrument in His hands, and being an instrument implies following the Protestant ethic. These typifications are aspects of religious cultures, and are appropriated, maintained and handed down by specific social groups (just as in the case of the social system). This view is also supported by the matrix theory of religious beliefs that correctly maintains that one can experience God only if one has a framework or the necessary concepts that help to interpret experiences, and to distinguish religious from other experiences:[79] for instance, Muslims have visions of Mohammed and not of Krishna. Consequently, there is no spontaneous interpretation of the God–man relationship. In other words, typologies and modes of interaction with God are not directly read off private individual experiences. And what may appear as a private individual interpretation to the casual observer may be nothing but the manifestation of one mode of interaction that is taken from a whole range of alternative modes of interaction, present within the given typologies of specific social groups.

In addition to typifications, there are intermediaries[80] who have special knowledge and access to superhuman beings. Hence, they can be approached to resolve the difficulties resulting from interaction with superhuman beings, e.g. the Calvinist pastor advises the Protestant ethic as the way out of the dilemma in which the ordinary Calvinist finds himself when oriented to his God. These intermediaries are of two kinds: superhuman intermediaries who are less than the supreme deity, e.g. angels, and human intermediaries who have special training or charismatic gifts that result in the special ability to translate divine signs, symbols and communications for other human actors, e.g. priests, holy men, diviners, etc.[81]

Then finally, we have language. The language and vocabularies of direct social action are used for describing the interaction with superhuman actors. For instance, the terms love, friendship, enmity, dependence, etc., which enable the performance of social tasks and actions, e.g. making proposals, comments, refusals, observations, etc., are also used for interaction with supernatural beings.[82] In other words, religion has no language of its own. It is parasitical on ordinary human language. It also uses the dominant mode of human interaction within a particular society, e.g. domination, to describe interaction with the supernatural being or God. Thus, the status inequalities between men are used to describe the status inequalities between God and man, e.g. the master-slave relationship. And inasmuch as the dominant mode of interaction within society changes, the description of the God-man relationship also changes, e.g. God may be called a superstar where relationships are highly commercialized. Thus, human social systems provide the material that enables human actors to conceptualize the problematic relationship between human and superhuman actors. In Marx's words,

> ... religion has no content of its own and lives not from heaven but from earth, and falls of itself with the dissolution of the inverted reality whose theory it is.[83]

To summarize: Religion is not a cognitive system, but a system of meaning whose working is similar to the human social system. Religion is similar to the human social system in that both are appropriated, maintained and handed down by specific groups, and both are the basis for interaction among social actors. Further, religion uses the vocabularies and concepts of ordinary human language to describe the roles of the supernatural and human actors, and for actually interacting with the supernatural actor. Then, religion uses the dominant patterns of human social interaction to describe the interaction with supernatural actors. And finally, the mode of interaction between human and superhuman actors is similar to the mode of interaction used in indirect human social interaction, i.e. typifications and stereotypes. Then God, even though non-empirical in Himself, is empirically demonstrable in the theologies (collection of typifications) of specific social groups. They give the type of God that is encountered in religious experience, the sort of relationship that the human actor can expect with such a God, and the forms of the interactional styles that are appropriate for interaction with Him.

NOTES

1. Annemarie Schimmel, *Mystical Dimensions of Islam* (University of North Carolina Press, Chapel Hill, 1975, pp. 102-5; also cf. M. Mujeeb, *The Indian Muslims* (George Allen and Unwin Ltd., London, 1967), pp. 113-36.
2. Anne Marie Schimmel, p. 101.
3. Jafar Sharif, *Islam in India: Qanun-i-Islam*, G. A. Herklot (ed. and tr.), (Oxford University Press, London, 1921), pp. 283-6. The detailed account accurately describes the rite as it takes place even today.
4. Dr. Zahurul Hassan Sharub, *The Mystical Philosophy of Khwaja Moinuddin Hassan Chisti*, (Khwaja Publishers, Ajmer, 1959), p. 43. This is true on many occasions in the Nizamuddin Dargah.
5. Annemarie Schimmel, op. cit., pp. 102-5.
6. Ibid.
7. Ibid., p. 101.
8. Ibid., pp. 102-5.
9. cf. Abu al-Najb al Suhrawardi, *A Sufi Rule for Novices*, Sheikh Muzaffer Ozak al-Jerrahi al-Halveti, *The Unveiling of Love*, pp. 155-72; Dr. Zahurul Hassan Sharib, op. cit., pp. 68-74; Barbara Daly Metcalf (ed.), *Moral Conduct and Authority: The place of Adab in South Asian Islam*, (University of California Press, London, 1984), pp. 243-5.
10. Annemarie Schimmel, op. cit., pp. 102-103. This is a very common saying among the *pirs* and *murids* of the Nizamuddin Dargah.
11. Barbara Daly Metcalf (ed.), op. cit., pp. 243-5.
12. Khan Sahib Khaja Khan, *The Secret of Ana'l-Haqq* (Sh. Muhammed Ashraf, Lahore, 1976), pp. 88-90.
13. Ibid., p. 180.
14. John A. Subhan, *Sufism, its Saints and Shrines*, (Lucknow Publishing House, Lucknow, *c.* 1938), pp. 88-90; also cf. Muhammed Enamul Haq, *A Study of Sufism in Bengal* (Asiatic Society of Bangladesh, Dacca, 1975) pp. 105-6, 140.
15. cf. Sheikh Muzaffer Ozak al-Jerrahi al-Halveti, op. cit., p. 158. The *pirs* in the *dargah* sometimes increased the stages of annihilation to include annihilation in the *pir's pir* and annihilation in Ali.
16. Bikram N. Nanda and Mohammed Talib, "Soul of the Soulless: An Analysis of Pir-Murid Relationship in Sufi Discourse", in Christian W. Troll (ed.), *Muslim Shrines in India: Their Character, History and Significance*, (Oxford University Press, 1989) pp. 24-43.
17. Ibid., p. 128.
18. Ibid., pp. 128-9.
19. Ibid., p. 129.
20. Ibid., p. 133. I would prefer that the reader divests the term 'master-slave' of the connotation that has been attached to it in the modern mind.
21. Ibid., pp. 141-2.

22. Ibid., p. 129.
23. Ibid.
24. Ibid., pp. 129-30.
25. Ibid.
26. Ibid., pp. 130-1.
27. Ibid., pp. 131, 136.
28. Imaginal in contrast to imagining which is self induced, is the reception of a message from outside and in the form of a symbolic image, i.e. it is not self-induced. cf. William C. Chittick, "Death and the World of Imagination". in *The Muslim World*, LXXVIII (1), January 1988, pp. 51-82.
29. cf. Bikram N. Nanda and Mohammed Talib, op. cit., p. 132.
30. Ibid., p. 137.
31. Ibid
32. Ibid., pp. 137-9.
33. Ibid., p. 138.
34. Ibid., pp. 133-4.
35. Ibid., p. 134.
36. Ibid.
37. Ibid., p. 139-40.
38. Ibid., p. 140.
39. Ibid., pp. 140-1.
40. Ibid., pp. 134-5.
41. Ibid., pp. 141-2.
42. Ibid., pp. 127-31.
43. Ibid., p. 129.
44. Ibid., pp. 127-31.
45. Ibid., p. 141.
46. Ibid., pp. 127-31, 141-2. 'God and yet not God' is a very common phrase in Sufi usage and will be dealt with later.
47. Mohammed Ajmal, "A Note on Adab in the Murshid-Murid Relationship", in Barbara Daly Metcalf (ed.), op. cit., pp. 241-54.
48. Ibid., p. 241.
49. Ibid., pp. 241, 248-251.
50. Ibid., pp. 241-51.
51. Ibid., p. 241.
52. Ibid., p. 248.
53.
54. Ibid., p. 243.
55. Ibid.
56. Ibid., pp. 243-50.
57. Ibid., p. 243.
58. Ibid., pp. 243-5, 249-50.
59. Ibid., p. 247.
60. Ibid., p. 241. Here the *pir* is defined as the one who "represents and

transmits...the reality of..." The term "reality of" refers to God in Sufi terminology. cf. William C. Chittick, *The Sufi Path of Knowledge: Ibn Arabis Metaphysics of Imagination* (State University of New York Press, Albany, 1989), pp. 37-8, 134-5.

61. Ibid., p. 241. Ajmal says that the *pir* creates "a gash in the *murid's* heart" Heart, on p. 248 is symbolized by a mirror. The function of a mirror is to reflect something which is not itself. And at the moment of reflection the mirror is not seen. It is only the image that is seen. Now, when the mirror is perfectly clean it reflects perfectly. This perfection in reflecting is called awareness of dependence on God. But when the mirror is dirty or covered with rust (as in the case of a metal mirror), the mirror does not reflect or reflects only dimly. One could say here that the mirror is unaware of its function to reflect. This state may be called independence. Coming back to the heart: its function is to reflect God. When it does this to perfection, the person may be said to be aware of his dependence on God. But when man is unaware of this function, to reflect God, he is independent. Consequently, the expression "gash in the *murid's* heart" would mean that the *pir* destroys the independence of the *murid* in order to make him aware of his true function to reflect God. Hence, the *pir* gives the *murid* an experience whereby he becomes aware of his dependence.

62. Ibid., p. 241.

63. Ibid., pp. 241-2.

64. Ibid., p. 242.

65. Ibid., pp. 245-6.

66. Ibid., pp. 241-2.

67. Ibid., p. 242.

68. Irina Tweedie, *Daughter of Fire: A Diary of Spiritual Training with a Sufi Master*, (Blue Dolphin Publishing, Nevada City, 1986). Also cf. the abridged version, Irina Tweedie, *The Chasm of Fire: A Woman's Experience of Liberation through the Teachings of a Sufi Master* (Element Books, Dorset, 1979).

69. This work does not use the term *pir*. Instead it uses the terms *guru bhai, guru*, and *sheikh*. In the course of my field work I found *murids* using the terms *Pir, Guru, Murshid, Pir-o-Murshid*, synonymously. The term *shyshia* was also used for *murid*. Hence, I use the term *pir* when summarizing her work.

70. Hasan Dehlawi, "Fawa'id-ul-Fu'ad", Ziya-ul-Hasan Faruqi (tr.), in *Islam and the Modern Age*, May 1980, Aug. 1980, Feb. 1981, May 1982, Aug. 1982, Nov. 1982, Feb. 1983, Aug. 1983, Nov. 1985, Nov. 1987, May 1989 56.

71. Bryan S. Turner, *Weber and Islam: A Critical Study* (Routledge and Kegan Paul, London, 1974).

72. ibid.; also cf. Max Weber, *The Sociology of Religion*, Ephraim Fischoff (tr.), (Beacon Press, Boston, 1963).

73. Also cf. Emile Durkheim, *The Elementary Forms of Religious Life*, Joseph Ward Swain (tr.), (The Free Press, New York, 1965), p. 62.

74. Bryan S. Turner, also cf. Emile Durkheim, *Elementary Forms of Religious Life*; pp. 39 ff.

75. cf. Peter Worsely, *The Trumpet Shall Sound* (McGibbon Kee, 1986), pp. 30-5.

76. cf. Bryan S. Turner, op. cit.; also cf. Max Weber, *The Protestant Ethic and the Spirit of Capitalism,* Talcott Parsons (tr.) (George Allen and Unwin, London, 1978), pp. 103 ff. cf. Talcott Parsons, *The Structure of Social Action: A Study in Social Theory with Special Reference to a Group of Recent European Writers* (Amerind, New Delhi, 1974), pp. 516-33.

77. Bryan S. Turner, op. cit.; also cf. S. N. Eisenstadt, *Max Weber on Charisma and Institution Building* (University of Chicago Press, Chicago, 1974), pp. 3-45; also cf. Max Weber, *The Theory of Social and Economic Organization*, A. M. Henderson and Talcott Parsons (tr.) (The Free Press, New York, 1964).

78. Ibid.

79. Also cf. Frederick E. Crow, SJ (ed.), *A Third Collection of Papers by Bernard J. F. Lonergan, SJ* (Paulist Press, New York, and Geoffrey Chapman, London, 1985) pp. 113-65.

80. Bryan S. Turner, op. cit. also cf. Clifford Geertz; *Islam Observed: Religious Development in Morocco and Indonesia* (University of Chicago Press, Chicago, 1971).

81. Also cf. Fredrick E. Crow, op. cit.

82. Also cf. Fatna A. Sabbah, *Women in the Muslim Unconscious*, Mary JoLakeland (tr.) (Pergamon Press, Oxford, 1984).

83. Karl Marx, *Capital*, taken from Bryan S. Turner, Ibid., p. 51

SECTION ONE

GOD, MAN AND THE UNIVERSE IN SUFI (or Muslim mystical) THEOLOGY (or typology)

In the introduction we presented a theoretical and methodological basis for explaining sociologically the *piri-muridi* relationship in terms of the relevant typifications that describe God and the human being as social actors, gave the kind of relationship that the believer can expect and hope for, and the interactional styles that are considered appropriate. In this chapter we shall attempt to present one such Sufi typification.

Very often, in the course of my field work, the respondents used to refer to Ibn al-Arabi and Rumi. On rare occasions, they would also refer to other mystical writers like Hujwiri and say that one must understand them in order to understand *piri-muridi*.[1] It appears that Rumi knew of al-Arabi's mystical theology and used it in his own mystical thinking and poetry.[2] And I have been able to understand Rumi only after going through al-Arabi's mystical theology. Islamic scholars have also pointed out that Ibn al-Arabi still remains the greatest synthesizer of Muslim mystical thought (i.e. he did not add anything new to Muslim mysticism, but put together into a systematic whole all the mystical knowledge that had been accumulated prior to him), and has had a profound and lasting influence on all later mystical development and practice.[3] Hence, in the course of this chapter, I refer mainly to Ibn al-Arabi and his mystical theology.

THE MYSTICAL SOCIAL SYSTEM (VALUES AND NORMS)

In the mystical social system, the values are the ninety-nine divine names. They are mentioned in the Quran, either singly, in pairs, or groups,[4] e.g. Allah, all-Merciful, King, Just, Protector, Light, Gentle, Severe, Exalter, Abaser, Honourer, Humiliator, Life-Giver, Slayer, etc.[5] It is these ninety-nine divine names and not the narratives or the rules of conduct (the laws) that form the connecting thread in the Quran.[6] They are known as the attributes of God to the Muslim philosophers, as the relationships between God and the universe (which includes man) to the Sufis or the Muslim mystics, and as the divine names to the Muslim theologians.[7] Besides the ninety-nine names, there are other values or meanings in the Quran and *hadith* (traditions of the prophet). They are called roots, supports and realities.[8] These are similar to the divine names in the sense that the divine names can also be called roots, realities and supports and, vice versa, the roots, realities and supports can also be called divine names. But this is not normally done, out of courtesy for divine revelation.[9] These roots, supports and realities are given in phrases, sentences, verses and, sometimes in whole *surahs* of the Quran, and in individual *hadiths*.[10] Hence, the need to meditate on them or recite them in special postures with specially prescribed movements of the head and the use of special breathing techniques in order to predispose oneself to receive the meaning.[11] An easier way of arriving at the meaning is to rely on the knowledge of specialists. Fortunately, there are many such specialists (commentators of the Quran, *maulvis*, saints, *pirs*, mystical writers, etc.) who are able to give these meanings. Ibn al-Arabi too gives some of these meanings. For instance, he mentions a *hadith* that says: On the last day, God will appear successively in different forms to the believers. And the believers will reject Him in all these forms because they will fail to recognize Him in them. Then, finally, God will appear to each of them in the form that each believer recognizes as Him. Consequently, the believers accept God. But, then, God will again reappear in the first form, and then in the other forms which were rejected by them.[12] According to al-Arabi, the meaning or value given in this *hadith* is transmutation. This meaning, he further explains, is supported by the Quran sentences, "everything is annihilated except its face" (Q.28/88) and "each day He is upon a new task" (Q.55/29).[13] Another Quranic phrase, "uplifter of degrees" (Q.40/15) gives the meaning, hierarchy or levels (relationships of higher and lower).[14] *Surah* an Naba (Q.78) according to the *malfuzat* of Nizamuddin Aulia, gives the meaning, captivated by love.[15] *Surah* Maryam (Q.19), according to a *pir* in the *dargah* gives the meaning, creation, and effects pregnancy in sterile women. And so it goes, even to the extent of giving such meanings to every sentence, phrase, and even word of the Quran, as my informants in the *dargah* made it a point to tell me. These meanings are also found in the invocations prescribed by saints.[16]

These divine names, roots, realities and supports have two types of referents:[17] First, empirical referents, e.g. the divine name, King, has as its empirical referent, the role of an earthly king, and the role of the spiritual king, the saint whether dead or alive. Holy has its empirical referent in the saint, the mosque, and the *dargah*. Gentle may have as its empirical referent the role of mother. Slayer may have the executioner as its empirical referent, etc. Other types of empirical referents of the divine names can be emotions, like happiness, sadness, anger, etc.; qualities like intelligence, stupidity, etc.; actions, etc. The second type of referent is non-empirical. Non-empirical referents are of two kinds. The first kind consists of all those non-empirical things (*jinns*, ghosts, spirits, *parits*, *hamzas*, etc.) which are not God. They are referents in the same way as empirical things. The second kind is God in that He exercises various roles in His relationship with the universe: He is Merciful, the Life-Giver, the Slayer, etc. In existent things, these roles, emotions, qualities, etc. are considered as the effects and properties of the names.[18] For example, a *murid* once said,

> How do we know what we are? How do we know what other people are? How do we know the meaning of ourselves and other people? We know or come to know by observing the person's behaviour: How does he behave, how does he speak, does he greet people warmly, does he bring blessing and good fortune to the people he comes in contact with, or does he make other people angry, afraid, etc.? In this way we make out whether his meaning is good or bad. If he brings destruction, spoils people's name, makes fun of them, or laughs at them behind their back, he is an evil man. I also find your meaning by looking to see whether you are healthy or sick, happy or sad.

If you are healthy and happy, you have a good meaning. But if you are sad, dejected and/or sick, you have a bad meaning. This body of ours gives witness to the meaning we have in ourselves.

Then, I can also find your meaning by looking at your history. If you were rich yesterday and used to eat pure ghee in your house, but today have to eat dry *chapati* (unleavened bread), then I know that you have come closer to hell. But if you were poor yesterday with nothing to eat and very little to wear, and go about today in good clothes, by a car, and eating good food cooked in ghee, then I know that you have come closer to heaven. Wealth, happiness, beauty, etc. are things of paradise. Sickness, dejection, anger, etc. are things of hell. There is still another way of finding a person's meaning. If he is very rich but does not give any money to the poor and, worse still, insults them, then I know that his meaning is bad. Why? Because wealth is given by God in order that it may be distributed among the poor. And if the man goes on refusing to give anything to the poor, then one day, God will take away everything from him and give it to someone else. Or, God may punish him in another way. He will allow him to keep all his wealth, but not to enjoy it. He will have health problems and, thus, he will not be able to enjoy even a good meal. What use is all his wealth then? In a similar way, I come to know my own meaning. Now, if a person comes and sits next to me, and even if I say nothing to him, I find that he begins to experience peace, and that all the anger and frustration that he felt so far slowly begins to disappear, then I know that my meaning is good. But if I insult him, or drive him away with hard words, or answer his angry words with angry ones of my own, then I know that my meaning is bad.

A *pir* also said,

I come to know the real meaning of a person by looking at his virtues, accomplishments, habits and defects. But sometimes I make mistakes and give him the wrong name because the person is an expert at deceit. That is why I call the person again and again and thus, verify whether the name I think fits him is his actual name.

Another *murid* told me,

> How do I know whether a *pir* is good or bad? I live with him and observe the effects of his words on the people who come to him. If they bring peace and help them to give up their evil ways, then I know that the *pir* is good.

It must be remembered, however, that the names do not exercise their effects and properties on God, who is completely different from created things.[19] Rather, God delimits Himself, or freely restricts Himself by the names and their effects and properties when dealing with the universe.[20]

These divine names are meanings that have no existence in themselves (i.e. they are not ontological),[21] but they are very real in their effects.[22] That is why they are called names, relationships and attributes, and not existent things. They make intelligible the ways in which existent things (whether empirical or non-empirical) interact with each other.[23] In other words, the divine names are that (the values) in terms of which interaction takes place between men, and men and non-human empirical and non-empirical existent things; that by which existent things interact with each other (i.e. all things in the universe, whether living or non-living, are believed to interact with each other in terms of these names),[24] and that by which God interacts with the universe.[25] A *murid* told me,

> You may have noticed that, when my *pir* gets angry with me I keep quiet, even when he is in the wrong. I remain calm and forgiving so that my *pir* and his family may continue to experience peace and happiness. I know that if I get angry with my *pir*, he and his family will lose all the peace and happiness that they now have, and begin to experience nothing but difficulty and trouble.

Proof of interaction between existent things in terms of these names is seen in the effects one existent thing has over another. For example, one *pir* said,

> Green walls in a house lead to peace of mind and happiness in all those who live in it. Red walls, on the other hand, are the cause of rising tempers and fights between the occupants of the house.

Once, a *murid* came to his *pir* and told him that his business was failing. The *pir*, after a brief conversation with him in a very low voice, asked for his full name and that of his mother. These names were reduced to a single number which helped the *pir* to interpret the influence of the stars and planets on the *murid*. Then the *pir* turned to his *murid* and told him that his business was failing because of the adverse influence of the planets. In order to negate this evil influence, he would have to buy a dark red stone and bring it to him to pray over. Then he should have it embedded in a silver ring and wear it at all times on his finger. The stone would ensure that only the good influence of the planets would reach the *murid*. Consequently, his business ventures would become successful.

One existent thing can exercise effects and properties of the divine names on other existent things because each existent thing is the institutionalization of a particular name.[26] For example, a school gives knowledge and education because it is the institutionalization of those values. The divine names, thus, serve to explain the nature of existent things in roughly the same way as human values explain the nature of institutions and roles;[27] for example, the values knowledge and education help to explain and make intelligible the nature of a school, a university, the roles of teacher, professor, etc. In the mystical social system, the divine name or value, Allah, is supposed to explain the nature of the saints, the prophets, the perfect men, the perfect *pirs*,[28] etc. All existent things, without exception, are the institutionalized forms of the divine names;[29] for example, man as an existent thing is supposed to be the institutionalized form of the name

Allah. One *murid* told me,

> Allah is in all of us. Your name is Allah, and my name also is
> Allah. You and I do not know how both our names can be Allah.
> But this does not mean that Allah is not our name. It is like this.
> Do you know musk? Musk is that precious thing found in a
> certain kind of deer. It is very rare and expensive and used only
> by kings. It has a lovely smell. Once, a deer who had this musk
> within himself smelt it. He liked it very much and went in search
> of it. He roamed everywhere for years on end, but did not find
> it. Then, when it was time for him to die, he realized that the
> source of that fragrance, that musk, was in himself. That was
> why he smelt it wherever he went, but never found it. In the
> same way, Allah is in you and in me, but we do not know this.
> It is the *pir* who will teach us this knowledge.

As institutionalized forms of the divine names, existent things
demonstrate the effects and properties of the divine names with
varying degrees of perfection;[30] for example, the saint is supposed to
institutionalize and manifest the effects and properties of the name
Allah in all its perfection.[31] An earthly king institutionalizes the same
name in less perfect form.[32] Other men may institutionalize it in
varying lower degrees of perfection in the same way as a village
school with only one teacher, no building, no blackboard, etc. (as is
common in north India) institutionalizes the values knowledge and
education to a far lesser and inferior degree than an elite school in
Delhi. As institutionalized forms of the divine names, the existent
things display the properties and effects of the names in two ways:[33]
First, in a passive way, i.e. the existent thing receives the effects and
properties of the divine name. And second, in an active way in the
sense that the existent things influence other existent things in terms
of the effects and properties of their ruling name; for example, respect
and obedience is given by subjects to a king because he displays the
effects and properties of the name King, or, one might say, the effects
and properties of the name King bring about the effect and properties
of obedience and respect in his subjects.[34] I have been told many

times in the *dargah* that it is enough for the *pir* (who institutionalizes
the name Guidance) to look at his *murid* only once, and the *murid*
changes his whole life-style. He no longer robs, tells lies, gets drunk,
avoids praying the *namaz*, etc. (i.e. he begins to display the effects and
properties of the name Guidance). This is further explained with
stories.

> Once, when Nizamuddin Aulia was returning to his *khanqah*
> (monastery), he found a *murid* in a drunken state. He got very
> angry with him, and catching hold of him by the scruff of his
> neck demanded an explanation for this terrible behaviour. The
> *murid* tried to defend himself by saying that he came from a
> community that was habitually given to drunkenness. Hence,
> it was but natural that his community's effects and properties
> were displayed in him. This justification only served to make
> Nizamuddin more angry. He demanded to know whether his
> own company had no effect on the *murid*. Then he looked long
> and deep into the eyes of his *murid* and left him. From that
> moment onwards, the *murid* gave up liquor and became a model
> *murid* for the rest of his life.

The respondents in the *dargah* also believe that people communicate the properties and effects of their ruling names to things,
which in turn communicate them to other persons. A *pir* once put
a *chaddar* on a girl of marriageable age, the daughter of one of his
murids. Then he turned to her parents and told them that she would
be safe. She would always experience success in whatever she put her
hand to. She would never suffer failure, nor would she experience
fear. She would be a good and obedient daughter and remain far
from the evil influence of other people. And all this, because he had
put on her a *chaddar* that had been lying on the grave of Nizamuddin.
The *pir* further explained that the blessing of Nizamuddin would be
communicated to the girl whenever she put the *chaddar* around
herself, and as long as she kept it with her. Hence, she should never
lose it or give it away.

Another *pir* explained to the wife of one of his *murids*:

The *chaddar* carries the blessing of the saint and the *pir*. And it transmits this blessing to the one who has it. Hence, it must be treated with respect. If it is thrown away, trodden underfoot, or given to someone else without the permission of the saint or the *pir*, then all the blessing that one experienced while it was with one will also go away. Moreover, one will begin to experience the effects of a curse: one's children will become disobedient, one's husband will meet with failure, there will be sickness and unhappiness in the home, etc. All this actually happened to one family I know well. They live in London and have a very big cloth business. Once, when they visited me, I gave them a *chaddar* from the tomb of Nizamuddin. I too prayed over it. When they returned to London, they wrote saying that everything was going very well, and they thanked me for the gift of the *chaddar*, and for my prayers. Two years later, however, they suddenly walked into my office and, with downcast faces told me that their business had failed, and that they had suffered one calamity after another. I immediately asked them whether they had the *chaddar* with them. They told me that someone had come to their house a year before and asked for it, and that someone in the house had given it to him. Then I asked them when their problems began. And they told me, one year ago. See, they experienced trouble ever since they gave away the *chaddar*. By giving it away, they gave away the blessing of the saint and my blessing.

People are also demonstrated as influencing each other in terms of the effects and properties of the names in stories that the respondents prefer to call incidents.

Once, Mohammed was travelling on foot with his companions. They came across a large graveyard and began to cross it. Halfway through, Mohammed suddenly saw huge flames leaping up from a grave. He walked towards it and found a dead youth moaning and groaning in agony. On seeing this,

Mohammed went to the nearest village and inquired whether anyone knew of the youth buried in that grave. The people knew him. Mogammed then asked if the man's mother was still alive. On being informed that she was, he asked them to lead him to her. When he met her, he asked her whether she had been happy with her dead son. She replied, "How could I be happy with him when he used to beat and torture me and find every possible excuse for giving me trouble? I seek vengeance, and have called down the wrath of God upon him. "Mohammed pleaded with her to forgive him." But she refused saying that nothing would ever bring her to forgive him. So Mohammed asked her to follow him to her son's grave. When she saw the flames, and the agony of her son, the love of a mother took over in her heart. She could not bear to see her suffering son, and immediately forgave him. And as soon as she forgave, a stream of milk shot out of her breasts and fell on the flames and began to extinguish them, and this did not stop until all the flames had died out and her son was in peace.

Since all existent things are believed to be institutionalized forms of the divine names, and since the relationship between the names and the existent things is believed to be necessary[35] (i.e. the relationship is not arbitrary, nor the result of consensus as in the case of human values and their referents), the divine names are believed to have a determining influence on the existent things.[36] Thus, knowledge of the divine names and their effects and properties is considered as the knowledge of the true nature of things.[37] In other words, if there is no divine name, then existent things would not exist in a much more drastic way than the way in which a hospital does not exist for a social group that does not have health as a value; if the divine names did not manifest their effects and properties, then there would be nothing, no existent thing.[38]

Nevertheless, very few things, if any, are the institutionalization of only one name or value;[39] for example, a school is not only the institutionalization of the value knowledge, but also of values like discipline, social order, social organization, etc. Similarly, existent things may be the institutionalization of more than one name. And just as in the case of a school, one value or divine name may have more prominence than another in the existent thing.[40] Man, for instance, by virtue of being the institutionalization of the value "Allah" is also the institutionalization of all the other divine names which are included or contained in the divine name "Allah".[41] And each individual human being cannot, or normally does not display all the values or divine names to the same extent or degree at any given moment.[42] This is true even of the perfect men (the prophets and the saints).[43] This prominent or ruling name may also belong to any of the two main categories or paradigms of the divine names, the names of mercy (e.g. Forgiveness, Gentleness, etc.) and the names of wrath (e.g. Vengeance, Slayer, Overpowering, Punisher, etc.).[44] In normal Sufi practice in the *dargah*, the process of isolating a ruling name consists in, first, trying to locate the paradigm, i.e. does the person display the effects and properties of the names of wrath, or the names of mercy? Once the paradigm is located, the individual ruling name is very easily isolated. For instance, once a *murid* brought a friend to his *pir* saying that the friend experienced great difficulty and many impediments in his business life. He (the *murid*) wanted to become a partner with him in a new business venture and, hence, he had brought him along in order to see if anything could be done to remove the difficulties and impediments. The *pir* (as he explained soon after the *murid* and his friend left) observed the *murid's* friend carefully. Repeated failure in business meant that the man was under the influence of the names of wrath. The fact that his *murid*, who was a very shrewd businessman, wanted to become his partner, discounted stupidity. The influence of the names of wrath had to be verified by observing the general temperament and behaviour of the man. As the conversation progressed, the *pir* found the man cheerful, generous in that he was very willing to pay for the tea ordered by the *pir*, and devout in that he was more than willing to go and pray at the shrine of Nizamuddin as soon as the *pir* suggested the idea. These traits (the *pir* explained) are not the effects and properties of the names of wrath. Hence, the need to know more about the man. When the man got up to go and pay his respects to Nizamuddin, the *pir* asked the *murid* to stay back. Then he asked him what sort of man this friend of his was. The *murid* told him that the man was very rich, yet not stingy because he always helped out his friends financially and always gave something to the poor. He was a good friend, a dependable and respected father and husband, and had no bad habits like visiting prostitutes, running after women, drinking, etc. Further, his business failures were a recent phenomenon. On hearing this the *pir* concluded that the name of wrath that led to business failure was not the ruling name of the man. If he had the name of wrath within him as a ruling name, then he would have to display its effects and properties in his behaviour. His behaviour, however, manifested the names of mercy. Hence, the ruling name of wrath was in some other person. Drawing on his experience and the fact that the man was rich, handsome and successful, he concluded that the ruling name of wrath that exercised its effects and properties in the business life of this man was the divine name "Jealousy". When the man returned from the shrine of Nizamuddin, the *pir* told him that his problem could be easily solved as the cause of the sickness was not in himself but in some other person. He would pray for him and, thus, remove the influence of the evil eye. Then the *pir* recited something silently. This done, he asked his servant to bring two eggs. Then he recited something over the eggs. One of these he gave to his *murid* and asked him to revolve it thrice around his head and then throw it away. This would ensure that he would not be affected by the evil eye through his association with his friend. The other egg he gave to the friend telling him to revolve it seven times around his head before throwing it away. He told him that as soon as he did this, he would find the failures and impediments disappearing (i.e. the egg would absorb the effects and properties of the divine name, "Jealousy"). He could now take his leave fully confident that he would be successful in whatever he put his hand to.

On another occasion, an elderly woman brought her daughter to the *pir* saying that she was very badly possessed by an evil *jinn*. The *pir* (as he explained after they had left and on my subsequent visits) told them to sit closer to him so that the others sitting in the office could not hear what they were saying. In this way he got them to come close enough so that he could smell the girl (if she smelt bad then she was possessed by a *jinn*, but if she had no bad smell then she was not possessed). This girl had no bad smell. That meant that she was looking after herself, having a bath, changing her clothes, etc., and that she was not possessed. Further, he found that she was educated, held a job, and was of marriageable age. Drawing on his experience and knowledge of what goes on with such girls, he came to the conclusion that, far from being a case of possession, it must be a case of love that could not find fulfilment in marriage. The problem could not be solved by having the mother around; he had to get rid of her in order to make the girl talk. Hence, he told the mother to go to the shrine of Nizamuddin and pray for her daughter. The daughter, he informed her, could not accompany her because she was unclean and would remain so as long as she was possessed by the *jinn*. As soon as the mother left, the *pir* confronted the girl. He told her,

> You are not possessed by a *jinn*. So why are you pretending to be possessed by one? Tell me the real nature of your problem and I will try to help.

But the girl refused to answer. Hence, he took a risk (as he told me) by saying with great confidence,

> I know your real problem. I asked you to tell me because I wanted to give you a chance to be open with me. But you refuse to open up. So I shall tell you what your problem is. You are in love with someone and cannot get married. That is why you are making trouble at home, and pretending to be possessed by a *jinn*.

The girl was taken by surprise and agreed that what he said was true. "Now tell me the full truth," ordered the *pir*, "otherwise, I shall tell your mother everything." So the girl (a Muslim) told the *pir* that she had fallen in love with a Hindu shopkeeper. Her mother and family were against her marrying him. But since she was earning and independent, she was capable of and willing to leave her family and marry him. They had not been able to marry until then (the affair had carried on for two years) because the boy was attached to his parents. He had told her that he was looking out for the right moment to explain his love in such a way that they would accept her into the family. He had also told her that, in case he failed to convince them, he would leave them and marry her. Finally, she told the *pir* that she was not willing to give up the boy, whatever anyone might say. The *pir* asked her whether she had sexual relations with the boy. She told him that they had indulged in heavy petting. The boy also wanted to have intercourse, but she had resisted. The *pir* told her that it was quite possible that the boy really loved her and wanted to marry her, but he had reasons to doubt his love and sincerity. To find out who was right, she should give the boy a test. She had to tell him that she want to get married to him within two weeks. He had to tell his parents. If they disapproved, they had to get married in court since she loved him enough to give up her mother and family and he had told her that he loved her in the same way. If she succeeded, he (the *pir*) would later on help her mother to understand; perhaps, help even the boy's parents to understand. But if the boy refused to marry her within the two weeks, then he (the *pir*) was right. It would also mean that the boy was only after her body, and once he tired of her, he would discard her like an old coat. Here the *pir* stands for the name guider, the boy for misguider, and the girl for love or desire that can be respected or abused.) She agreed to test the boy, fully confident that she would win. But, the *pir* told me, she returned two weeks later and told him that he had won. The boy refused to have a court marriage, and also found one excuse after another to keep her away from his parents. She had begun to suspect that he was not interested in marriage, that he was only using her. Then, the *pir* told me he explained to her, that the boy was rich while her family was poor. Why should he want to marry a poor girl, and that too against the wish of his parents, when he could choose from any number of rich and educated girls who were more acceptable to his parents?

The divine names, as the reader may have already realized, are also moral traits that human beings have to develop, i.e. they are normative.[45] They exist potentially in all human beings by virtue of man being the institutionalization of the name Allah, and have to be activated.[46] Further, as seen above, the divine names are divided into two major categories, the names of mercy and the names of wrath. The rule or the norm is that individuals should develop the names of mercy, and not the names of wrath, which are believed to be already well developed in man. Besides this, the names of wrath lead to undesirable effects and properties not only in the individual person, but also in everything they come in contact with.[47] Then, while developing the names of mercy, individuals have to learn to balance them with each other in order to prevent the occurrence of the effects and properties of the names of wrath. For instance, too much justice and no generosity leads to tyranny, too much forgiveness and no justice leads to chaos, etc.[48] Balancing these moral traits is possible because, first, they are balanced in the supreme name Allah,[49] and second, the perfect men (the prophets and saints) are demonstrated as having balanced them in their lives and actions. These perfect men are consequently the role models for the believers.[50] They also indicate something else: that the ones who do balance the divine names or moral traits have the highest spiritual status with respect to other men.[51]

Besides the ninety-nine divine names, the roots, supports and realities found in the Quran and the *hadiths*, there are other names which may be infinite in number. Each object in the universe has its own name which appears to be different from the ninety-nine names, the roots, supports, and realities; for example, cow, goat, stone, etc., the individual names of men and women, etc.[52] Hence, the question: What is the connection between the divine names (the indefinite variable or the cause of all existent things) and these infinite other names?[53] These infinite other names are considered as symbols of the divine names, i.e. they can be reduced to the divine names, the roots, supports and realities[54] by the chosen few (the perfect men or the perfect *pirs*) who have been blessed with the gift of esoteric knowledge.[55] Consequently, all names can, and very often are taken as divine names and thought of as manifesting their effects and properties in the persons who bear them.[56] But, they are not called divine names out of courtesy for God who has given only the ninety-nine divine names in the Quran.[57] For instance, one *murid* told me,

> All names are divine names. Even the names of my parents are divine names. And I do *dhikr* of my parents' names. After all, are not my parents the ones who brought me into this world? They are my real masters. When I recite their names, I find that I cannot do anything evil. To do evil in their name is equal to forsaking paradise and one's religion.

Once, when I was sitting in the office of a *pir*, a woman came in with a male infant in her arms. She was accompanied by three daughters. They told the *pir* that they wanted help in choosing an appropriate name for the baby. He asked for and received the following information: date of birth, 29th November; day of the week born, Sunday; time of birth, 12.00 midnight. Therewith the *pir* made a calculation to determine the influence of the stars and the planets on the child. Then he lifted up his head and announced, "His name should be Ahmad." The woman protested that his father's name was Nazir. "Is his father's name Ahmad?" asked the *pir*. "No," she replied. "Then name the child Ahmad. It is a good name and will be beneficial to him." But seeing that the woman was not happy, he asked, "Is Ahmad not a good name?" "It is a good name," she replied. "Then what is the problem?" asked the *pir*. "May be you want some high sounding name or a majestic name," exclaimed the *pir* (Majesty is another term for the name of wrath). And he continued,

> You can give him a majestic name, but then you and your husband will have to suffer the consequences: He will not pray the *namaz*, not read the Quran, refuse to keep the fast, and when he grows up he will throw his father aside and refuse to respect and look after you. Ahmad, on the other hand, is a cool name (a name of mercy). If you give him this name, even though it may not sound very grand, it will have good consequences on the child. He will be God-fearing, respect his parents and look

after them.

On hearing this, the woman and her daughters began to laugh. "What, are you laughing at my advice!" exclaimed the *pir*. Then he continued,

All right, go and give him a majestic name and suffer the consequences. Or go to some big person, like the *imam* of Jama Masjid. Ask him to help you.

"No, no", protested the woman in a frightened voice, "We were not laughing at you. We were laughing at something that occurred to us while you were speaking. We are very sorry." They left soon after. As soon as they left the enraged *pir* began to say,

"See what kind of people we have in today's world. They do not understand the all-powerful influence of the name. All right they will learn through hard experience."

Another *pir* was telling a visiting *pir* who was reading his palm,

You see, I have changed my name. When my name was Ahmad, I had a lot of trouble. And very many difficulties came one after another. Then, I consulted my stars and found that my problems could be solved by changing my name. So I changed it to Nizami. And what to tell you, ever since then I have experienced only blessing in every aspect of my life.

The divine names, roots, supports and realities are arranged in hierarchies of higher and lower,[58] on the basis of two criteria: First, the divine name that denotes the wider and greater reality is higher in the hierarchy. The divine names Allah and All merciful occupy the highest position in the hierarchy of names. These two names, unlike other names are equal and, hence, are interchangeable.[59] They include all other realities and names.[60] Below them come the other names. For instance, life occupies a higher level in the hierarchy than knowledge because there is no knowledge without life (i.e. life denotes a wider and greater reality, or a more inclusive reality or meaning than knowledge).[61] Then knowledge is higher than desire since one needs to know what to desire before one can desire anything.[62] Power is lower than desire because one must desire something before one can exercise power or do something to attain the desired thing,[63] and so on. The lower the level, the more limited and specific the scope of the name.[64] Second, the names come under paradigms that are hierarchically related, for instance, the names of mercy and the names of wrath. This is a basic distinction between the names and has also been called the names of transcendence and imminence, the names of harmony and disharmony, etc.[65] The names that come under the paradigm of mercy (e.g. Life, Light, Knowledge, Unity, Forgiveness, etc.) are superior and, hence, occupy higher levels in the hierarchy than the names of wrath (e.g. Death, Darkness, Ignorance, Multiplicity and Dispersion, Vengeance, etc.).[66]

The levels have no existence (i.e. they are not ontological) in the same way as the divine names are not ontological.[67] But they are very real in their effects.[68] Further, they are the relationships between the names.[69] Usually the lower name leads to the higher one which includes it,[70] e.g. mercy precedes wrath in the hierarchy not only because wrath is lower in the hierarchy, but also because wrath is an offshoot, or an aspect of mercy in the sense that the effects of wrath (burning, punishment, chastisement) are meant to lead to the final effects of mercy (paradise and felicity). This can be explained with another example: a surgeon operates (gives pain) in order to make one healthy again.[71] Every level in the hierarchy is occupied by only one name.[72] As levels the divine names are the stations of the spiritual path.[73] While there is agreement on having the names of Allah and All merciful occupy the highest level, and on having the names of mercy occupy higher levels in the hierarchy than the names of wrath, there may be confusion as to which particular name within the paradigms of mercy and wrath occupies a higher or lower level (this is the same controversy as the one regarding the hierarchical position of the individual stations, as seen above).[74] This hierarchy or the levels, are the effects of the root given in the Quranic phrase, "Uplifter of degrees" (Q.40/15).[75] And these effects are not restricted only to the divine names. The levels have their effects in existent things.[76] The existent thing that displays the effects and properties of a particular ruling name occupies the same level with respect to other existent things as that occupied by the ruling name in relation to other divine names;[77] for example, man, as the institutionalization of the name; Allah, occupies the highest place in the universe. He is higher than the angels, *jinns*, etc., the animals, the plants and inanimate things. Thus, he can bring all existent things under his sway and rule over them.[78] On the other hand, since Allah includes all the divine names, individual persons also display the effects and properties of one or the other divine names which are divided into the names of mercy and the names of wrath. This prominently displayed name is called his ruling name; for example a saint has knowledge as his ruling name (knowledge means knowing the names, their relationships and their effects and properties). Consequently, the saint's level is higher than that of the king who may institutionalize or have powerful as his ruling name, and so on.[79] When it comes to having one of the names of wrath as one's ruling name, besides being lower in spiritual status than those who have the names of mercy as their ruling names, the spiritual status of the person with a name of wrath as the ruling name may be even lower than that of non-human existent things, which themselves are lower than the human level;[80] for example if adultery is a person's ruling name, that person may be said to be on the level of an animal because animals display that kind of sexual behaviour. For instance, a *murid* in the *dargah* told me,

> If I do not recite the divine names (the names of mercy are recited, not the names of wrath), I become a small man. My whole mentality changes and I become another sort of man. I become a donkey, an animal. But when I recite the divine names, I find that I can behave like a human being among human beings. People come to me and I can also go to them. I can speak

nicely to people and promote peace among them. I feel like speaking words of peace and love. Anger, deceit, and the crookedness of mind that I suffer from, when I do not recite the divine names, goes away. I am no longer angry and, hence, do not suffer any more from sickness in any way. Also, if after I have recited the divine names, someone who is angry comes and sits next to me, I notice that after some time his anger disappears. The sickness that is in him slowly disappears. And he begins to experience peace, my peace, and further, he takes that peace with him when he leaves me. I do not analyse or ask questions why or how this happens. I only know that it happens when I have the divine names within me.

This does not mean that the person who displays the effects and properties of wrath at only some moments of his life has a low spiritual status. He has low spiritual status if the effects and properties of wrath are a predominant feature of his life. For instance, a saint can display the effects and properties of wrath at some moment of his life without thereby losing his position as saint. Nizamuddin, for example, is believed to have killed three kings who were bent on getting rid of him. In such cases the norm is that the effects and properties of the names of wrath must be seen by the person who displays them as leading to the effects and properties of the names of mercy.[81] But then this norm may be expressed in a way that seems to contradict it. For instance, one *pir* repeatedly told me,

If someone wants to harm or kill another, then one is justified in harming or killing him even before he sets out to do what he intends, e.g. a snake—one does not wait to see whether the snake will bite one before killing it. One goes ahead and kills it as soon as one sees it.

Some *murids* express the same norm in a story about Moses and al-Khidr.

In the course of their journey by boat, they once came across a very handsome boy who was immediately killed by al-Khidr for no apparent reason. Moses was shocked and protested but was told to hold his peace because there was much that he did not understand. (Much later in the story,) Moses is told that the boy was killed because al-Khidr saw into his future. He saw that he would commit many murders and do much harm to the faithful of Islam. It was better to get rid of him before he set out to commit evil. Killing him was, therefore, a form of mercy. And his death would have no adverse effects on his parents because they would beget another son who would be a saint and lead many people to Islam.

The divine names, as one may have already noticed, are arranged in binary opposites.[82] Some of these binary opposites are more important than others, e.g. the binary opposite of mercy and wrath referred to above. Another important binary opposite is that of Guider and Misguider. The name Guider is also another name for the paradigm of mercy and leads likewise to felicity and paradise. It is institutionalized in the roles of saints, prophets, and the friends of the prophets and saints. The name Misguider is another name for the paradigm of wrath and leads to burning, chastisement, and punishment. It is institutionalized in the role of Satan, and the friends of Satan. As aspects of mercy and wrath, Guidance is superior to or higher in the hierarchy than Misguidance. Misguidance is an aspect of Guidance and leads finally to Guidance. But all the same the paradigms of wrath and misguidance must be avoided if one wants to prevent their effects and properties from becoming present in oneself. Another major binary opposite is harmonious–disharmonious. Harmonious is another name for the paradigm of mercy, for example, compassion, forgiveness, gentleness, etc. come under the paradigms of mercy, the harmonious and guidance. Disharmonious is another name for the names of wrath, e.g. Avenger, Terrible, Punisher, Overpowering, etc. come under the paradigms of wrath, the disharmonious and misguidance. These binary opposites, like the divine names, and their different levels display their properties and effects in existent things.

As binary opposites, these names are the roots of all conflict in and between existent things.[83] And as roots of conflict, these binary opposites are also the root of all change and transformation in the universe.[84] The conflict begins with the fact that each name demands the removal of the properties and effects of its binary opposite in order that its own effects and properties may be displayed in the existent thing. For instance, compassion demands the removal of vengeance, forgiveness demands the removal of the effects and properties of punishment, gentle demands the removal of the effects and properties of overpowering and vice versa.[85]

Finally, the names are personified.[86] This personification, it must be stressed, does not in any way imply that the names exist in themselves. Nor does it imply that the names are semigods.[87] Personifications just make it easier to demonstrate the effects and properties of the names in existent things, and help to focus attention on the names, e.g. it is easier to conceive of a person as the cause of anger in another rather than a name being the cause of the anger in a person. Ibn al-Arabi expects this understanding when he calls the names the family members of God. Also, while discussing the creation of the world, he portrays the divine names as sitting together and discussing how they can make their effects and properties manifest. The names come to the conclusion that their properties and effects can be manifest only in existent things. Hence, the different names approach the higher names in the hierarchy for help to bring their effects into existence. The higher names refer the lower one to the still higher one, and so on until the lower names are referred to the name Powerful. Powerful refers them to Desire, Desire refers them to Knowledge, and Knowledge refers them to Allah, the highest name in the hierarchy. Allah agrees to take the plea of the names to God, who agrees to make the properties and effects of all the names manifest in existent things.[88]

Conflict between the opposite names is also personified.[89] The divine names are described as competing with each other to make their effects and properties present in a given existent thing. But since the existent thing already manifests the properties and effects of one name (also called the ruling name), the opposite name or the new name has to make the ruling name vacate before it can manifest its own properties and effects in it. This it attempts to do by calling out to, or by attracting the existent thing in such a way that it demonstrates its properties and effects rather than those of the ruling name. Hence, it is labelled as the calling name. The winner of the battle between the calling name and the ruling name will be the stronger name. But then all the names are in themselves equal in strength. To make one name stronger than the other an additional factor is needed. The situation is this additional factor. If the situation is conducive to the effects and properties of the calling name, the latter becomes stronger and forces the ruling name to vacate. It becomes the new ruling name of the existent thing. But if there is nothing in the situation that strengthens the hand of the calling name, the ruling name remains strong by virtue of the previously existing situation, i.e. it already manifests its effects and properties in the existent thing.

For instance, a woman accompanied by her mother-in-law once walked into the office of a *pir*, and when he turned his attention to them, the woman told him that her husband had run away. She did not know where he was or what she could do to get him back. She had come to him for help. The *pir* told her to recite *ya wadudo*, which means come beloved, three thousand times. Then he gave the two women a huge *tasbih* and sent them into a small dark room to recite. When they had finished, he called them out and asked them what they had seen. They told him that they had seen nothing. He proceeded to upbraid them,

> You did not keep your eyes closed while reciting, and you did not concentrate on him (the husband) while reciting, nor on the spirit whose name you were reciting. How will you see anything? Anyway, you must continue to recite *ya wadudo* (come beloved) three thousand times every afternoon. [Another *pir* had told me that *ya wadudo* was a *jinn* of the afternoon, while a good number of other *pirs* had told me that it is a divine name]. And buy a *tasbih* so that you will find the counting easier.

The woman told the *pir* that she was working and that the lunch break was not long enough to recite three thousand times. The *pir* told her to divide the recitation. She was to recite a thousand times in the morning before leaving for work, another thousand times during the lunch break, and another thousand times as soon as she returned home from work. He too would recite while sitting in his office. Every time she finished reciting, she would have to say "obey me" three times. Also, she would have to take some of the clothes her husband had left behind and keep them immersed in a bucket or tin of water (the clothes were a symbol of the husband) until he returned home. Then the *pir* wrote out eight similar *tawizes* (charms). She had to burn one *tawiz* every evening and as it burnt call out to her husband by name. The *pir* explained:

> I will make your husband wet [receptive to the calling name] when you put his clothes into water. He is possessed by an evil spirit [the ruling name, most probably, the opposite name, hatred], and your recitation of the name *ya wadudo* [the calling name] will cause great shaking and trouble [the conflict between the ruling and the calling name] in him. As you recite the name and concentrate on him, you yourself may feel fear [the effects of the husband's ruling name, hatred]. But do not worry. When you come next time, bring some sugar along, and I will recite something over it. Then when you eat it all the fear will go away. For the present take this lime. I have prayed over it and it will help you to overcome the fear. Squeeze a few drops into black tea and drink it. Do this for three days.

The woman asked how long it would take for her husband to return. The *pir* replied,

> Do not worry. You have already begun the work with your three thousand recitations. I too will recite. He is already feeling troubled. He will surely come one day. But before he comes you will see him in imaginal form. He will appear to you with joined hands and touch them to your feet. Then he will ask for

your forgiveness. After that he will surely come.

In the Nizamuddin Dargah, the *pirs* and *murids* and the clients of the *pirs* appeal to and invoke *maukils*, spirits, *jinns*, angels, *parits*, *hamzas* (spirits of the shadows of persons) ghosts, the saints and *devas* (gods of the Hindu pantheon like Kali, Lakshmi, Radha, Ganesh, Shankar, Hanuman, etc.). In course of time it dawned on me that these entities are nothing but personifications of the divine names. They are all similar because all of them serve as advocates. Further, they are believed to bring about certain effects and properties in and for their human clients. Their descriptions, however, vary and are very confusing.

Maukil is the most common personification used in the *dargah*. One *pir* told me that they are the four angels, Israel, Izrafeel, Michael, and Raphael, who act as mediators and advocates for man. At another time, the same *pir* said that there are lakhs and lakhs of *maukils*, that they are not the angels, and that they are the advocates that plead man's case before God. On still another occasion, he again said that the *maukils* are the four angels. Some other *pirs* denied that the four angels are *maukils*, but stressed the role of the *maukils* as advocates. Some *murids* and *pirzade* (custodians of the Nizamuddin Dargah) agreed that the four angels are also *maukils*. But, as they said,

> They are very big *maukils* and not normally approached. People usually approach the smaller *maukils*. But we cannot tell you their names because this is part of the secret knowledge. Much harm and much good can be done with this knowledge.

A few *pirs*, however, gave me some of the names of the *maukils*: *ya wadudo, ya aziz kul aziz, ya Rahimo, ya Ghafaro*, etc. Some other *pirs* said that these are the divine names. One *pir* said,

> There is no difference between *maukils, hamzas, jinns, devas*, etc. They are all the same thing. They plead man's case before God. Even a saint is a *maukil*—after all, does he not plead one's case before God! Hence, calling them *maukils, jinn* or by any other

name is a matter of personal taste.

Another *pir* said,

> *Maukils* and *jinn* are holy beings. If one does anything wrong while one possesses them, they will kill one. To have a *maukil* one must be holy.

But another *pir* said that *maukils* are not necessarily holy.

> Some *maukils* are holy and some are evil. It all depends on what one wants from them. These *maukils* can be made slaves of men by doing certain things, like *wazifa* (recitation of the divine names) and by giving *zakat* (a form of payment that leads the *maukil* to agree to become a slave of a person). *Zakat* for the good *maukils* consists in giving many lakhs of *tawizes* that one writes while reciting the *wazifa*. The *tawizes* are put into a tin, and then either thrown into an empty well, buried at the foot of a tree in a lonely place, or thrown into the river. Also one has to lead a pure life and avoid foods that leave a bad smell (one of the effects of the names of wrath) in the mouth like onions, garlic, meat, fish, etc. The evil *maukils* can be captured in a similar way. One recites a *wazifa* in the proper way. One may also write it down and give the *tawizes* as *zakat*. In addition, one has to perform filthy practices like eating fasces, drinking urine, blood and doing some other unmentionable things. These evil *maukils* are not possessed by us. They are possessed by those who practise satanic magic. We possess only good *maukils*. Once the *maukil* becomes one's slave, he will do whatever one tells him to do. For instance, Hassan Nizami (he is dead) had a *jinn* as his slave and he made it do a lot of work for him. That is why he was such a great *pir*. But then it is troublesome to have *maukils*, *jinns* or *hamzas* as slaves because they constantly trouble one to give them work. One cannot even sleep properly because they wake one up in the middle of the night and demand work. Hassan Nizami used to get so fed up that he used to give his *jinn* a sieve and tell

him to fill it with water and bring it to him. In this way the *jinn* was kept occupied day and night—how can one fill water in sieve! He was a very clever man. There was another *pir* who used to sit just outside the *baoli* (water tank). He had many *hamzas* as his slaves. They too used to worry him day and night for work. After some time he grew weak and tired and died. If the possessor of a *maukil* wants to be free from the trouble they give one has to spend twenty-four hours of the day in prayer and worship. It is a very difficult life indeed.

These *maukils* and *jinns*, said another *pir*,

can be transferred to other people whether to help them or to create havoc in their lives. To do this we either give a *tawiz* or put the *maukil* into food or water that is then given to them. If we cannot put it into their food we put it into something else which is left at a crossroads they are sure to pass. Then when they pass that way, the thing enters them and begins to demonstrate its effects and properties in them. They get sick, suffer failure, etc. and do not know why these things are happening.

Then a *murid* said,

Maukils, *jinns*, etc. are things possessed by a *pir*. If I had them, then I too would be a *pir*. It is true that one can get these *maukils* by reciting *wazifa*, but then it is not all that easy. These things are so powerful, that they can injure one, or drive one mad. One needs the help and power of one's *pir*, if one is to make them one's slaves.

This was further illustrated by a *pir* who said,

Three years ago, a man came to meet my father. He wanted to learn from him how to capture a very powerful *jinn*. Unfortunately, my father was out of town. The visitor said that he wanted to become my father's *murid*. So I told him to spend the night in the office along with the other guests. He did not tell me that he wanted to learn the *wazifa* that would enable him to capture that *jinn*. In the evening he met a *pirzada* who knew the *wazifa* and willingly taught it to him. That night while he lay down in my father's office, he began to recite the *wazifa*. At around two in the morning, he suddenly felt something lift him up and throw him down violently. In the fall he broke his arm. When I saw him in the morning with his broken arm, I asked him whether he had had a fight with someone. He said that he was reciting that *wazifa*, when the *jinn* came and threw him down and broke his arm. I cautioned him that he should never attempt such a thing again without the permission and aid of a *pir*. Who knows, next time he might go mad or even die.

This experience is also the effect of the divine names' might according to al-Arabi.[90] Some other *pir* lifted up his *lungi* and showed me the scars on his shin. These he said, evidence of the fights he had with the *jinns* he captured and then set free. But then he said with great force,

No one has seen a *jinn*, or a *maukil*. If they say they have seen them, they are lying. One cannot see these things. One can see only the different forms that they take, either in one's dreams or in the outside world. And one can only experience their influence in one's life. No one has ever seen a *jinn*. Show me one man who has seen a *jinn*, and I will go and challenge him. And if he satisfies me in his description of what he has seen and knows, then I will become his *murid*.

The description is very similar to the divine names that have no existence in themselves but are very real in their effects and properties. Another *pir* said,

When the *jinn* or the *maukils* are about to be captured, they appear before one and ask what one wants. If one tells them to become one's slave, they may agree or refuse. If they refuse and one really wants to capture them, one must fight with them. If one loses, the consequences are bad. One may be severely injured, or one may become their slave. Hence, it is dangerous to try it alone. One needs the help of a *pir*. When they come before one, they may appear in different forms. They may appear as a lion, or as a very holy man with a lovely and shining white beard or in some other form, or they may appear to one in one's dreams.

One *pir* said that a man had once come to him and asked him to pray for his wife who was dying. Doctors had given up on her. He told the man to sit down in one corner of the office and recite, ya Baba Farid (Baba Farid is the *pir* of Nizamuddin Aulia), until told to stop. Later, he sent him away telling him to continue reciting. A few days later the man joyfully returned and asked him to visit his wife as she had begun to recover. When the woman saw the *pir* she thanked him for all that he had done for her, and turning to her husband told him that this was the same man who used to visit her at about 1 o'clock every morning, mix medicines and then give her the mixture to drink in a small glass. Her recovery had begun with the first visit of the man. The *pir* remarked to me,

I listened to her with utter astonishment. I never visited that woman and had never seen her before. So who was this person who looked like me? Was he Baba Farid, or was it something else? I don't know. All I know is that it appeared to her in my form.

Another *pir* was telling a Hindu visitor who had come to ensure that he would not be transferred, but retain his job in the home ministry (the new Government had just come to power and many transfers were taking place),

I have done the *jap* (recitation) of Shankar, Ganesh and Hanuman. And they have all come before me and become my slaves. I have them in me. No one can fool around with me, and whatever I say happens. See, I still carry something of Ganesh with me (he took out something and showed it to him). So don't worry. Nothing will happen to you. I got Rajiv Gandhi out and if I want I can also make this government fall as well.

One *pir* advised his female *murid,* who was having trouble with her husband,

Recite the name Radha (consort of Krishna) before going to sleep, and don't worry. Everything will be all right. If you have a dream come and tell it to me. If you cannot come tell it over the phone.

Then a *pir* told me,

Once, when I was sitting here in this office, someone came and offered me a book saying, take this book and you will know everything. I asked him his name. He asked me if he could pray the *namaz* here. I told him he could pray. As he prayed the *namaz*, I closed my eyes. When I opened them again, he had finished his *namaz* and was walking away. I had not taken the book from him, so I called out to him. He did not turn back. I tried to follow him, but he disappeared in the crowd. I never saw him again. Who knows what kind of things come to one! One must be ready to receive them and what they have to give when they come. Otherwise the opportunity is lost. Also, one must have the ability to distinguish guidance from misguidance immediately. I still take time to do this and, therefore, miss some of the opportunities that come my way.

Another *pir* said,

Each and everything has its own *jinn.* One has to learn to recognize them.

Still another *pir* said,

> Why do you ask me about *maukils*? Everything and everyone has
> a *maukil*. There is nothing in this world that does not have a
> *maukil*. Even you have *maukils* within you. But do you know
> your *maukil*? No, you don't. That is why you are asking me,
> what is a *maukil*? If you knew your *maukil*, you would be a very
> powerful *pir* indeed, and you would also know the *maukils* of
> other things and other people without having to ask questions.
> The photographs that you take—they too have *maukils*. But can
> you tell me what their *maukils* are? No, you cannot. If you
> could, you would be a very powerful *pir*.

The confusion resulting from these different and even contradictory explanations may be brushed away by looking at what is
central to them.

All the respondents agreed that *maukils*, *jinns*, *hamzas*, and *devas*
are powers that are central to the effectiveness and power of a *pir*.
These powers, they also explained, are active in the *tawiz* (amulet,
charm or talisman). It is through the *tawiz* that the *maukils* and other
powers work on and in people and events. Hence, as the respondents
informed me, explanations of *maukils* and other such things are given
in books of *tawiz* or *naqsh*. An examination of the *tawiz* may
therefore, help to explain the nature of the *maukils*, *hamzas*, *jinns*,
devas, etc. The *tawiz*, as a number of *pirs* and *murids* explained, is the
written form of the *wazifa*; as the written form of the *wazifa* it is called
naqsh. *Wazifa*, everyone agreed, is the recitation of a divine name,
a phrase, verse or a *surah* of the Quran or a *hadith* (which very often
includes the saying of saints) for a given number of times, at a specific
time of the day or night, and in one specific place. (It must be
remembered here that all names of all things, as explained above, are
also considered as divine names). For instance, the name *ya wadudo*
(which was called a *jinn* of the afternoon by one *pir*, and a divine name
by many other *pirs* and *murids*) has to be recited 3,000 times in the
afternoon. *Wazifa*, as the respondents explained, is different from
dhikr which consists in reciting the same things, but for any number

of times at any time of the day or night, and in any place. The
recitation of the name in *wazifa* is believed to result in observable
effects of the name that is recited. For instance, *ya wadudo* means
come beloved, and in the example given above, it is believed to effect
the return of the deserter husband. These effects can be brought
about by someone who does not want the benefits for himself but for
another person, e.g. the *pir's* clients. A *pir* said,

> When I don't want the effect of the name for myself, I say, before
> and after reciting—I do not want the benefits for this recitation
> for myself. I want the benefits to be experienced by so and so
> for whom I am reciting this *wazifa*.

Besides bringing about effects and properties in other people, the
wazifa is used to bring about the effects and properties of the name
being recited in oneself. A *pir* siad,

> When I recite a *wazifa*, I go on reciting it until one day I suddenly
> see a bright light entering me and lodging itself in my heart. Or
> I see an old man coming to me and asking me what I want, and
> then telling me that I have it. Together with this experience
> comes the knowledge that I now have the meaning and the
> effects and properties of that thing in myself. They are mine and
> no one can take them away from me. This knowledge is similar
> to knowing that one is wealthy or poor. I also know then that
> if I recite the *wazifa* for making the effects and properties present
> in someone else, e.g. the person sitting in front of me, the effects
> and properties will become manifest in him. The quickness with
> which these properties become manifest depends on the purity
> of my intention—I must not desire to gain personally for this
> service to the other person. This name, then becomes a power
> within me. And it is this power that enables me to write effective
> *tawizes*. Some say that to communicate the effects and properties
> of the name to someone else it is enough to recite the name. But
> I know from experience, and from the advice of my *pir*, that to
> have additional power one must write down what one recites.

One must write for the same number of times as one recites. (The written form of the *wazifa* may consist in filling magical squares with numbers, or writing words into the outline of a face, etc.) If one does both things—recites with one's tongue and writes with one's hand—the power in one becomes so much that one only has to recite it once, and the effects are manifest; for example, if one recites *ya wadudo* and writes down the corresponding *naqsh*, then even as one is writing it, the runaway will change direction and head for home. If one recites *ya Azizo*, others will stop troubling one, and so on. But to persevere in the recitation is difficult. Most people do not get this power halfway. *Wazifa* is not some kind of idolatrous practice. The names of the *maukils* that we recite are taken from the words, phrases, verses and *surahs* of the Quran. It is the recitation of the divine names and very praiseworthy.

Another *pir* said,

The names of the *devas* also are divine names; they also are found in the Quran. You don't know how to find them there and I won't tell you because you are not a *murid*. These names and meanings and the work that they can do is the secret knowledge that is given only to those who are fit to shoulder such a responsibility. It is given to very few people.

Here, it may be instructive to recount what someone who is outside the Sufi tradition had to say about her mother-in-law, who was a devout Muslim. She said,

My mother-in-law used to take great pains to recite each word of the Quran correctly, even to the extent of calling experts to instruct her. She was a kind of female *pir* whose words were effective, i.e. what she said came about. When the family members were ill, she used to recite the Quran [obviously, not the whole Quran but certain parts of it] after observing ritual and intentional (or inner) purity. Then she would hold her breath and go and blow over the sick person. She believed that this would help to make the sick well again.

This part of the account demonstrates that she knew the effects and properties of the passages of the Quran, and how to make them present or communicate them to other people. Keeping this in mind may help to understand what follows. The informant said further,

> She was widowed when she was quite young, at the age of twenty-six, and when her children were very young. She had great financial difficulties with no one to help out. But one day she saw a young girl wearing bells on her anklet enter the house. She went after her, but the girl disappeared. Now and then, she would either get a glimpse of the girl or hear her anklet the bells jingle. She knew that the girl had come to stay. She was a welcome guest because ever since she entered the house, the household entered upon better times. The mother-in-law found a job and could educate and bring up her children properly. She called this little girl who entered her house Lakshmi, the Hindu goddess of wealth.

The informant did not give any explanation, but the meaning, in the light of what we have just discussed, is obvious: The little girl whose presence brought about the effects and properties of wealth was the imaginal form of the divine name Wealthy or Enricher. Lakshmi is another name (or divine name) for wealth and also the imaginal form of it (According to Ibn al-Arabi, imaginal forms are one of the cardinal ways in which the divine names and other meanings or values, which produce their effects and properties in us, make themselves known to us[91]).

To summarize: The divine names, the roots, supports and realities given in the words, phrases, verses and *surahs* of the Quran and in the *hadiths*, and the names of all existent things are the values, in terms of which all existent things interact with each other and with God. These values also explain the nature of existent things because all things are the institutionalized forms of these names and display their effects and properties. These values are arranged in hierarchies, in paradigms and in binary opposites. These interrelationships among the names explain inequality and are the source of all transformation and change in the universe. Finally, knowledge of these divine names, their interrelationships, and their effects and properties in existent things is the real knowledge and the secret esoteric knowledge.

But as in the case of the social system as explained by Durkheim and structural functionalists, one is faced with the problem of human freedom and creativity. Here too we have a similar problem: If everything is determined by the divine names and their effects and properties, where is the freedom of the person, and why should he be held accountable and punished for any wrong that he does?[92] Ibn al-Arabi's answer is that the real problem is of ignorance:[93] the ordinary person does not know that he is influenced by the divine names nor how. Consequently, he thinks that he is the cause of the effects and properties displayed in himself and other things in the universe. This ignorance is not the effect and property of any divine name: it is the result of non-existence.[94] It is this ignorance, and not the effects and properties of the divine names, whether judged as good or evil, that is punishable.[95] And it is in knowing the divine names, their interrelationships, and their effects and properties, and in acting in accordance with this knowledge, that human freedom is exercised and demonstrated. This explanation may become more understandable when we examine the ways in which God and man are social actors.

NOTES

1. ' Cf. Muhyiuddin Ibn Arabi, *Ismail Hakki Bursevi's Translation and Commentary on Fusus al-Hikam*, 3 vols., Bulent Rauf, R. Bràss, H. Rollemache (tr.) (Muhyiddin Ibn Arabi Society, Oxford, Istanbul and San Francisco, 1985); also cf. William C. Chittick, *The Sufi Path of Knowledge*; cf. Toshihiko Izutsu, *Sufism and Taoism: A Comparative Study of Key Philosophical Concepts;* (University of California Press, Berkeley, 1984); cf. Reynold Alleyne Nicholson, *Studies in Islamic Mysticism* (Cambridge University Press, London, 1921), Hujwiri, The Kashf al Mahjub.

2. Cf. William C. Chittick, *The Sufi Path of Love: The Spiritual Teaching of Rumi,*

(State University of New York Press, Albany, 1983); cf. K. Khosla, *The Sufism of Rumi*; cf. Annemarie Schimmel, *The Triumphal Sun: A Study of the Works of Jalaloddin Rumi* (East West Publications, London and Hague, 1978).

3. Cf. Annemarie Schimmel, *Mystical Dimensions of Islam*, pp. 63-74. cf. William C. Chittick, *The Sufi Path of Knowledge*, pp. xii-xv.

4. Cf. William C. Chittick, op. cit., pp. 33-46. cf. Toshihiko Izutsu, op. cit., pp.99-109

5. Cf. William C. Chittick, op. cit., pp. 33-46; and by the same author, *The Sufi Path of Love*, p. 46; cf. Toshihiko Izutsu, op. cit., pp. 99-109, cf. Shaykh Hakim Abu Abdullah Gulam Moinuddin, *The Sufi Book of Healing*, pp. 171-8.

6. Cf. William C. Chittick, *The Sufi Path of Knowledge*, pp. 33-46.

7. Ibid.

8. Ibid., pp. 37-8.

9. Ibid.

10. Ibid,. pp. 33-46; cf. Hasan Dehlawi, "Fawa'id-ul-Fu'ad", in *Islam in the Modern World*, February 1983, pp. 73-4.

11. Cf. Sheikh Muzaffer Ozak Al-Jerrahi, *The Unveiling of Love*, pp. 67-81; cf. Hasan Dehlawi, op. cit.; cf. Mohammed Enamul Haq, *A History of Sufi-ism in Bengal*, pp. 103-106

12. Cf. William C. Chittick, op. cit., pp. 99-104.

13. Ibid., pp. 101, 102.

14. Ibid., p. 48.

15. Hasan Dehlawi, op. cit.

16. Ibid. p. 73.

17. William Chittick, op. cit.

18. Ibid.

19. Ibid.

20. Ibid.

21. Ibid.

22. Ibid.

23. Ibid.

24. Ibid.

25. Ibid.

26. Ibid.

27. Ibid.

28. Ibid., pp. 28-30, 356-81; also cf. Toshihiko, op. cit., pp. 247-81

29. Cf. William C. Chittick, op. cit., pp. 33-139; also cf. Toshihiko Izutsu, op. cit., pp. 99-151.

30. William C. Chittick, op. cit., pp. 255-334; cf. Toshihiko Izutsu, op. cit., p. 263.

31. Ibid.

32. William C. Chittick, op. cit., pp. 3-30.

33. Ibid.

34. Ibid.

35. Ibid., pp. 79-144.
36. Ibid.
37. Ibid., pp. 147-90.
38. Ibid., pp. 33-144.
39. Ibid., pp. 33-76.
40. Ibid.
41. Ibid., pp. 12-18, 58, 66-7.
42. Ibid., pp. 47-58, 66-7.
43. Ibid., pp. 336-75.
44. Ibid., pp. 33-76.
45. Ibid., pp.21-2, 104, 172, 286-7, 304-9.
46. Ibid.
47. Ibid.
48. Ibid.
49. Ibid. pp. 351-2.
50. Ibid., pp. 21-2.
51. Ibid., pp. 358-81, cf. Toshihiko Izutsu, op. cit., pp. 247-60.
52. William C. Chittick, op. cit., pp. 41-4.
53. Ibid.
54. Ibid.
55. Ibid.
56. Ibid.
57. Ibid., pp. 47-51.
58. Ibid.
59. Ibid.
60. Ibid.
61. Ibid.
62. Ibid.
63. Ibid.
64. Ibid.
65. Ibid., pp. 19, 23-6, 120, 130, 225-6, 291.
66. Ibid.
67. Ibid., pp. 47-51.
68. Ibid.
69. Ibid.
70. Ibid.
71. Ibid.
72. Ibid., pp. 274-90.
73. Ibid.
74. Ibid.
75. Ibid., p. 48.
76. Ibid., pp. 47-58.
77. Ibid.
78. Ibid., pp. 16-17, 188, 235, 274-5, 296.
79. Ibid., pp. 188, 195, 286, 296, 312.

80. Ibid.
81. Ibid., pp. 47-56.
82. Ibid.
83. Ibid.
84. Ibid.
85. Ibid., p. 52.
86. Ibid.
87. Ibid., pp. 53-4.
88. Ibid. pp. 55-6, 67.
89. Ibid., pp. 255-73.
90. Ibid., pp. 218, 227-8, 262, 271, 251, 324; cf. William C. Chittick, "Death and the World of Imagination: Ibn al-Arabi's Eschatology", in *The Muslim World*, 78 (1), Jan. 1988, pp. 51- 82; cf. William C. Chittick, *The Sufi Path of Love*, pp. 125, 248-67.
91. William C. Chittick, *The Sufi Path of Knowledge*, pp. 20, 56, 60-1, 205, 328, 330-1.
92. Ibid.
93. Ibid.
94. Ibid.
95. Ibid.

GOD AS A SOCIAL ACTOR

God, like man, can be viewed from different angles. Man can be considered as man in himself, as man the organism. He can also be considered as a social actor. Similarly, God can be considered in two ways: First as God in Himself. And second, in relation to and acting in terms of the expectations of existent things, i.e. God can also be considered as a social actor. We shall first examine what God in Himself is to the believer because this aspect is essential to prevent him from the misconceptions that arise in the course of treating God as a social actor.[1] Further, it helps us to understand the common Sufi description of God, "Everything is He, not. He."[2]

Philosophically, and in Ibn al-Arabi, God in Himself is the Necessary Being. The term "Necessary Being" implies that God cannot be considered, thought of, or spoken about apart from His existence because His existence or "whatness" is identical with His essence,[3] i.e. He has no potentialities that are not actualized. As Necessary Being, God is essentially unknowable since He is completely different from non-necessary beings and the only such Being (i.e. there is no other, and no empirical reality of a Necessary Being that can be used by us as a basis for understanding God). Thus, God in Himself, or the Necessary Being is usually referred to in negative terms, for example, the first half of the Muslim profession of the faith, "There is no God but God..." (for example, Q.47/19).

The Quran, as revelation, explicitly refers to God the Necessary Being through some of the divine names. The divine names that denote distance, transcendence, and difference (i.e. the names of majesty which are also called the names of wrath, disharmony and misguidance, as seen above) stress the fact that God in Himself is incomparable, and unknowable.[4] Hence, they are also called the names of darkness[5] (darkness is associated with our ignorance). Examples of such names are Independence, Free, Magnificent, Overbearing, Overwhelming, Inaccessible, All High, Great, King, etc.[6] Consequently, these divine names, besides being the values in terms of which interaction takes place between existent things, and between God and existent things (as explained above) also denote the Necessary Being in its essential unknowability and distance from non-necessary beings.[7] All the other divine names (the names of similarity, beauty or mercy) are supposed to do this implicitly.[8] And inasmuch as the divine names denote the Necessary Being, they do not give the attributes or qualities of the Necessary Being (or God in Himself);[9] for example, calling a man father does not describe or qualify his essence which is human being, or man (animals and plants also beget). The role of father qualifies a specific orientation to another person and points to the level (or essence) at which this orientation takes place, at the level of human being. In the same way, the divine names serve to make one aware of God as infinitely above and beyond us without qualifying His Essence.

Ibn al-Arabi makes this very clear in his treatment of the divine name, Independent (Q3/97, 35/15) or Free.[10] This name, he says, tells the believer that God is non-delimited (free from all restraints and limitations), and even free from the limitation of being free from non-delimitation. Independence also implies that God is not related to creatures and the universe in any way, that He has no need for the universe, that He cannot be influenced by anything in it in any way, that He transcends all levels and relationships, and cannot be described, known or judged by anything in the universe. Hence, the divine name Independent stresses that only God knows Himself, and that this knowledge of God (as He is in Himself) is impossible to all existent things (non-necessary beings) including man. Ibn al-Arabi explains here that, not even the mystics (those who are described as, or who describe themselves as having attained union with God), nor the perfect men (who are described in divine terms) know God in this way.[11] Consequently, humans have constantly to declare that God is independent (Q.57/1, 64/1),[12] the Incomparable and the only Incomparable, that He has no attributes or qualities in Himself (Q.23/91, 37/180, 10/32),[13] that He has no name (i.e. knowing the name of someone implies knowledge of the "whatness" or the essence of the person), that He is unattainable (Q.37/164),[14] and that humans have no access to Him as He is in Himself. Finally, humans must constantly remember that reflection on God as Necessary Being (or on the Essence of God) is forbidden (Q.2/28, 42/11),[15] and that man can only worship God (Q.51/56).[16]

But then, this is not the only way in which God can be considered in Islam. If it were, the claims of the Muslim mystics of having attained union with Him, and the purpose of *piri-muridi*, would be meaningless, if not false. Their claims are not false, however, because God can be considered as also similar to man. And this similarity, far from contradicting His incomparability and independence, stems from that very same independence and incomparability.[17] God's independence and incomparability also means that He is not limited by non-delimitation: He is free from non-delimitation, and again, free from the freedom from non-delimitation. In other words, Ibn al-Arabi explains, God can delimit (set boundaries and limits) to Himself as and when He pleases;[18] for example, He has obligated Himself to act in accordance with the divine names (or values) of mercy in His dealings with the universe (Q.6/54).[19] Freedom from non-delimitation also means that God cannot be prevented from being delimited in any form by the limitations and boundaries of existent things (or non-necessary beings). Hence, God can choose to impose on Himself the delimitation of any non-necessary being in the universe, i.e. He can become similar to non-necessary being as and when He chooses. And this making Himself similar (or delimiting Himself) does not result from the influence of non-necessary beings (or delimited things), nor is it restricted by them. He is delimited only by Himself and nothing else (Q.15/85).[20] Hence, He remains the Necessary Being in the very act of becoming delimited. Consequently, the delimitation does not take place with respect to His Essence (or with respect to what He is in Himself).[21] The delimitation concerns the divine names which, besides being values, are also the relations or roles that God assumes with respect to non-necessary beings (Q.11/123).[22] It concerns God as a social actor, for example, when a human being acts as father, his essence does not thereby undergo a change. He assumes the limitations and restrictions included in the role while retaining his essence in its immutability. God's delimiting Himself, or God becoming a social actor and thus, similar to us is witnessed to, according to Ibn al-Arabi, in the Quranic verse, "Fulfil My covenant and I will fulfil your covenant" (Q.2/40),[23] and in those verses that describe God in anthropomorphic terms. The Quran describes God as sitting, hearing, seeing, laughing, mocking, etc.[24] Ibn al-Arabi further explains that this aspect of God has been ignored or explained away by the rational philosophers and theologians who cannot reconcile the incomparability and independence of God with Quranic descriptions of similarity because they are contradictory and, hence, mutually exclusive as far as the faculty of reason is concerned. Hence, they prefer to retain one aspect, the incomparability, and to reject the other aspect, His similarity.[25] This refusal to accept God as also similar, al-Arabi says, is equal to rejecting the Quran, Mohammed the Messenger of Islam, and also equal to preventing the mercy of God from reaching them (Q.18/104),[26] i.e. those who reject God as also similar are non-believers. God as similar to us is denoted by the divine names of similarity, seen above as the names of mercy, for example, Gentle, Loving, Forgiving, etc. Moreover, since the names of wrath are supposed to lead to mercy, the names of wrath can also be included among the names of mercy.[27] Hence, God is both incomparable and similar. This is attested to by the Quranic sentence, "Nothing is like Him, and He is the Hearing, the Seeing" (Q.42/11).[28] Thus, true knowledge of God can be attained only by calling Him both, incomparable and similar, and by asserting that He is both, unknowable and knowable. Once this is firmly established in the believer's mind, he can go about accumulating knowledge about God as similar to us. This is the only knowledge that humans and other non-necessary intelligent beings can attain about God since it is only at this level, the level of similarity, that God can be discussed, conversed with and about, and understood. Hence, this knowledge can be considered as the real knowledge of God even though it is only partial and incomplete. But one has always to take the precaution of remembering that God is also incomparable and, hence, essentially unknowable.[29] The Sufis take this precaution by saying, "Everything is He not- He."

This level of similarity is also called the level of divinity (*ilah*).[30] Divinity is that by which God in Himself becomes, or takes on the role of, a god. As divinity or in the role of a god, God is also called Allah and/or the All-merciful.[31] Divinity has also been referred to in mystical thought by other names: Non-delimited Imagination, the Cloud, the Breath of the All-merciful, Universal Reality, Nature, and the Reality of the Perfect Man.[32] The divine names, Allah and All-merciful, however, are the most common ways of referring to God as divinity (or social actor). They refer to the Essence in the same way as father, administrator, and other human roles refer to the essence of human beings. They do not qualify the essence, but the action that is oriented to other social actors. Further, God in Himself is not the institutionalization of the divine names as existent or engendered things are and He does not have their effects and properties as human beings and all other existent things have them.[33] Since the Essence of God is unknowable, the divine names are said to refer to the Essence in a way that is unknown (Q.11/123).[34] As already seen, the divine names, Allah and All-merciful, are equal and interchangeable, and contain all the other divine names, the roots, the supports and realities, and the names of all creatures. Hence, each of them refers to the Essence in the same way as the divine names, Allah and All-merciful, and like them qualify, not the Essence, but the roles that God assumes as a god who is oriented to the universe. The norms of courtesy dictate, however, that only the ninety-nine divine names be ascribed to God, since He has ascribed only these ninety-nine names to Himself.

Ibn al-Arabi says that these divine names, as roles of God, are influenced by the expectations of the creatures in the universe in the same way as the human role of father is influenced by the expectations of a son and/or a daughter, the role of king is influenced by the expectations of subjects, etc.[35] This is also seen in his advice on how to pray. He says, when one is hungry, one should appeal to God in His role as Sustainer with the expectation that He will somehow give one a meal, and not in His role as Allah. The divine name Allah contains all the divine names (or divine roles) that can be divided into negative and positive ones (This distinction has been described above as the names of mercy and the names of wrath). Hence, to address God as Allah is to create confusion that may result in God acting in an unwanted role.[36] God is not independent as divinity, or in the role of a god, or as similar to us. As social actor He is dependent on the expectations of other social actors just as the role of father is dependent on children, the role of king is dependent on subjects, and in such a way that if there were no children, and no subjects there would be no role of father and no role of king. Thus, God as Allah needs the expectations of other social actors. God as Sustainer needs someone or something that expects or demands to be sustained, God as Forgiver needs someone who expects forgiveness, God as En-richer needs someone who expects to be enriched, and so on. Thus, creatures or non-necessary beings can be considered as exercising constraints on the Necessary Being when He acts in the role of a god (cf. Q.3/181, "God is the poor and we are the independent"),[37] and the independent Necessary Being exercises properties and effects in existent things only in His role as a god, or as a social actor.

Hence, it has been said that God cannot exist apart from the universe, and that He exists only through the cosmos while at the same time giving the cosmos its substance. This has also been called the immanence of God.[38] God the social actor, as described so far, is still distant in the sense that one cannot see Him and assess His moods and responses to one's actions. The immanence of God in the Quran implies that He is closer to one than one's very life—"We are nearer to him than the jugular vein" (Q.50/16).[39] Taking this as true, al-Arabi tries to show how God is very close and immediately available to us. He does this by turning to the existent things as the institutionalizations of the divine names. The divine names, besides being values are also the roles of God, the social actor. Hence, all existent things, inasmuch as they institutionalize the divine names and influence other existent things in accordance with the effects and properties of these divine names, can also be considered as the concrete manifestation of the roles of God. The effects of these existent things on and in us can be considered as the responses of God to our actions.[40] The existent things can be considered or looked at from two points of view: They are things in themselves; and as such they have their own properties that result in institutionalizing the divine names in different ways. Secondly, they can be considered as the roles of God; and as such, they are also called the loci of manifestation, and as the loci of divine self-disclosure.[41] They may also be called God, the social actor. But since there are many, perhaps infinite, such existent things in the universe, this type of description of God is problematic in that it appears to make God many and— appears to contradict the Muslim profession of faith that asserts that God is one (cf. Q.51/51).

How can the many be the One, and the One the many? For an answer, Ibn al-Arabi goes back to God as the Necessary Being. As seen above, only the Necessary Being can be said to truly exist. Everything else is potentiality that is still being actualized and, hence, still in the process of finding existence. Ibn al-Arabi reasons: Since only God can be said to truly exist, and since the existence of non-necessary beings cannot come from nothingness, their existence is actually the existence of God.[42] Further, inasmuch as their existence is God's they can be said to exist only through God. Hence, their existence is called the outward radiance or the manifestation of God.[43] Al-Arabi goes on to show how existent things are even dependent on God for their very essences. He begins with a Quranic verse that says, "There is no thing whose treasuries are not with Us" (Q.15/21).[44] The "treasuries" of a thing is interpreted as the essence of a thing. Consequently, the Quranic statement means that the essences of all things are with God. They are found in the knowledge of God (Q.7/89).[45] This may be understood by having recourse to the way in which ideas and images exist in our minds. We have images and ideas of machines like watches, cars, cycles, etc., of buildings like houses, offices, theatres, mosques, temples, churches, etc. These images and ideas are essences to which we can give existence. Further, they may be said to have a type of existence in our minds when compared with those essences that are not in our minds, even though they have no existence of their own. Similarly, the essences of all existent things exist in the knowledge of God. And since God is eternal, the essences of all things are eternal as existing in His knowledge.[46]

These essences are not God, just as the essences in our minds are not ourselves. They have identities of their own, and are possible in the sense that even if they do not have existence, they can be given existence. Giving them existence does not result in their disappearance from the knowledge of God, in the same way as the essences to which we give existence do not disappear from our minds even after they have been given existence.[47] Further, since they have to be given existence, they do not have the power to reject the existence that is given to them. For this reason, they are described as equidistant between existence and non-existence.[48] This state of possibility is a form of existence because in this state the essences have the ability to hear and obey the command "Be" (Q.16/40, 36/82)[49] that brings them into existence. Inasmuch as the essences receive the existence given to them they can also be described as helping God against non-existence (Q.47/7,61/14),[50] even as they seek existence from God. Thus, in the very act of bringing them into existence, God is thought of as acting in accordance with their expectations.[51] Further, these possible things have identities of their own with respect to other possible things in the knowledge of God; for example, the essence of a chair is different from the essence of a car, which in turn is different from the essence of a watch, and so on. They are different because they may be said to have different sets of potentialities and abilities for receiving values that are given to them in the course of bringing them into existence. For instance, human craftsmen may use common values like beauty, utility, comfort, precision, etc. while bringing chairs, cars, watches, etc. into existence. But then the different essences, for example, those of chair, car, watch, will display the properties of these common values in different ways. The different ways in which the common values are displayed may be said to be a function of the properties of the different essences, not of the craftsman. Similarly, when God gives the possible things existence, He gives them the divine names. The different ways in which they display the effects and properties of the divine names may be said to be a function of the properties of their essences, not a function of God. Hence, inasmuch as each

divine name is also a role of God, each existent thing is said to colour
the self-manifestation of God with its own properties and
preparedness to receive the divine names.[52] Then each universal
essence, for example, a chair or a car or a watch has an infinite
number of ways in which it can combine the different values that
are given to it. This results in different kinds of existent things that
come under a common name, for example, chair. Some chairs may
display the effects and properties of the value beauty more prominently than comfort and utility. Another chair may display comfort
prominently, and beauty not at all, and so on. We may consider
each of these specific entities as having specific essences, which are
so many variations of the universal essence.

Each and every universal essence and each and every specific and
individual essence is supposed to exist in the knowledge of God;[53]
for example, human beings by the nature of their common essence
are able to accept all the divine names. But there is an infinite variety
of ways in which the effects and properties of these divine names
may be displayed. One man may display the effects and properties
of gentleness prominently, and the effects and properties of justice
to a very small extent. Another may display justice prominently, and
so on until we come to the one or to the few individuals who display
all the divine names as perfectly balanced with each other. These
are the saints and the prophets.[54] Even among them, one divine
name may be given more prominence than the others, depending
on the situation they found themselves in when they were living.[55]
Not only the universal human being or man, but the essence of each
individual person is in the knowledge of God.[56]

The individual person changes from one moment to the next.
He may now be forgiving, vengeful, and then punishing, and so on.
At each of these moments the individual is supposed to have a
different specific essence that is able to receive a different combination of the divine names. Each of these essences within the
individual person is supposed also to exist in the knowledge of
God.[57] And, inasmuch as each of these specific essences is believed
to receive existence, God can be said to be constantly creating,
or bringing these specific essences into existence.[58] Proof of this

continual creative action of God is seen in the Quranic verse that says, "Each day He is upon some task" (Q.55/29).[59] Each day is interpreted as the indivisible moment (Q.54/50) and not as the 1,000-year day or the 50,000-year day (Q.32/5, 70/40).[60] The divine tasks are interpreted as the essences, states and situations found in engendered existence when understood as the loci of manifestation. This continual creative action of God is also seen to be supported by the *hadith* on transmutation, given above, and another Quranic verse that says, "God created you and what you do" (Q.37/96).[61] Further, since the manifestation of a new aspect of the wider essence of an existent thing, or the manifestation of a new specific essence of an existent thing requires that the previous specific essence disappear, each existent thing in the universe, and indeed the whole universe, is believed to be constantly (or at every moment) in the process of being annihilated and brought into existence (Q.13/39).[62] Hence, what we see at two consecutive moments is not the same existent thing, but similar existent things. And, inasmuch as each existent thing is also a role of God, or a self-disclosure, God is thought to be constantly responding to our actions.[63]

Besides seeing the existent things as roles of God, one can also see the existent things as things in themselves with their own properties. When one sees things in this way, one does not see God as similar. One sees Him as incomparable.[64] Both aspects, God as similar and God as incomparable, may be found in the existent thing at one and the same moment, i.e. the thing is God (in the sense of a divine role) and yet not God.[65] But the believer, or the observer cannot see both aspects at the same instant.[66] He sees the existent thing as either a role of God, or as a thing in itself. Sufis illustrate this by using a mirror: When one sees the reflected image in the mirror, one does not see the mirror, and when one sees the mirror, one does not see the reflected image.[67] Further, depending on what one sees, the existent thing in itself, or the existent thing as a role of God, one sees a different aspect of God. When one sees the existent thing with its properties, one is said to see God as the non-manifest, since this way of looking at the existent thing leads to knowledge

of the essence of the thing. And knowing the essence of an existent
thing is equal to knowing this essence as it exists in the knowledge
of God.[68] Hence, this knowledge can be used to understand how the
properties of the essence colour the manifestation or the role of God
through their different preparednesses to receive the divine names
offered to them;[69] for example, the mirror may reflect the same object
as smaller or bigger, with a big head and a small body, etc.: these
different reflections are a function of the properties of the mirror and
not of the object reflected. Looking at the existent thing in this
way leads to God revealing Himself to the intelligence, or
epistemologically.[70] Whichever way one chooses to look at the
existent thing, one sees God. As the Quran says, "He is the First
and the Last, the Manifest and the Non-manifest" (Q.57/3);[71]
"wherever one turns, there is the face of God" (Q.2/115);[72]
"He is with you wherever you are" (Q.57/4);[73] "Sight perceives
Him not" (Q.6/103);[74] and "Everything is annihilated except His
Face" (Q.6/103).[75]

So far, we have discussed how God is immanent (or discloses
Himself as social actor) in the outside world, i.e. in all existent
things including human beings who are not oneself. Each of them
manifest God as acting in a particular role (the divine name). Ibn
al-Arabi explains that God can also be conceived of as immanent in
one's own self, or as disclosing Himself to us in our own persons.[76]
But before going into this aspect of God's self-disclosure we shall
have to take a brief look at al-Arabi's structure of the universe.
The universe as a whole, according to al-Arabi, can be considered
as an institutionalization of the divine name, Allah.[77] Consequently,
the universe as a whole contains all the roles of God. If one wants
to see God as Allah, one has to see all the different roles of God (or
the effects and properties of all the individual divine names in
everything that exists).[78] Everything (all existent things) exist in
the universe in three ways. Accordingly, the universe has been
divided into three worlds: the first is the spiritual world, where the
angels and other non-necessary beings that have no corporeal
bodies dwell; second comes the imaginal world; and, finally, the
corporeal world, or the world of matter. The corporeal world is

where we dwell, and which we see around us. The imaginal world, as standing between the spiritual and corporeal worlds, separates the two worlds while containing the characteristics of both. This is where spirits, *jinns* and other non-necessary beings, which have no corporeal bodies, can be seen with corporeal bodies. The inhabitants of the spiritual world take forms in this place that we may see them.[79] (It must be remembered here that the term 'place' is used here only analytically and has no particular spatial significance. The three worlds exist within one another. Further, the basic division into three worlds can be further divided to make 8,000 or more worlds.)[80] According to al-Arabi, to see God as Allah one must be able to see His roles in all three worlds, and in the past, present and future— an impossible task.[81]

But the task has been made easier with the creation of another universe, which is much smaller—the microcosm—and mirrors entirely the macrocosm. The microcosm also contains the spiritual, imaginal and corporeal worlds within itself and also in its totality represents God as Allah. This microcosm is the human being.[82] By coming to know oneself in all one's aspects (spiritual, imaginal and corporeal) one comes to know God in His totality as social actor, or as Allah, and, hence, also the macrocosm.[83] This is supposed to be attested to by the Quranic verse that says, "We shall show them signs and horizons in themselves until it is clear that He is the Real" (Q.41/53). Consequently, man in his very own being manifests the roles of God to himself, and in a similar way to the macrocosm. Hence, the Muslim mystics try to see God as interacting with them through themselves, and in the same way as they see Him interacting with them through other existent things.

To summarize: God can be considered in two ways: as God in Himself and as God the social actor. As God in Himself, He is unapproachable and unknowable. But as God the social actor, He is not only knowable but observable in all existent things and even in ourselves as constantly responding to our actions. Nevertheless, even when considering Him in this aspect one has to constantly remind oneself that He is the independent, the incomparable and unknowable. In practice, this assertion helps to make one aware that God, however similar He may appear, is always the Master, never the servant.

NOTES

1. Cf. William C. Chittick, *The Sufi Path of Knowledge*, pp. 77-144; cf. Toshihiko Izutsu, *Sufism and Taoism*, pp. 23-35; cf. Annemarie Schimmel, *Mystical Dimensions of Islam*.
2. Cf. William C. Chittick, *The Sufi Path of Knowledge*.
3. Ibid., pp. 77 ff.; also cf. Toshihiko Izutsu, op. cit., pp. 23-35.
4. Ibid. pp. 31-76.
5. Ibid., p. 58.
6. Ibid.; also cf. William C. Chittick, *The Sufi Path of Love*, p. 46.
7. Ibid.
8. Ibid., p. 145.
9. Ibid.
10. Ibid., pp. 41-86.
11. Ibid., pp. 333 ff.
12. Ibid., pp. 245, 311, 307.
13. Ibid., pp. 71, 75, 95, 376, 380.
14. Ibid., pp. 19, 295, 299.
15. Ibid., pp. 62-74, 155, 165, 233.
16. Ibid., pp. 65, 150, 311-12.
17. Ibid., pp. 79-94.
18. Ibid.
19. Ibid., pp. 110, 214.
20. Ibid., p. 85.
21. Ibid.
22. Ibid., pp. 46, 73, 301, 302, 303.
23. Ibid., p. 110.
24. Ibid., pp. 59-77.
25. Ibid.
26. Ibid., pp. 74, 248, 257, 275.
27. Ibid.
28. Ibid., pp. 73-5, 104, 111-13.
29. Ibid., pp. 59-77.
30. Ibid.
31. Ibid.
32. Ibid., pp. 125-44.
33. Ibid., pp. 33-144.
34. Ibid., pp. 46, 73, 301, 303
35. Ibid., pp. 59 ff.
36. Ibid., pp. 65-7, 91-2.

37. Ibid., p. 318.
38. Ibid.
39. Ibid., pp. 12, 154, 249, 330, 364-5.
40. Ibid., pp. 89 ff.
41. Ibid.
42. Ibid.
43. Ibid.
44. Ibid., pp. 57, 96, 103, 173.
45. Ibid., p. 148.
46. Ibid., pp. 81 ff.
47. Ibid.
48. Ibid.
49. Ibid., pp. 87-102, 128.
50. Ibid., p. 87.
51. Ibid.
52. Ibid.
53. Ibid.
54. Ibid., p. 333 ff.
55. Ibid.
56. Ibid.
57. Ibid., pp. 96 ff.
58. Ibid.
59. Ibid., pp. 18, 38, 96-104.
60. Ibid., p. 98.
61. Ibid., p. 114.
62. Ibid., p. 381.
63. Ibid., pp. 96-111.
64. Ibid., pp. 77-190.
65. Ibid.
66. Ibid.
67. Ibid.
68. Ibid.
69. Ibid.
70. Ibid.
71. Ibid., pp. 67, 89, 102, 115, 125.
72. Ibid., pp. 4, 12, 20, 51, 89, 111.
73. Ibid., pp. 125, 264, 343.
74. Ibid., pp. 89, 223, 368.
75. Ibid., pp. 18, 39, 88, 102, 118, 127, 195.
76. Ibid., pp. 77-190.
77. Ibid., pp. 12 ff.
78. Ibid.
79. Ibid.
80. Ibid.; also cf. Zahurul Hassan Sharib, *The Mystical Philosophy of Khwaja Moinuddin Hassan Chisti*, p. 19.

81. William C. Chittick, op. cit.
82. Ibid., pp. 16 ff.
83. Ibid.
84. Ibid., pp. 43, 92, 164, 245, 359.
85. Ibid., pp. 253-413.

MAN AS A SOCIAL ACTOR

As seen earlier, the universal essence of man, which may be called man, human being, or mankind, is the microcosm because it is able to institutionalize the supreme and all-inclusive divine name, Allah.[1] This belief is an interpretation of Q.2/31 which says, "God taught Adam all the names".[2] The microcosm, cannot however, be considered apart from the macrocosm, since the microcosm is found within the macrocosm.[3] As within the macrocosm, or as an element within it, the microcosm is the most superior element within the macrocosm because no other essence of the existent things in the macrocosm is able to institutionalize the divine name, Allah (or all the divine names).[4] All other beings within the macrocosm, including angels, can institutionalize only some of the divine names.[5] The only other thing that can institutionalize the divine name, Allah (or all the divine names) and, hence, equals the microcosm, is the macrocosm itself.[6] This equality between the microcosm and the macrocosm results in an inverse situation: the microcosm not only is within the macrocosm, but while being within it, contains within itself the whole macrocosm.[7] This is usually expressed in figurative language. The microcosm is said to mirror or reflect the whole macrocosm.[8] But this reflecting of the macrocosm (or the containing of the macrocosm within itself) does not imply that the microcosm contains within itself all the forms of the existent things as they are seen in the macrocosm.[9] For instance, cows, sheep, dogs, goats, buildings, etc. do not exist in the microcosm (or man). Hence, these things are thought to be contained in the macrocosm as universal essences:[10] Since all the essences can be reduced to the different capacities and preparednesses to receive various combinations of, and different effects and properties of the divine names, the microcosm in its ability to receive all the divine names in all their various combinations, and all their effects and properties, may be said to contain all the existent things in the macrocosm or universe.[11] Further, all the existent things in the macrocosm exist in either the spiritual, the imaginal, or the corporeal world, and all these three worlds, as seen before, are also present in the microcosm.[12] Then the microcosm has all the basic elements, hot, cold, dry, and wet which in various combinations are a very important factor in concrete existence within the three worlds of the macrocosm.[13] Hence, the microcosm, while being an element of the macrocosm, is also a kind of essence of the macrocosm.[14] As essence of the macrocosm, it may be considered to exist in the knowledge of God prior to the macrocosm.[15] And as existing in the knowledge of God who is eternal, it is also considered to be eternal.[16] Thus, the microcosm, besides being the most superior essence within the macrocosm, is also said to be the epitome of the universe,[17] the spirit of the world of Being,[18] and the gathering up of all the elements manifest in the universe.[19]

So far, the divine names have been considered as values. The divine names, as seen earlier, are also the roles of God the social actor. Since the microcosm and the macrocosm institutionalize the supreme and all-comprehensive divine name "Allah", it is said that both manifest God the social actor fully (or they manifest Him in all His roles).[20] Hence, the macrocosm and also the microcosm can be called God the social actor. Since roles need their objects (just as father needs children and king needs subjects)[21] and since a social actor, to be considered as a social actor,[22] needs another (or the other) social actor, the microcosm as God the social actor and the macrocosm as God the social actor need another (or the other) social actor and objects to receive their roles. The macrocosm is the other social actor when the microcosm is considered as God the social actor; and the microcosm is the other social actor when the macrocosm is considered as God the social actor. The macrocosm is that which receives the roles when exercised by the microcosm, and the microcosm is that which receives the roles when exercised by the macrocosm.[23] Since the macrocosm is dispersed over vast spaces and large spans of time, however, and spread over basically three worlds, the macrocosm can never be fully seen by existing man.[24] To see the macrocosm, man has to look into himself or at his own universal essence (the microcosm).[25] That is why, when speaking of God as

Allah the macrocosm is usually seen as exercising only the individual roles of God.[26] The microcosm, on the other hand, as Allah, or as containing all the roles of God the social actor, is displayed in collected form in each of its existent forms, the individually existing human persons.[27] Thus, we usually find statements that the microcosm is the fulness of God's orientation to the macrocosm[28]—and as such, the microcosm is said to be the divine consciousness that manifests God to Himself as He is in His state of absolute Unity.[29] The microcosm is not God, Necessary Being: it appears, in the form of Allah and inversely, Allah appears in the form of the microcosm or man.[30] In more figurative language, God becomes the hearing, the seeing, the hands, and the feet of the microcosm; and inversely, the microcosm becomes the seeing, the hearing, the hands and feet of God.[31] Consequently, it is said that the microcosm (as God the social actor) is the reason for the creation of the macrocosm.[32] Also, the microcosm is that through which the universe is maintained and that to which the universe tends.[33]

The microcosm, though closely associated with God, is not God. Of itself it is not Allah, or the Necessary Being. The divine name "Allah" does not refer to the microcosm in the same way as it refers to God in Himself but refers to it in two other ways: (a) as receiving the effects and properties of the supreme divine name and all the other divine names; and (b) as manifesting God the social actor (or the effects and properties of all the divine names) to the macrocosm.[34] In the first instance, the microcosm is the slave or the servant that receives everything because it has nothing of its own except poverty[35] (i.e. possibility, or the ability to receive). And since it has nothing but the ability to receive, it cannot reject what is given to it.[36] It has no option but to be perfectly content with what it receives. It may receive the effects and properties of the names of wrath; or it may receive the names of mercy. In either case, it must remain perfectly content. Having no will of its own it is entirely dependent on the will of God, who decides what to give.[37] In the second instance, the microcosm is the Master. It is God the social actor who manifests Himself to the macrocosm and affects its essences in accordance with the effects and properties of the divine names. Here, the macrocosm is the slave that has nothing in itself except poverty (i.e. the ability to receive the effects and properties of the divine names). Since the microcosm gives what it receives, and gives everything in the same way as it receives what it receives with its own will, its giving to the macrocosm can be considered as God Himself giving to the macrocosm.[38] Further, since God has committed Himself to act in accordance with mercy, the names of wrath can be considered to be given only to the extent (or only in such a way) that they lead to mercy.[39] The microcosm which gives in this way, is called the vice-regent that protects the treasures of the macrocosm or the cosmos (i.e. it is seen as preventing the names of wrath from dominating over the names of mercy, thus avoiding chaos and keeping the world in existence).[40] Most important here is the dual aspect of the microcosm: it is poor or the slave in its relationship with God; and the Master and independent, or God the social actor, in its relationship with the macrocosm or the universe. Further, even as Master it is servant, because it is not giving of itself, but through itself.

This microcosm, which is a universal essence, is also called the Perfect Man or the Universal Man.[41] The Perfect Man (as the microcosm) is said always to act as a servant with respect to God, and as Master with respect to the macrocosm.[42] He is always aware of his poverty or servanthood even when acting as Master towards the macrocosm (i.e. he is always aware of receiving everything from God, of giving only what God gives and as God gives it to him).[43] Inasmuch as he is always aware of his servanthood, he is said to know God:[44] he knows how God is oriented to him through the divine names and how he interacts with God in terms of these divine names (he always receives the effects and properties of the divine names). And inasmuch as he is Master, he is aware of how God is oriented towards the macrocosm or the world through himself. He is also aware of the way in which the macrocosm interacts with God in terms of these divine names, and of the ways in which the existent things in the cosmos interact with each other and manifest God to each other and to himself in terms of these divine names. Hence, he is said to be all-knowing, or to have perfect knowledge.[45] Since this knowledge also includes acting in accordance with it, the Perfect or

Universal Man (or the microcosm) is also the perfect social actor with
respect to God, on the one hand, and with respect to the macrocosm
on the other. The Perfect Man is a perfect social actor because he
is always aware of being servant (of receiving everything from God),
and aware of manifesting only God (he does not attribute the effects
and properties of the divine names to himself). He, thus, displays
complete lack of self-will.[46]

This perfect social actor (or the Perfect Man, the Universal Man,
the microcosm, or Allah) is also called the reality of Mohammed. Ibn
al-Arabi uses *hadiths* and a Quranic verse to justify this claim. In one
a *hadith* Mohammed is believed to have said about himself, "I was a
prophet even when Adam was between clay and water";[47] another,
Mohammed says, "The first thing that God created was my light".[48]
The Quranic verse about Mohammed (Q.8/17) says, "thou were
not the one who threw when thou threwest, but God it was who
really threw".[49] In the Nizamuddin Dargah, the *pirs* and *murids*
express this belief in other ways: One *murid* said,

> There is no difference between Mohammed, the Prophet and
> God. This is because God brought forth the Prophet from His
> own Light. The Prophet and God are one. They are different
> only in the eyes of the world. For instance, Mohammed once
> asked this question of Hazrat Gabriel: From where do you get
> the messages that you come and give me? Gabriel answered, "I
> hear God giving me those messages from behind a curtain."
> Mohammed asked, "Have you ever seen God talking to you?"
> Gabriel replied, "I have never seen God talking to me. He
> always talks to me from behind that curtain." Mohammed
> ordered the angel Gabriel to go and lift the curtain and see for
> himself who it was that was talking to him. Gabriel protested
> saying, "If I do that, my feet will get burnt". Mohammed
> repeated, "I order you to lift the curtain and take a look". So
> Gabriel went and did as Mohammed ordered. Now, at the
> moment when he left Mohammed, Mohammed was tying his
> turban around his head. When Gabriel lifted the curtain with
> great fear and trembling, lo and behold, he saw Mohammed

tying his turban around his head. Then Mohammed said to
Gabriel, "If I give you permission you can enter my house. But
if you enter my house without permission, you will get burnt or
you will be beaten because others will think that you are a
robber." Heaven is Mohammed's house. That was why he
could tell the angel Gabriel to lift the curtain and enter. Ali, the
son-in-law of the Prophet, himself said that God was roaming in
Mecca for 40 years but no one recognized Him. He was
speaking about Mohammed. Look at the whole thing from the
point of value. Mohammed was made the *imam* (the leader) of
the prophets. One hundred and twenty-four lakh prophets
came before him. They were made messengers. But why did
Mohammed come in the end if he is the greatest of the prophets?
He should have come at the beginning, if he is the greatest of the
prophets. The meaning of what I have said is that Mohammed
was made in the form of God. That is why he is the *imam* of the
prophets. What is God? God is Light, which no one can
understand. And a bad man cannot even look at this light. If he
does, he will go blind. Coming back to what happened to the
angel Gabriel, he saw Mohammed the Prophet down on earth,
and then he saw him in heaven behind the curtain performing
the same action. So what happened to Gabriel? He realized that
Mohammed and God are one, that Mohammed himself is God.
God made him from His own Light.

A *pir* said,

God divided His Light into two equal parts. He divided Himself
into two parts, and He kept the other part before Himself and
began to look at it, and continued to look at it for 70,000 years.
This other part was the light of Mohammed. Then He divided
that light that was before Him into two equal parts. In a similar
fashion He continued to divide one of the resulting halves into
two halves until He got an infinitely small half. Then He took
this infinitely small half and made the world and all that you see
in it, the stars, the sun, the sky, the earth. But after God made

all these things, He found that He was still alone. He used to
continue looking at the light that He had taken out of Himself
(at Mohammed). The angels, Izrafeel, Michael, Israel, Israfil,
Gabriel were all made by God. And He started looking at them.
He made all these things, but then who would want all these
things, who would eat what He had made? Hence, He took
some of Mohammed's light and made a *putla* (form). You have
a body, and I have a body. This body is made of mud. It has five
things in it: air, water, mud, wood and fire. Out of the wood
God made the bones, with the water He moulded the mud, and
out of the water He made the blood. The *putla* was ready. Then
He put air into it. The air is the spirit. But then, God found that
the air would not go into the *putla* because it is dark within us—
completely black. So He took the light of Mohammed. Then
He took out a little from it and put that little bit on the head of
the *putla* and ordered it to go within. Then He was happy. Then
God made one lakh and fourteen thousand prophets. Then He
put a ban on any prophet coming after Mohammed. Mohammed
went directly to God. The meaning of this is that he had a
meeting with God. Mohammed was resting in the house of
Mome Hanni at that time. He had covered his head with a sheet.
On seeing this Allah got worried. "What is happening to him?"
He began to wonder. God loved Mohammed. Anyone who
loves begins to smell like scent. Love and scent go together and
cannot be separated. On seeing Mohammed with a sheet over
his head, Allah got worried and called to Mohammed. And in
front of the angel Gabriel, He kissed Mohammed on the
forehead and on his eyes. Now Gabriel is by nature cold. So
when God told him to bring Mohammed by carrying him on his
back, Gabriel refused saying, "I will get burnt." So Mohammed
went to Allah on a flying horse. But before flying to heaven the
flying horse took him to a graveyard. And when he landed in
the graveyard, all the dead people rose from their graves, saluted
Mohammed, became Muslims and prayed the *namaz*. Then the
flying horse took him through the seven heavens until he met
God.

Another *pir* said,

> The difference between Mohammed and God is the letter *meem*.
> God's name is Ahad. And Mohammed's name is Ahmad. There
> is the curtain of *meem* between them. Otherwise both are the
> same. Mohammed has come from the Light. And the first thing
> that Allah did was to take out some Light from Himself. He
> made a picture of Himself and started looking at it. He fell in love
> with it. It is a question of the heart. This picture was Mohammed.
> But He sent him after all the prophets.

Still another *pir* said,

> Mohammed is greater than Allah. What can one get from Allah?
> Nothing. One can get what one wants only if one goes to
> Mohammed. Mohammed and Allah are one. But there is a
> difference between them. The difference is the letter *meem*.
> From this *meem* has come the world and all that you see around
> you. If we Muslims ask of Allah we will get nothing from Him.
> We will get what we ask for only if we ask of Mohammed. Allah
> Himself has said, "Those who ask of Me cannot be Muslims until
> and unless they accept Mohammed." And if one is not a Muslim
> then one will get nothing. Further, Allah says, "If you worship
> Me, but do not remember Mohammed, I will give you noth-
> ing." Everything comes from Mohammed. From the letter *alif*
> comes Allah, and from the letter *meem* comes Mohammed. If
> you do not remember Mohammed, your prayers will not be
> answered. But if you remember Mohammed, then Allah will
> have to listen to your prayers. There is a curtain made of very
> fine cloth between them. Allah sits on one side of the curtain and
> Mohammed on the other. If you remember Allah only, then
> Mohammed knows, and none of the things you ask for will be
> granted. But if you remember Mohammed, and even if you do
> not remember Allah, then Mohammed will tell Allah, "You
> have to give this person what he asks for. So what if he has not

remembered you! After all, when he remembers me, he
remembers you also." So Mohammed and Allah are one. They
are sitting together. The curtain between them is the letter
meem. If you pray directly to God, God will not care for your
prayers. But if you pray to Mohammed, then Allah will give you
what you ask for immediately. No one can go directly to God,
not even the greatest *pir*. He too has to go to God through
Mohammed. And only Mohammed can take one's prayer to
Allah. Without Mohammed nothing ever happens.

A *murid* in answer to my question, whether Mohammed is greater
than Allah, said,

Mohammed is not greater than Allah. Whoever told you this
told you something wrong. See, it is like this. Allah has kept
nothing with Himself. He has given everything to Mohammed.
And what did Mohammed do? He gave everything to Ali. Then
what did Allah do? He robbed back all that He had given to
Mohammed and all that Mohammed had given to Ali. And then
He gave it to Moinuddin Chisti. Moinuddin Chisti brought it
to Ajmer. Then Allah came and again took away all that He had
given to Moinuddin Chisti.

Another *pir* said,

Allah is with me, and I am in Allah. Mohammed is in me and
I am Mohammed. Every man is Allah. The greatest thing is to
know this.

A *murid* kept on reiterating,

The *pir* takes his *murid* to his *pir*. Then his *pir* takes him to his
own *pir*, and so on until the *murid* is taken to Ali. And Ali takes
the *murid* to Mohammed. And when the *murid* has reached
Mohammed, he has reached Allah. What more is there to gain?
He has gained everything.

To summarize: The reality of Mohammed, inasmuch as it is considered or believed to be the microcosm (or the Perfect Man, the Universal Man, or Allah) is believed to be the divine consciousness that God manifests to Himself in His state of absolute Unity,[50] the essence of the universe,[51] the unifying principle of the cosmos,[52] the active principle on which depends the existence of all other universal essences,[53] the hearing, seeing, hands and feet of God, and finally, the universal essence of each and every existing human being.[54] It stands before God as the servant who receives from God; and when it stands before the cosmos, it stands as the Master, or as God's orientation to the universe since it does not mix God's giving of Himself (God as social actor and not as God in Himself) with its own will.

All men have this universal essence, whether it is called the microcosm, the Perfect Man, the Universal Man, the Reality of Mohammed, or Allah. Hence, it is said that all men are endowed with the same ontological comprehensiveness.[55] Not all men are, however, aware or conscious of this ontological comprehensiveness to the same extent. The extent of this consciousness depends on their individual capacities and preparedness.[56] Different levels of consciousness result in different kinds of men.[57]

At the highest level are the perfect men who are fully conscious of their ontological comprehensiveness.[58] They are like polished mirrors.[59] Their minds have an other-worldly structure, and can see through existent things, or grasp the underlying reality (or meaning) of all existent things[60] (i.e. they see all existent things as the effects and properties of the divine names and also as the roles of God). They are people who know God through unveiling or immediate tasting and not through reason[61] (i.e. they know God through direct experience and not theoretically). Also they are people with pure minds and hearts, free from bodily or this-worldly desires and are servants of God[62] (i.e. they have no will of their own). The most general attribute of this category of men is sainthood.[63] Sainthood implies ultimate knowledge about God, the world, and the relationship between God and the world.[64] This knowledge further implies that they have gone through the process of self-annihilation (*fana* and baqa), which results in giving up self-will so that one wills only what God wills.[65] They can say and believe with a clear conscience that they manifest God (even though God is the One, the Incomprehensible) and not themselves; and also say that all phenomena are the self-manifestation of God.[66] This is also called the consciousness of the essential oneness of Being.[67]

Perfect men have what is called *himmah*.[68] *Himmah* is a kind of magical power. It is the ability to display the effects and properties of the divine name "Free Disposal", and also the divine names "All-powerful" and "All-knowing".[69] It is believed that the Quran attests to the existence of this power in men, especially in the perfect men, in the verse (Q.31/20) that says, "And We have subjugated to you all that are in heaven and in earth."[70] *Himmah* is of two kinds. The superior kind consists in just commanding a thing to be for it to come into existence. Solomon alone had this power.[71] The other kind of *himmah* is more common and possessed by all the prophets, saints and perfect men.[72] This common *himmah* consists in concentrating on an essence, or on the image of a thing in one's mind. This concentration is believed to bring about the existence of the thing in the outside world. This power is also shared by imperfect men to a limited degree in that they too can imagine and concentrate on the images in their minds. But unlike the perfect men, they cannot being about the existence of the thing through mere concentration because they are not yet aware of being Allah (or they are not aware of their ontological comprehensiveness). Even perfect men can keep the thing in existence only as long as they concentrate on it. if the concentration wavers, the thing disappears.[73] But then—there are different levels of consciousness (also called presences)—the presence of the sense, the presence of the image-exemplars, the presence of the spirits, the presence of the intellect, and the presence of the essence. A perfect man who is more perfect than other perfect men can retain the thing in existence by retaining awareness of it on any one of the levels of consciousness.[74]

The dynamics of this activity is explained by referring to the individual essences within the wider individual essences as they exist in the knowledge of God, the continuous creative activity of God, and the universal essence of time.[75] God, as seen earlier, is constantly in the process of bringing these individual essences within the larger individual essences into existence. Consequently, what we see at two consecutive moments is not the same thing, but two similar things, not the same person, but two similar persons These individual essences can be brought into existence only when (or only at that moment of time when) they are ready to receive the effects and properties of the divine names. Hence, they exercise restraints on God through their preparedness.[76] The perfect man, by virtue of knowing the Perfect Man (the universal essence of man, or the microcosm) which is also the essence of the macrocosm, knows all the individual essences.[77] Further, he knows the continuous creative activity of God and the exact moment when the individual essences are prepared to receive the effects and properties of the divine names. In other words, he knows what God is going to do and can do at the next moment (i.e. there are also essences that are prepared for existence, or prepared to receive the effects and properties of the divine names, but which are not given existence).[78] All that the perfect man does when exercising *himmah* is to influence God to make the thing appear in another place rather than at the place where it habitually comes into existence, or he influences God to make an essence that normally does not receive existence, existent.[79] This magical power is, thus, a participation in the continuous creative activity of God.[80] Since the perfect man has no will of his own, he cannot contradict the will of God while exercising *himmah*, though he may appear to do so in the eyes of the world. By making a thing appear in the corporeal world he is actually doing the will of God and, acting under this influence. Hence, *himmah* does not change the fate of existent things: it only appears to do so. And in the final analysis *himmah* is useless as a means of correcting the state of the world, or as a means of overcoming what has been foreordained or predestined.[81]

At the lowest level of the consciousness of ontological comprehensiveness—the other pole of this continuum—are persons who are said to be completely opaque: they are not at all aware of their ontological comprehensiveness.[82] As opposites of the perfect men,

they are people whose minds have a worldly structure. They are
deeply involved with bodily attachments, and are completely under
the sway of desire. They depend on reason in order to know God,
to such an extent that they are consciously the slaves of reason and
not of God.   They do not accept anything as true unless it is
acceptable to reason and declare as absurd and impossible mystical
truths. For instance, they would describe as absurd the Quranic verse
that says about Mohammed, "thou were not the one who threw
when thou threwest, but God it was who really threw" (Q.8/17).[83]

In between the two extremes, of perfect men and opaque
persons are the people of faith.[84] They do not understand the imagery
given by the prophets (i.e. they do not know how the existent things,
which includes themselves, institutionalize and interact in terms of
the values, the divine names, nor do they know of the ways in which
the existent things are the roles of God, or manifest God).   The
deeper significance of the message of the prophets escapes them. But
they do not dare to contradict the given imagery, and hence, believe
in it blindly; for example they believe that God threw—when—
infact Mohammed threw—even though they do not know how
God can throw.[85]

Human beings differ, as stated earlier, on account of the different
degrees of awareness of ontological comprehensiveness, which again
is the result of different capacities or preparednesses. This preparedness does not concern existence, since ontological comprehensiveness belongs to all men in equal measure.[86] It concerns awareness or
knowledge of this ontological comprehensiveness. Hence, it may be
said that the difference between human beings results from the
different abilities or inabilities for being aware of personal servanthood
or poverty before God, and from different abilities for being aware
of the ways in which one manifests God. The levels of inability to
know one's ontological comprehensiveness result from a particular
way of exercising the faculty of reason.[87] Human reason demonstrates
to the individual that he is master of all that he surveys, that he can
be the author, sustainer and destroyer of all the things in this world,
and that the effects and properties of the divine names are his own.
In other words, reason demonstrates that man is everything and that

God is nothing.[88] Further, when reason concentrates on God, it is able to understand only His incomparability and independence. Consequently, it rejects God's similarity and nearness and, thus, prevents actual contact with Him, i.e. God becomes something that is too far away to really concern man.[89] Thus, reason results in the ignorance of God. This ignorance of God, which demonstrates itself in man's attributing to himself what he should be attributing to God, is called the ego.[90] The ego, besides being a false picture of the nature of things, is also the veil that hides God from man.[91] Having this false picture of the nature of things, or having an ego is a terrible state of affairs because, besides hiding God from oneself, it results in damnation.[92] Damnation cannot be avoided as long as one believes in life after death because reason and the ego do not give man the power to postpone death indefinitely. In the measure that one believes that one's fate after death depends on one's relationship with God, that this relationship is assessed by how well one follows God's supreme command to know Him (i.e. the term 'worship' in Q.51/56, " I created the *jinn* and mankind only to worship Me", has been traditionally interpreted as knowledge),[93] and to the extent that one believes that, not God in Himself, but God as social actor (or God as similar to us) can be known, salvation or damnation after death depends on knowing Him as social actor and immediately available to oneself.[94] Knowledge of God the social actor implies coming to know how one receives the effects and properties of the divine names, how one manifests God to others through their effects and properties, and how other existent things institutionalize the divine names and manifest God to oneself and to each other. This knowledge (or awareness) cannot be attained as long as one has the ego, which prevents one from attributing anything to God.[95]

Hence, great importance is attached to giving up the ego. The process of giving up the ego is called the spiritual path, which is essentially a process of annihilation and finding (self-subsistence), usually called *fana* and *baqa*.[96] This process has to be undergone many times, or at each station of the spiritual path. It can also be considered apart from the stations.[97] *Fana* or annihilation consists of two stages. The first stage is explained as a slow process of giving up one's attributes and taking on the attributes of God.[98] Since there is nothing in existence that is not the effects and properties of the divine names, all human attributes are the effects and properties of the divine names. Giving up the ego is equal to giving up the false awareness of possessing attributes (or of being Master); and taking on the attributes of God is equal to being aware that, far from being master (or possessing attributes), one is actually servant (or receiving and only manifesting attributes that are not one's own, but God's). A person tries to begin experiencing this by displaying the attributes (or the effects and properties) of servanthood, and not the effects and properties of the names of Majesty, or Master, which are also seen as the names of wrath because so far they have been exercised as belonging to oneself, and when exercised thus, lead to damnation. Displaying the attributes of servanthood, which is equal to taking on the attributes of God, is equal to trying to manifest the effects and properties of the names of mercy, like gentleness, forgiveness, poverty, obedience, repentance, etc.[99]

When one is successful in this endeavour, one moves on to the next stage of annihilation, called the annihilation of one's own essence in the Essence of God.[100] Here the person tries to come to the realization that God alone truly exists. Everything else, or everything that is not God, including oneself, is imaginary and essentially non-existent.[101] As non-existent imagery, all existent things, including oneself, are found in the knowledge of God as essences that have to be continually given existence with the aid of the divine names: hence the realization that all existent things possess nothing of their own, except the ability to receive (or poverty); and even in the receiving, they cannot reject the effects and properties of the divine names and, hence, have no will of their own. This realization results in the complete annihilation of the ego[102] and the person moves on to the stage of *baqa*, or self-subsistence. In this stage of *baqa* the person follows a direction opposite to that of his earlier state.[103] He regains himself, in the sense that he again begins to recognize in himself all the attributes of majesty that he had earlier negated from himself. But he takes them up as a servant, as one who receives the effects and properties of the divine names. And when displaying them, he knows that they manifest God in His orientation to the universe, and not himself. As he is able to see this process in himself, he is also able to see it in all the other creatures. Further, since he has no will of his own but wills only what God wills, he has become a perfect man, or the perfect social actor with respect to God and the universe.[104] He has become the hearing, seeing, hands and feet of God and God has become his hearing, seeing, hands and feet.[105] At this stage he is constantly aware of acting in two ways: "you are highest and so is God with you" (Q.42/35), and "Praise the name of the Lord, the Highest" Q.87/1),[106] i.e. as master and as servant.

This process of annihilation, or of giving up the ego may be described in another way: When contrasted with the Perfect Man, who has no ego, the person with ego is considered to be at the lowest level of creation. He is lower than the animals, the plants and inanimate matter. As he gives up his ego, he climbs to the level of animal, which is believed to have less of an ego than man. Then he ascends to the level of plant, which is believed to have less of an ego than animal. And finally, he reaches the level of inanimate matter, which is the highest level because inanimate matter has absolutely no ego, or no will and desire of its own, and with perfect contentment allows itself to be moulded and used by another as and how the other wishes.[107]

To summarize: Man as the perfect social actor is represented by the concept of the Perfect Man. This concept is also called by other names: the Universal Man, the microcosm, the Reality of Mohammed, and Allah. The concept of the perfect social actor is attainable by existing men who are then called perfect men, prophets, and saints. An existing perfect man has no ego, or personal will or desire of his own. Consequently, he is constantly aware of receiving everything from God at every moment (i.e. he is aware of his servanthood), and also aware of constantly manifesting God the social actor to others (i.e. he is aware of being Master, without allowing this knowledge to interfere with his awareness of his servanthood). He is also aware of the ways in which all existent things receive the effects and properties of the divine names and manifest God to each other and to himself. Finally, since he has no will of his own, but wills only what God wills, besides being the hearing, seeing, hands and feet of God, and besides God being his hearing, seeing, hands and feet, he is perfectly content with his concrete situation, whatever that might involve—riches or poverty, honour or insults, being well fed or being hungry, etc. and even paradise or hell.[108] He also follows the external law, the *sharia*.[109] Such a person be easily recognized, and is described as hidden while existing in this world.[110] This stage is the highest in Muslim mysticism. It is the much sought after union with God.

Freedom, then, is not the ability to take away all the obstacles that prevent one from exercising one's own will. Freedom is the ability to remove all the obstacles, especially one's ego, that prevent one from doing the will of God, or that prevent one from being aware of how one receives everything from God and manifests only Him. Punishment is due not to the displaying of the effects and properties of the divine names, be they the names of mercy or the names of wrath.[111] Punishment is due to the lack of constant awareness that one is nothing but servant since one is only an institutionalization of the divine names, and a locus of the manifestation of God the social actor at every moment of one's existence.[112]

NOTES

1. William C. Chittick, *The Sufi Path of Knowledge*, pp. 12-17; also cf. Toshihiko Izutsu, *Sufism and Taoism,* pp. 218-43; also cf. Abd al- Karim al Jili, *Universal Man*, Titus Burckhardt and Angela Culee-Seymour (tr.), (Beshara Publications, Paris, 1983).
2. Cf. Toshihiko Izutsu, *Sufism and Taoism*, p. 226.
3. Ibid., pp. 218-24; also cf. William C. Chittick, *The Sufi Path of Knowledge*, pp. 12-17.
4. Ibid.
5. Cf. Toshihiko Izutsu, op. cit., pp. 229-30.
6. Cf. William C. Chittick, *The Sufi Path of Knowledge*, pp. 12-17.
7. Cf. Toshihiko Izutsu, op. cit.; pp. 218-43, also cf. William C. Chittick, *The Sufi Path of Knowledge*.
8. Ibid.
9. Cf. Toshihiko Izutsu, op. cit., pp. 218-34.
10. Ibid.
11. Ibid.

12. Cf. William C. Chittick, *The Sufi Path of Knowledge*, pp. 12-17.

13. Shaykh Hakim Moinuddin Chisti, *The Book of Sufi Healing*.

14. Toshihiko Izutsu, op. cit., pp. 224-34; also cf. William C. Chittick, *The Sufi Path of Knowledge*, pp. 12-7.

15. Toshihiko Izutsu, ibid.

16. Ibid.

17. Ibid.

18. Ibid.

19. Ibid.

20. Ibid., pp. 218-34; also cf. William C. Chittick, *The Sufi Path of Knowledge*, pp. 12-17

21. Cf. William C. Chittick, ibid., pp. 35 ff.

22. Cf. Bryan S. Turner, *Weber and Islam*, pp. 39-55

23. Cf. William C. Chittick, *The Sufi Path of Knowledge*.

24. Ibid.

25. Ibid.

26. Ibid.

27. Toshihiko Izutsu, op. cit., pp. 224 ff.

28. Ibid.

29. Ibid.

30. Ibid.

31. Ibid.

32. Ibid.

33. Ibid.

34. William C. Chittick, *The Sufi Path of Knowledge*, pp. 77-190.

35. Ibid.

36. Ibid.

37. Toshihiko Izutsu, op. cit., pp. 218-46.

38. Ibid.

39. Cf. William C. Chittick, *The Sufi Path of Knowledge*, pp. 110, 214.

40. Toshihiko Izutsu, op. cit., pp. 234-35.

41. Ibid., pp. 218-48; cf. also William C. Chittick, *The Sufi Path of Knowledge*; also cf. Abd al-Karim al-Jili, *Universal Man*.

42. William C. Chittick., *The Sufi Path of Knowledge*, pp. 277-8, 321-4, 319, 368-9, 327, 329.

43. Ibid.

44. Toshihiko Izutsu, op. cit., pp. 218-46,

45. Ibid.

46. Ibid., also cf. William C. Chittick, *The Sufi Path of Knowledge*, pp. 366-9.

47. Toshihiko Izutsu, ibid.

48. Ibid.

49. Ibid.

50. Ibid., pp. 236-8.

51. Ibid.

52. Ibid.

53. Ibid.
54. Ibid.
55. Ibid., p. 247.
56. Ibid.
57. Ibid.
58. Ibid., pp. 263-74.
59. Ibid.
60. Ibid.
61. Ibid.
62. Ibid.
63. Ibid.
64. Ibid. pp. 247-62.
65. Ibid.
66. Ibid.
67. Ibid., pp. 275-82.
68. Ibid.; also cf. William C. Chittick, *The Sufi Path of Knowledge*, pp. 104, 218, 279, 276.
69. Toshihiko Izutsu, ibid.
70. Ibid.
71. Ibid.
72. Ibid.
73. Ibid.
74. William C. Chittick, *The Sufi Path of Knowledge*.
75. Ibid.
76. Ibid.
77. Ibid.
78. Ibid.
79. Toshihiko Izutsu, op. cit., pp. 275-82.
80. Ibid.
81. Ibid., pp. 247-61.
82. Ibid.
83. Ibid.
84. Ibid.
85. Ibid.
86. Ibid.
87. Ibid.
88. Cf. William C. Chittick, *The Sufi Path of Knowledge*, pp. 145-90.
89. Toshihiko Izutsu, op. cit., pp. 247-61.
90. Ibid.
91. Ibid.
92. Cf. William C. Chittick, *The Sufi Path of Knowledge*, pp. 145-56.
93. Cf. Toshihiko Izutsu, op. cit., pp. 247-61.
94. Ibid.
95. Ibid.
96. William C. Chittick, *The Sufi Path of Knowledge*, pp. 219-20, 253-333.

97. Cf. Toshihiko Izutsu, op. cit., 247–61.
98. Ibid.
99. Ibid.
100. Ibid.
101. Ibid.
102. Ibid.
103. Ibid.
104. Ibid.
105. Ibid., pp. 240, 241.
106. Ibid.; also cf. K. Khosla, *The Sufism of Rumi.*
107. Cf. William C. Chittick, *The Sufi Path of Knowledge,* pp. 364–81.
108. Ibid., pp. 289–333.
109. Ibid. pp. 364–81.
110. Ibid. pp. 253–333.
111. Ibid.
112. Ibid.

PIRI-MURIDI

All things have to return to God in the sense that all living existent things die and disappear (Things that are considered to be inanimate are also believed to have life, but to such an inferior degree that it cannot be recognized as such by the normal run of men).[1] As seen earlier while discussing the continuous creative activity of God, this process of returning to God takes place at every moment for all existent things. Here, however, we are more interested in the larger going back to God, the death of the living organism—"O man, you are laboring towards your Lord laboriously and you will encounter Him!" (Q.84/6).[2] When going back to God, all existent things, except man and *jinn*, go back in the same way as they came into this world. Even angels will go back in this way (Q.37/146 says about them, "None of us there is but has a known station").[3] Going back to God is interpreted as meeting God in the after life in one or more of His social roles (the divine names) and experiencing their effects and properties.[4] It is further believed that the role of God that the existent thing will encounter when it returns to Him will be the same as the one it displayed while in this world—"Whithersoever you turn, there is the Face of God" (Q.2/115).[5] Since all existent things, except man, display God in only one or a few of His roles (or in the effects and properties of one or a few of the divine names), and since they do not have an ego (or the capacity to attribute to themselves the effects and properties of the divine names or the roles of God), they are said to be constantly aware of being the loci of manifestation.[6] Consequently, it may be said that they know the role in which God manifests Himself to them now, and the role in which He will appear to them when they return to Him.[7] With man, it is different. Man, unlike any other existent thing in the universe, has the ability to institutionalize all the divine names, or the ability to manifest God in all His roles, or in His fulness as social actor. This poses no problem for the perfect men who have no ego and, hence, are constantly aware of manifesting God in all His roles at each successive moment of their lives.[8] They know that they will encounter God as Allah, which besides being God the social actor in His fulness, is also the locus of the perfect balancing of all the divine names and roles as All-merciful.[9] But as seen earlier, one has to become a perfect man by going through the process of annihilation and self-subsistence (*fana* and *baqa*). This is because man, unlike other existent things, possesses and habitually exercises the ability of attributing the roles of God and the effects and properties of the divine names to himself. He has an ego. Ego has also been called by other names—the evil or base *nafs* (or soul), the dulled intelligence, the dirty or impure heart, the rusty or dirty mirror, and the independence of man.[10] This ego results in not only a false picture of the universe and himself (i.e. the inability to see the universe as the effects and properties of the divine names), but also in ignorance of God. Hence, men inasmuch as they possess egos (or are imperfect), do not know God as constantly manifest in themselves and in other existent things. They do not know what divine role they manifest now, nor the divine role they will encounter at death. But to the believer this divine role is of supreme importance because it determines his fate in the after-life. As seen earlier, the ninety-nine divine names can be divided into the names of mercy and the names of wrath, and also into the roles of mercy and the roles of wrath. God's role of mercy is manifest in the after-life in paradise with its felicity. And the role of wrath is manifest in hell with all its burning, punishment and chastisement.[11] Consequently, to encounter God the social actor at death is to experience paradise or hell, which is also called the reward and the punishment.

Reward or punishment for one's actions implies responsibility, and responsibility implies freedom. As seen earlier, freedom concerns the ability to take away all the obstacles, especially one's ego, that prevent one from seeing oneself as constantly manifesting God the social actor (or that prevent one from being constantly aware of one's servanthood). It does not concern the ability to take away all the obstacles that prevent one from doing one's own will, or that prevent one from attributing the effects and properties of the divine names, and all the roles of God to oneself (i.e. freedom does not concern the strengthening of the ego, or increasing the awareness of being Master). Further, freedom also implies choice. Given the Muslim mystical social system, the choice can only concern choosing between being aware of manifesting either God or oneself. Since awareness of manifesting God is equal to awareness of one's servanthood before God, which in turn is equal to displaying the effects and properties of the divine names of mercy, and since awareness of manifesting oneself is equal to awareness of being Master, which in turn is equal to displaying the effects and properties of the divine names of Majesty or Wrath, freedom as the ability to choose may also be described as the ability to choose between displaying the effects and properties of either, the names of Mercy or the names of Wrath.[12] For the present, however, it is enough for us to consider freedom as the ability to choose between either being aware of manifesting God, or being aware of manifesting oneself. In so far as a decision is made to be aware of manifesting God, there is a problem when it comes to executing the decision because human beings as habitually aware of manifesting themselves, do not know God. And further, as ignorant of God, they do not know the mystical value system and how they are social actors within that system. Hence, the extremely important question, how is one to become aware of oneself as manifesting God? The question implies an experience of God which is attained by going through a process: First, one has to find God. But to find God, one must know where and how to search for Him. Since God is everywhere, in all existent things that are found in the macrocosm (the universe) and the microcosm (man), and in the spiritual, imaginal, and corporeal worlds which are present in both of them, finding God does not consist in travelling to a special place that God inhabits.[13] Finding God consists in learning to interpret reality (all existent things, the concrete situation in which one is placed, one's actions and oneself) with a different ideology.[14] Since ordinary human beings do not know this ideology (this ideology, as seen earlier, is the secret knowledge) in all its details, and habitually use the opposite ideology to give meaning to the concrete conditions of their existence, they have first to give up the habitually used ideology before they can get socialized into the new one. This socialization process, of giving up the ego-centric ideology and then accepting to be socialized into the new theo-centric one, has been traditionally institutionalized only in the *piri-muridi* relationship, even to the extent that it is universally believed that setting out and progressing on the spiritual path cannot take place outside *piri-muridi*, or outside the special relationship with a *pir*.[15]

The basic reasons for the importance of the *pir* in this process of finding God (or in this socialization process) are traditionally given as the following: First, the path to God, or the spiritual path, is unknown before it can be traversed since God, the end of the path, is unknown to the traveller.[16] Second, the path is full of dangers and pitfalls that cannot be prepared for because, again the path is unknown to the traveller.[17] Third, the Quran says, "Enter houses by their doors" (Q.2/185). These doors, according to al-Arabi, have been set up by God and Mohammed.[18] And only the delegates of God and Mohammed are believed to be qualified to open them. These delegates are those who have received the *khilafat* (or the mandate to lead others to union with God) and are part of the chain of transmission, the Sufi orders that are believed to have come down from Ali.[19] Trying to enter the house without going through the door, or without a *pir*, then, is interpreted as showing the greatest discourtesy or disrespect for God and Mohammed.[20] And since the end is union with God (the reality of Mohammed is also described as God the social actor, as seen above), disrespect or discourtesy to Him cannot lead to Him or to union with Him.[21]

The *pir* then, is the one who belongs to a Sufi order and has been given the *khilafat*. As *pir* or as the one who can open the door that leads to union with God, he is the perfect man (the one who institutionalizes the supreme divine name Allah by manifesting God as Allah or by manifesting God in all His roles).[22] He stands in the place of God, as the deputy of God in the cosmos, the inheritor of the messengers. Like them , he asks nothing of God, except God Himself.[23] He also has knowledge of the sources and origins of the people's actions (i.e. the divine names), and possesses the science of incoming thoughts, both the praiseworthy and the blameworthy[24] (i.e. he knows how God manifests Himself to the person at each moment in his spiritual, imaginal and corporeal aspects). The *pir* knows the meanings that are displeasing to God (i.e. the divine names that can be attributed only to God and not to man, the names of Majesty or Wrath) and those that are pleasing to Him[25] (i.e. the divine names that man can attribute to himself, the names of Mercy or servanthood). Consequently, he knows when a person truly sees the manifestation of God and when he merely imagines that he is seeing the manifestation of God[26] (i.e. the person cannot see God manifesting Himself while at the same time being aware of himself as Master). The *pir* also knows the method for training since he, himself, has gone through it, the dangers of the path (i.e. acquiring other effects and properties of the divine names may strengthen rather than deflate the ego), when to stop exercising control over the nature (bad habits or the manifestation of the awareness of the self as Master in concrete action) of the *murid* and when to begin exercising control over his reasoning faculty (i.e. the *murid's* awareness of himself as Master in his private thoughts).[27] Further, the *pir* knows how to cure illnesses, both physical and mental (which are believed to result from imbalances between the effects and properties of the divine names and the four basic compound elements, air, water, earth and fire) in order to facilitate progress on the path. He also knows the properties of the soul (as the locus of the divine manifestation) and satan (as the ego), and what the *murid* unknowingly hides from him[28] (i.e. aspects of the ego that the *murid* has not yet learnt to recognize). Consequently, the *pir* combines in himself everything that the *murid* needs in his state of training or wayfaring in order to lead him to the stage when he too can become a *pir*[29] (or the perfect man). He preserves the *sharia* (the external manifestation of man's servanthood before God) for everyone and helps the elect to observe courtesy towards God.[30]

Consequently, showing reverence to the *pir* is equated with reverence for God.[31] The *pir* is the freedman (or the perfect man) of God and, hence, His hearing, seeing, hands and feet and inversely, God is the hearing, seeing, hands and feet of the *pir*.[32] All the *pir's* words are believed to come from God and the *pir* cannot be judged even if his behaviour and words contradict the injunctions of the law (or the *sharia*).[33] The *murid* is not allowed to copy the extraordinary behaviour of the *pir*, be it blameworthy or praiseworthy, without the explicit permission of the *pir* because what is allowed the *pir* is not allowed the ordinary believer.[34] The *pir* as a perfect man or as a saint, has no ego and, hence, does only what God wants, while the *murid* cannot act in this way because of his ego.

In actual life, however, one finds different levels of *pirs*.[35] Ibn al-Arabi has reduced these various levels of *pirs* to two categories: the perfect *pir* and the less than perfect *pir*. The perfect *pir* is the ideal *pir* because he is a perfect man. He is said to know the Quran and the *sunna* and to uphold both of them in his outward activity.[36] His most important attribute or quality is his constant awareness of his own servanthood before God.[37] This is displayed in the manifest observance of God's bounds, fulfilling of the covenant, taking cautiously what is given, avoiding people who mix levels (i.e. avoiding those who constantly act and think of themselves as Master when in actual fact they are servants, e.g. the kings), hating disobedience without hating the disobedient one, hating what God hates with God's hate and loving what God loves with God's love.[38] This kind of *pir* commands what is approved and forbids what is disapproved (i.e. he encourages the following of the law) and vies with others for doing good works.[39] He pardons people, venerates the old, shows mercy to the young, removes harm from the way of the people, invites people to come to God by first stressing what is most incumbent and only later what is less incumbent.[40] He behaves gently with all creatures, considering all of them members of his household. He interprets only his obedience as the work of God, and repents for his disobedience because courtesy demands that he attribute his disobedience only to himself and not to God. Finally, he reminds the believer of the presence of God through his mere presence.[41]

The less perfect *pirs*, like the perfect *pirs* have received the *khilafat* from one or more of the various *silsilahs* (or Sufi orders), but unlike them are not perfect men.[42] They are the ones who are most often seen to disobey the injunctions of the *sharia* and to work miracles. This is not because they wilfully intend to disobey God, but because they are under the influence of a state (or the manifest effects and properties of a particular divine name without having the ability to control those effects and properties).[43] People are advised not to become their *murids*. But even these *pirs* must be shown reverence, whatever their behaviour, since they stand in the place of God by virtue of their office. Reverence for them is equal to reverence for God.[44] Also, showing discourtesy to a *pir*, whatever his behaviour, is equated with losing one's way to God and showing heedlessness and discourtesy to Him.[45] The *pir* is the official locus of the divine self-disclosure. If one cannot show reverence to God in the official locus of manifestation how can one show reverence for Him (or come to know Him) in all the other unofficial loci of manifestation? Those who lose respect for a *pir* are advised to avoid him till they are able to regain respect for him, because visiting him with contempt in the heart is equal to working towards their own damnation.[46]

The respect accorded to a *pir* and his august position does not imply that the *pir* can be aware of himself as Master in his relationship with the *murid*. He has to be constantly aware that he is not Master, that he is not God, that like the *murid* he too is on his way to God and, hence, only a servant. He too has constantly to pray, "My Lord, increase me in knowledge."[47] Further, he has to see everything, including his *murid* as the locus of God's self disclosure to himself. Consequently, he should not be ashamed to accept God's teaching him through his *murid*. Also, he cannot exalt himself above the *murid* because of the *murid's* poverty (or dependence) towards himself because this will only serve to make the *murid's* poverty a barrier between himself and God.[48] He must rather consider the *murid's* poverty towards himself as an example and as a reminder of his own poverty before God. Finally, in his dealing with the *murid* he has to ensure that the *murid's* rights over himself are greater than his own rights over the *murid*, i.e. on the one hand, the *pir* has to consider the *murid* as his own *pir*[49] (or as the locus of divine self-disclosure), while acting as *pir* towards him. He has to be aware of his servanthood while displaying God as Master and Guider.

Murid means one who desires.[50] As one who desires, the *murid* has no free choice because free choice belongs to the will and not to desire.[51] Desire (also called love) moves blindly to attain that which satisfies it, or that which is its end. And when it attains the end (or when it is satisfied), it disappears.[52] The object of desire for the *murid* is the *pir*, since the *pir* is the official locus of God's self-revelation (i.e. God can be attained only in as much as He is a social actor, not as He is in Himself, and He is a social actor only through the effects and properties of the divine names or through the institutionalizations of the divine names—the existent things—which also are His roles). Since the *murid* desires the *pir* or seeks union with him, believing that this union is equal to or leads to union with God, his main task is to keep company with the *pir*.[53] This companionship with the *pir* is of two kinds: the first kind consists in undergoing training at the hands of the *pir*; the second kind consists in visiting the *pir* and acquiring his blessing.[54] Both aspects of the companionship with the *pir* are structured by the rules of conduct called *adab*. These rules teach the *murid* to behave towards the *pir* as if he is God (i.e. the *murid* is at all times aware that the *pir* is a man like himself, but he has to treat him as if he is God in order to become aware of the way in which God the social actor discloses Himself in this world, first in the *pir*, and then in all existent things which are the loci of divine self-disclosure and, hence the desired end, union with God). By forcing the *murid* to treat the *pir* as God, rather than teaching him the theory by which he will come to understand theoretically how the *pir* can be the locus of divine manifestation, *piri-muridi* follows the basic tenet of Islamic mystical thought, that true knowledge comes only after one has gone through the process of actual experience, or existence comes before understanding,[55] (i.e. *piri-muridi* is a socialization process). The rules of conduct teach the *murid* to treat the *pir* as God or as the locus of divine self-disclosure by giving him a set of beliefs that he should have about the *pir* and himself, and by prescribing appropriate behaviour in the presence of the *pir*.

The rules of conduct describe the *pir* as the perfect man. As perfect man he is the representative of Mohammed and God the social actor.[56] Hence, the *murid* is told that all the reverence, love, respect and trust that is given to the *pir* is actually given to Mohammed and God. Two *hadiths* say,

> To obey me is to obey God, Exalted is He. To disobey me is to disobey God, the Lord of Glory and Perfection. To disobey your commander is to disobey me.

and,

> A fall of seven floors is a gentle drop compared with falling from the heart and affection of the spiritual guide.[57]

The rules of conduct also describe the *pir* as all-seeing, all-knowing, all-merciful and as the Guider (i.e. as God the social actor or as Allah) who is above good and evil and, hence, above human judgment, and also completely independent of the *murid*.[58] Further, the *murid* must believe that he can have only one *pir*.[59] The relationship between him and the *pir* is everlasting and cannot be broken even by the *pir*.[60] The *murid* cannot go to or become the *murid* of another *pir*. If he does, all the graces and blessings, both spiritual and material, that he has so far received will disappear.[61] All spiritual blessings, even those which the *murid* sees in dreams as coming from another saint, must be accepted as coming from his *pir*, who has taken on the form of that saint in order to give him the blessings.[62] Similarly with material blessings. The *murid* must believe that his life, his property, his children, and everything else in his life has come to him only through his *pir*.[63] Hence, his *pir* and not himself is the real owner of these things.[64] Further, he must believe that the *pir* can see him wherever he is, whatever he is doing, and even his innermost secret thoughts.[65] He must also believe that salvation is possible only through that *pir* because it is only that *pir* who will come to his grave and answer the questions put to him by the angels, Munkar and Nakir, concerning his faith and conduct in this life and, thus, save him from what is due to him for his sinfulness.[66] Finally, the *murid* must remember that the only way he can show his love and reverence for the *pir* who gives him everything he has, even his own life and salvation, is through obedience and service.[67]

Adab, or the rules of conduct, also tell the *murid* how he should look at himself. The *murid* has to remember at all times that he is selfish, and that this selfishness keeps him in bondage to itself by making him adore himself.[68] To arrive at true knowledge of himself, he must strive to look at himself from the opposite point of view. He must constantly think of himself as the most inferior human being because his selfishness forces him to assume an air of superiority, haughtiness and arrogance, that actually makes him brutish and nasty, takes away all beauty from his life, and leaves him satisfied with ignoble human desires.[69] He must feel ashamed of his sinfulness and shortcomings, derive pleasure from distress and trouble by remembering God so that troubles become his pleasure and a preparation for further troubles, renounce all worldly objects and desires, never allow himself to feel sorry for himself because this shows that he is still under the influence of his selfishness or ego, and constantly control himself by eating less, sleeping less, talking less, trying to lead a life of seclusion, and constantly fasting. He must strive not to make others feel sorry or sad with his words and deeds, and try constantly to point the way to God through his hospitality, love, piety, respect for others, patience, perseverance, self-control and courtesy to everyone.[70] Finally, whatever he does, he should always consider his own judgment and knowledge as untrustworthy.[71] The only way in which he can truly overcome his ego is by placing his complete trust in God as manifest in the *pir*, his orders, his words, his actions and judgment, irrespective of whether the *pir* treats him well or like a doormat.[72]

The actions that are encouraged or prohibited with respect to the *pir* teach the *murid* how to give the greatest possible respect to him as the locus of divine self-disclosure. In the presence of the *pir*, the *murid* should always be in a state of ritual purity[73] and give all his attention to the *pir* irrespective of whether the *pir* is talking to him or not, and even if such attention prevents him from praying or attending to a guest.[74] He is prohibited from having his shadow fall on the *pir*, from using the *pir's* place of ablution, from using his utensils, from stepping on the *pir's* prayer carpet, from extending his feet in the direction of the *pir*, from spitting in the direction of the *pir*, irrespective of whether the *pir* is before him or not, from performing ablutions in his presence, from raising his voice in the

presence of the *pir*, from talking informally with him, from correcting him even though he may be undeniably in the wrong, and from
leaving the *pir's* presence without his permission.[75]

Prescribed behaviour requires an extremely polite tone when
talking to the *pir*, always seeking to serve the *pir*, both physically, and
financially, and being very grateful for the opportunity given to serve
him, keeping the promises made to the *pir* even if this requires the
sacrifice of the *murid's* life,[76] complete openness with the *pir* to the
extent of telling him all his dreams, doubts, sins and illnesses,
respectfully waiting for the *pir's* answers, explanations and advice,[77]
and justifying the *pir's* apparently scandalous and bad behaviour and
obscure utterances by telling himself that he is still too stupid to
understand the wisdom of the *pir*. Of course, if he does not
understand the *pir's* explanations, he may ask for an explanation as
politely as possible, but if he still does not understand, he must
consider himself too stupid and at too low a spiritual level to
understand the *pir's* wisdom.[78] Finally, the *murid* must trust the good
intentions of the *pir* completely, and obey him even when what is
ordered seems to contradict the law, or even seems to be sinful and,
hence, leading to damnation, because the *pir* possesses a wisdom that
is far above his understanding.[79] For instance, one *murid* who was
very proud of his sanctity was ordered by his *pir* to break the Ramdan
fast in public. Besides breaking the law, the breaking of the fast in
public would have resulted in public censure and possible imprison-
ment. The *murid* trusted his *pir* and obeyed; and he may have lost
his pride. After Ramdan was over, the *pir* ordered him to fast for sixty
consecutive days and for one additional day to make up for the day
on which he broke the fast in Ramdan.[80] Another *pir* who was close
to death and unable to decide which of his *murids* was submissive
enough and, hence, worthy of succeeding him, ordered each of them
to bring his wife to his room that night. All the *murids* agreed. But
on leaving the *pir* they all thought it an evil command that
contradicted the law. Hence, they did not find it necessary to obey.
One *murid*, however, recalled that the *pir* had never ordered him to
do evil. Hence, trusting in the *pir's* good intentions, he went and
fetched his wife and took her to the *pir's* room. The *pir* sent him out

to heat water, telling him that he wanted to perform general ablution, and closed the door. When the wife was alone with him, he told her that he was about to die. Then he lay on his bed and asked her to tie his toes together, bind his chin and lay a stone on his stomach as soon as he died, and to forgive him. Then he gave up his spirit. The woman rushed out of the room to inform her husband of the *pir's* death and found him busy attending to the fire. Subsequently, the *murid* was forced to take the place of the dead *pir* by the other *murids*.[81] The *malfuzats* record a *pir* ordering one of his young *murids* to marry an "old hag".[82] Irina Tweedie was ordered to donate all her money to the poor.[83] And after she had begun to liquidate all her assets in order to distribute her wealth as her *pir* desired, he told her that all *murids* have to pass such tests at some stage of the path. Some are told to bring their wives to the *pir*. If the *murid* does not trust the *pir* and begins to wonder what the *pir* will do with her and, thus, chooses to disobey, his progress on the path stops.[84] At another time the *pir* ordered Irina Tweedie to write down all the sins she had committed in her past life and to give the sheets of paper to him.[85] Rumi was told to throw all his books into the sea or river,[86] and so on.

By following this code of behaviour with the *pir*, the *murid* overcomes his ego, or the "selfishness" that makes him think of himself as Master rather than servant. The overcoming of the ego in the process of living out the code of conduct is seen in the transformation that is brought about in the *murid*. He finds that his arrogance (thinking of himself as superior to others) changes into modesty and humility, his hypocrisy (doing good and admirable things in order to be praised by others) changes into sincerity, his sanctimonious pride (considering himself more pious than others) changes into dissatisfaction with his own accomplishments, his reputation seeking (behaving admirably in order to acquire fame and popularity) changes into humility, his envy (jealous resentment at the merit of others) changes into gratitude and contentment with what God has given him, his irascibility (tendency to fly into a rage over every little thing) changes into mildness and docility, his sensuality (ruthless and unscrupulous pursuit of ambition and sensual lust) changes into subordination of his will and desire to the will of God, his material greed (love of wealth and the things of this world) changes into love of God and Mohammed, his status seeking (pursuit of worldly rank and status) changes into honour and dignity in the service of the Truth, and finally, his self–reliance changes into complete trust in and reliance on God.[87] But the *murid* must remember that this transformation (giving up his own attributes and assuming the attributes of God) has been worked, not by his own effort, but by the efforts of the *pir*[88] (i.e. the *murid* has to consider that the divine names of mercy are institutionalized in the *pir* and as institutionalized in the *pir*, display their effects and properties in himself because of his close relationship with him. And in the measure that these effects and properties are being displayed in him, he too begins to institutionalize the same values). The *murid* has also to believe that his ability to keep the *adab* is the effect and property of the *pir*[89] (i.e. the effect of the *pir's* deep awareness of his own servanthood before God).

The *pir* may give the *murid,* who is engrossed in trying to follow the *adab* spiritual task, like reciting the divine name, the forgiver.[90] The recitation of the divine name also involves arriving at a greater understanding of what it means to forgive and whom he should forgive (for instance, his enemies and those who have tormented him); coming to value forgiveness more than the dictates of his ego, laws, and even religious tenets like, "an eye for an eye and a tooth for a tooth"; trying to involve his emotions and feelings with the concept of forgiveness; and finally going out and forgiving enemies.[91] This process involves *fana,* the struggle to die to himself or his ego that encourages him to display the effects and properties of vengeance rather than forgiveness. Once forgiveness has triumphed over vengeance, he may be said to reside in the station of forgiveness, or to have at all times a forgiving attitude (*baqa*).[92] This process will be carried out with all the divine names of mercy.[93] Here too the *murid* must believe that his ability to institutionalize the values (or divine names) of mercy is the effect and property of the same values as institutionalized by the *pir*. The *pir* need not necessarily give the *murid* these spiritual tasks. Even so the effects and properties of the divine names of mercy begin to display themselves in the *murid* because the *pir* possesses them and the *murid* has surrendered himself to him.[94]

This keeping company with the *pir* offers opportunities for the *murid* to demonstrate his love in special acts of devout service which may draw the *pir's* attention towards him.[95] The *pir* may then reward the *murid* by asking him to attend the secret instruction (either in a closed room or at night) where the *murid* will be given the secret mystical and divine knowledge.[96] This knowledge can be no other than the knowledge of the mystical social system: the mystical value system, the way in which God can be considered and experienced as a social actor, and the way in which man is a social actor, as outlined above. Here too the knowledge is given by way of a practical exercise. The *murid* will be asked to give the meaning of an experience, a dream, etc. He will be instructed to give the first meaning that comes to his mind and not to rely on what comes after detailed reflection.[97] This is very similar to the way in which ordinary human beings are constantly giving socially acceptable meanings to their experiences. For instance, if a newspaper report tells us that a bus exploded because of a bomb that was planted in it, we immediately call it an atrocity without having to go through a lengthy process of logical reasoning. This is because we have learnt, in the course of a lengthy socialization process, to give this and other such instances socially acceptable meanings. Similarly in *piri-muridi*, the *murid* learns which meanings are acceptable, by watching the reactions of the *pir*. Later, he learns to see these meanings as divine names, and later still as the roles of God. Consequently, he progresses to a stage where he is able to see all existent things, including himself as a role of God that keeps changing moment to moment. He is able to see how God interacts with all things and with himself at every moment. Thus, each moment becomes an occasion for union with God, and the *murid* is ready to receive *khilafat*.

The *murid's* progress from the earliest stage, when he did not know God, to the latest stage when he begins to interact consciously with God at every moment, is also called the path of love.[98] As the path of love, it has a number of stages.[99] At the beginning, just before the person becomes a *murid*, he is understood as busy denying a love (or a desire) that he feels but cannot accept.   Nevertheless, he continues to visit a *pir*. He is like a man who falls in love with a woman but refuses to recognize the resulting emotions and actions as the manifestation of that love (or desire) for her.[100] This situation is unstable and forces a solution, the second stage of love. The person takes a bold step by making *bai'a* (the oath of surrender) at the hands of the *pir*. Once *bai'a* is taken the *pir* may begin to ignore, insult and humiliate the *murid* because the *murid's* ego still prevents him from accepting that his desire (or love) has made him lose whatever control he thought he had over himself. He has still to accept that he is now under the sway of the beloved, the *pir*.[101] This treatment by the *pir* takes the *murid* to the third stage of love. At this stage the *murid* begins to accept to some extent that he is no longer master of himself, and that he is in love with (or desires union with) the *pir*. Consequently, the *pir's* friends become his friends; the *pir's* enemies become his enemies; the *pir's* likes, his likes, etc.[102] The ego of the *murid*, however, still remains and begins to reassert itself. This reassertion of the ego takes the *murid* to the fourth stage of love, the stage of jealousy. The *murid* tries to reserve the *pir* for himself and begins to hate seeing the *pir* talking and attending to other *murids* and clients. The *pir* on his part, again begins to ignore and insult the *murid* and constantly finds some excuse or other to keep him at a distance.[103] This brings the *murid* to the fifth stage of love. He can no longer bear his separation from the *pir* and gives up his jealousy. And he makes up for the *pir's* distance by automatically seeing him imaginally in himself and in everything around him. He begins to find the *pir's* qualities, mannerisms, etc. in other people.[104] Then the *murid* moves to the sixth stage of love when he finds himself talking and acting like the *pir*. He has unknowingly taken on the qualities of the *pir* while giving up his own qualities.[105] Finally comes the stage of love where the *murid* finds that there is no difference between himself and the *pir*. He not only speaks and acts like the *pir*, but also finds himself thinking like the *pir* in that he can complete the sentences of the *pir* and even tell what the *pir* is going to say and do next.[106] Further, he may even be able to exercise the power or the *karamat* of the *pir*.[107] He has achieved union with the *pir*.

The power or *karamat* of the *pir* is extremely important to the *murid* at the early stages of love, and loses significance as he progresses to the later stages of love. *Karamat* is important because it encourages the *murid* to make progress rather than give up by convincing him that his *pir* truly has a special connection with God and, hence, knows what he is doing. It is not essential that the *murid* personally experience this *karamat*. But it is important that he believe in its existence. And when he does experience it, it is usually in the sphere of the imaginal and serves to change the attitude of the *murid*, rather than the situation in which he finds himself. Consequently, the *murid* works to overcome the situation in which he finds himself and attributes his success to his *pir's* power.[108]

As seen earlier, Ibn al-Arabi explains that once the end of a desire is achieved (or when the desire is satisfied), it disappears.[109] In *piri-muridi*, once union with the *pir* has been achieved, the *murid's* desire for the *pir* must disappear and give place to love of God.[110] This is explained with the aid of the Joseph-Zulaika love story. Zulaika, Potiphar's wife, gives up her marriage, her wealth and her beauty in her desire to be united with Joseph. And when she finally finds Joseph willing to marry her, she no longer wants to marry him because she suddenly realizes that Joseph was a veil between herself and God, i.e. all that she had done and given up for Joseph, she had actually done and given up for God, the true Beloved. Joseph consequently becomes one of the loci of divine self-disclosure.[111] So too in *piri-muridi*, the *pir* becomes one of the many loci of divine self-disclosure and loses his central position in the *murid's* life. Nevertheless, he is still given great respect because he remains a locus of divine self-disclosure, and will always be the one who helped the *murid* to achieve union with God.

To summarize: *Piri-muridi* is an institutionalized form of social-ization that aims at forcing the *murid* to give up his awareness of manifesting himself (his ego), and then to take on the new awareness of manifesting God at each and every moment of his life. It tries to achieve this by giving him an official locus of divine self-disclosure, the *pir*, and by prescribing a rite of self surrender (*bai'a*) and a set of practices and beliefs (*adab*) with respect to the *pir*. The living out of the *bai'a* and the *adab* inculcates in the *murid* a consciousness of complete dependency on the *pir* even for his own personal qualities, with the result that he finds himself manifesting not himself, but the *pir*. He has attained union with the *pir*. From here it is a short step to realizing that by manifesting the *pir*, he is actually manifesting God the social actor. He has attained union with God.

NOTES

1. William C. Chittick, *The Sufi Path of Knowledge*, pp. 3-30.
2. Ibid., pp. 19-21.
3. Ibid., p. 19.
4. Ibid., pp. 19-21.
5. Ibid.
6. Ibid.
7. Ibid.
8. Ibid., pp. 333-81; also cf. Toshihiko Izutsu, op. cit., pp. 218-86.
9. William C. Chittick, *The Sufi Path of Knowledge*, pp. 3-76.
10. Ibid., pp. 106-9; cf. Mohammed Ajmal, "A Note on Adab in the Murshid-Murid relationship", pp. 241-51; cf. Sheikh Muzaffer Ozak al- Jerrahi, *The Unveiling of Love*, cf. A. Reza Arasteh, *Growth to Selfhood: The Sufi Contribution* (Routledge and Kegan Paul, London, 1980); cf. Zahurul Hassan Sharib, *The Mystical Philosophy of Khwaja Moinud-din Hasan Chisti*; cf. Annemarie Schimmel, *Mystical Dimensions of Islam*; cf. Toshihiko Izutsu, op. cit.
11. William C. Chittick, *The Sufi Path of Knowledge*, pp. 19-21.
12. Ibid., pp. 60-1.
13. Ibid., pp. 3-31.
14. Ibid.
15. Ibid.
16. Ibid.
17. Ibid.
18. Ibid.
19. Ibid.
20. Ibid.
21. Ibid.
22. Ibid., pp. 270-2.
23. Ibid.
24. Ibid.
25. Ibid.
26. Ibid.
27. Ibid.
28. Ibid.
29. Ibid.

30. Ibid.
31. Ibid.
32. Shaykh Hakim Moinuddin Chisti, *The Sufi Book of Healing*.
33. William C. Chittick, *The Sufi Path of Knowledge*, pp. 270-2.
34. Barbara Daly Metcalf, *Moral Conduct and Authority: The Place of Adab in South Asian Islam*, pp. 241-51.
35. William C. Chittick, *The Sufi Path of Knowledge*, p. 272.
36. Ibid.
37. Ibid.
38. Ibid.
39. Ibid.
40. Ibid.
41. Ibid.
42. Ibid., p. 273.
43. Ibid.
44. Ibid.
45. Ibid.
46. Ibid.
47. Ibid.
48. Ibid.
49. Ibid., p. 274.
50. Ibid. p. 289, n. 8.
51. Ibid.
52. Ibid.
53. Ibid., p. 271; also cf. Annemarie Schimmel, op. cit., p. 102.
54. William C. Chittick, *The Sufi Path of Knowledge*, p. 271
55. Ibid. pp. 77-190
56. Sheikh Muzaffer Ozak al-Jerrahi, op. cit., pp. 155-74.
57. Ibid.
58. Ibid.
59. Barbara Daly Metcalf, op. cit., pp. 241-51.
60. Zahurul Hasan Sharib, op. cit., p. 35.
61. Barbara Daly Metcalf, op. cit., pp. 241-51.
62. Ibid.
63. Sheikh Muzaffer Ozak al-Jerrahi, op. cit.
64. Ibid.
65. Ibid.
66. Ibid.
67. Ibid.
68. Zahurul Hasan Sharib, op. cit., pp. 68-86.
69. Ibid.
70. Ibid.
71. Ibid.
72. Ibid., pp. 42, 68-86.
73. Ibid.; also cf. sheikh Ozak al-Jerrahi, op. cit., pp. 155-73.

74. Barbara Daly Metcalf, op. cit., pp. 241-51.
75. Ibid.
76. Sheikh Muzaffer Ozak al-Jerrahi, op. cit., pp. 155-86.
77. Ibid.; also cf. Barbara Daly Metcalf, op. cit., pp. 241-51.
78. Ibid.
79. Ibid.
80. Ibid.
81. Ibid.
82. Zahid Ali, "A Critical Study of Malfuzat Literature in Persian: Sultanate Period" (University of Delhi, Dept. of Persian, 1989), unpublished.
83. Irina Tweedie, *Daughter of Fire*, pp. 143-51.
84. Ibid., p. 187.
85. Ibid., pp. 122-30.
86. William C. Chittick, *The Sufi Path of Love*.
87. Sheikh Muzaffer Ozak al-Jerrahi, op. cit., pp. 173-5.
88. Zahurul Hassan Sharib, op. cit.
89. Ibid.
90. A. Reza Arasteh, *Growth to Selfhood*, pp. 54-6.
91. Ibid.
92. Ibid.
93. William C. Chittick, *The Sufi Path of Knowledge*, pp. 253-333.
94. Cf. Irina Tweedie, *Daughter of Fire*; also cf. Zahurul Hassan Sharib, op cit.
95. Zahurul Hassan Sharib, op. cit.
96. Ibid., p. 39
97. William C. Chittick, *The Sufi Path of Knowledge*, p. 224.
98. A. Reza Arasteh, *Growth to Selfhood*, pp. 119 ff.
99. Ibid.
100. Ibid.
101. Ibid.; also cf. Zahurul Hassan Sharib, op. cit.
102. A. Reza Arasteh, op. cit., 119 ff.
103. Ibid.
104. Ibid.
105. Ibid.
106. Ibid.
107. Bikram N. Nanda and Mohammed Talib, op. cit., pp. 125-44.
108. Ibid.
109. William C. Chittick, *The Sufi Path of Knowledge*.
110. Sheikh Muzaffer Ozak al-Jerrahi, op. cit.
111. Ibid.

SECTION TWO

PIRI-MURIDI IN THE NIZAMUDDIN DARGAH

THE *PIR* IN THE
NIZAMUDDIN DARGAH

The *pir* is usually a man with a long flowing beard, a long coat, white pajamas, a high quality cap, and a ring with a stone of a different colour on each finger of his right hand. He usually squats on a carpeted floor behind or next to a low table or desk which contains blank sheets of paper on which he writes *tawizes*, different kinds of inks, different kinds of pens, a book on *tawiz* and astrology, and some personal items. This outward appearance signifies a *pir*. The *pirs* do not give formal classes on Muslim mystical theory. The relevant books are in Arabic, Persian and English, languages most *murids* and clients either do not know, or cannot read fluently. Even otherwise, most *murids* seem to have little access to these books. Urdu translations do exist but it appears (from what the *murids* have to say) that they are very rare and treasured family heirlooms. Hence, these too are not easily available. Further, the *murids* display no interest in finding and reading these books because the *pirs* and the more advanced *murids* insist that their knowledge has not been gained from books: it has been passed on to them by word of mouth or from "heart to heart" by their *pirs*, and also attained through direct experience. The only books commonly read and easily available are the books on *tawiz*.

Consequently, the *murid* may not know exactly what a *pir* is supposed to represent. He has to give meaning to the *pir* by taking into account his own experience of him, his own personal needs and motives, and the beliefs given to him in the form of stories and simple statements of belief, which are regularly narrated by the *pirs*, the more advanced *murids*, the *pirzade*, and the *murid's* own family members and friends. Consequently, the *murids* do not have a common definition of the *pir*; and a given *murid* may revise his definition many times as he advances in the *piri-muridi* relationship. This ambiguity may be demonstrated in the words of three *murids*.

The *pir* is a secret. Secrets are not to be revealed, or explained to anyone. The *pir* is a riddle that each *murid* has to make an effort to solve and understand. The *pir* is a question to the *murid*. He has to search for the answer to this question. He has to search for the great and good things in the person of the *pir*. The *pir* will not tell him who he is. He will only hint at what he is by giving good advice. In the examination hall one gets a question, one or two lines long that tells one what is expected. The *pir* is like that question. The *murid* must try to answer that question. If he succeeds in answering that question correctly, the *pir* will give him the *khilafat*. If not, he will remain a *murid* all his life.

The *pir* is a lesson that has to be studied. He may appear to be doing wrong, but in actual fact he is not. He alone knows that he is not in the wrong, and why he is doing what looks wrong. The *pir* does not walk in a straight line. He twists and turns constantly. Hence, it is very difficult to know what a *pir* is and what he is up to.

Another *murid* explained that science is not the method for understanding the *pir*.

It is very difficult to understand what a *pir* is. Science will not enable you to understand. Science was born only recently. Mohammed *sahib* went on his *miraj* [ascension into heaven] fourteen hundred years ago. What rocket did he use? There was no rocket then. Hazrat Fazal was sitting on the bank of the Nile and listening to all the insults heaped on him by the king who was sitting in his palace in Persia. What kind of telex, telephone, or telegraph did he use? The *pir* cannot be understood through science. Science cannot bring a dead man back to life. Even if science succeeds in doing so today, it succeeds only because it kills another man and then uses his organs to make the first man alive again. A *pir*, on the other hand, has only to blow over the dead man and he becomes alive. What doctors cannot cure, the *pir* can cure with one look. All this happens because of the power of the *pir*. That lie detector ... that computer, it is true, can read the minds of men. But then it can only record what the man is thinking. If he keeps his mind blank, nothing will be recorded. And if he goes on repeating a lie in his head, it will record the lie and call it the truth. All these tricks do not work with the *pir*. He looks only once, and he knows everything, the good and the bad. Nothing is hidden from his sight. Science cannot help us to understand what the *pir* is. The only way to understand is through personal experience. But each one's personal experience is different. So how will you ever understand what a *pir* actually is?

As pointed out earlier, the *pir* is the official locus of the self-manifestation of God. The *murid* may not know this at the beginning nor how such a statement is to be understood. He has to come to this understanding in the course of watching, listening to and obeying the *pir*. The different definitions of the *pir* may, thus, point to the different levels of the *murids*, and also to those aspects of the *pirs* that the *murids* are more familiar with.

DEFINITIONS OF THE *PIR*

In order to put some order into the material at hand, I present some of the different representative definitions of the *pir* under different headings.

The *pir* is a guide, helper and teacher who takes one to God.

The *pir* is like the moon. He spreads his light in all four directions. Those who come under the influence of this light meet him and get what they want. He shows the way and brings them into the light.

He catches and saves the *murid* from falling by the wayside. He will not let him out of his grasp until he can stand on his own two feet. This catching and saving of the *murid* takes place through the light of the *pir*.

The *pir* shows the path. Without a *pir*, one's education is incomplete. The *maulvis* teach only the Quran. The *pir* tells you about your whole life. He tells you what to do, what is good and bad. When one is in trouble, the *pir* will tell one how to get out of it. The *pir* cannot take one to God. One goes to God by one's own effort; the *pir* will only show the way. It depends on oneself to walk on the path shown by the *pir*. The *pir* has only such power as enables him to show you the way.

The *pir* looks at the habits of the *murid*. He searches for those things from which he can save his *murid*. The *pir* is not an ordinary man like you and me. We are all sinners and, hence, do not know the way. The *pir* is very great. He is the one who saves and gives. If he likes you, he will give you everything. The *pir* can guide because he knows everything, who is good, who is bad. But one must make an effort to be connected with him.

The *pir* wants to make the *murid* like himself. He watches over the *murid* for twenty-four hours without the *murid's* knowledge in order that the *murid* may not go astray and continues to walk on the right path. Distance and physical obstacles do not come in the way of the *pir* because he has that special power that comes from true faith.

The *pir* is the guide who brings the *murid* on the way of the Quran and in such a way that the *murid* begins to live according to its injunctions.

The *pir* is just a guide. He is nothing in himself. He shows the way to God. All his power is derived from God. There are *pirs* who just by one look can bring about a person's conversion. He can change the person's life. This power is called *karamat*. It is not magic, but alchemy that changes base metals into gold.

The *pir* guides his *murids* through his words. These have a powerful effect on the *murids* because the *pir* practises what he and the *maulvis* preach. The *pir* also guides the *murid* through his power (We shall deal with the power of the *pir* later on).

When my *pir* says something, it has a great influence on me because he practises what he preaches. He is like Baba Farid. Baba Farid had a great weakness for sweets. Once, a mother brought to him her child who had the habit of eating sugar all the time. The mother asked the *pir* to do something to stop the child from eating so much sugar. He told her to come the next day, and then again the following day. On the third day, he called the child to him and told it to stop eating sugar as it was bad for its health. Then he sent them away. The mother complained loudly, "You could have told him that on the first day instead of making us come to you for three days." Baba Farid agreed, but explained, "I too like sweets. If my words are to have any effect on the child, I have to first practise and then preach. I have not eaten a single sweet for the last three days." The child stopped eating sugar after that. One can see God in the words of the *pir*. He is the one who leads me on the right path. And many times he has to talk indirectly.

The *pir* is like the *maulvi* who teaches the Quran, the *sunna*, the *hadith* and how to worship. He is also different from the *maulvi* because, besides these things, he teaches one to live like the great saints, those men who have made the world carry on. The *maulvi* preaches, but does not necessarily practise what he preaches. The *pir*, not only preaches, but also puts his preaching into practice. Hence, he can tell one how to put the Quran into practice. He knows all the difficulties involved and how to solve them.

You will understand this better with a story: A *maulvi* was preaching in the mosque, "If you have faith and pray the *namaz* with faith you will be able to walk on the river and cross over to the other side. You will not drown. You will walk on the water as if it were dry ground." In the audience was a man with a limp. He was a woodcutter. The forest, near which he lived, was on the other side of the river. He used to cut the wood, and carry it across a bridge over the river into the town. Because this covered a long distance, he could bring only a little wood at a time and with great difficulty because of the limp. When he heard the *maulvi* he believed fully and thought to himself, "The message is for me. The *maulvi* is telling me something contained in the Quran. What can be wrong with what he says? I have been a fool not to have been using this shorter route over the water. When he left the mosque, he recited the *kalima* with faith, and stepped on the water and began to walk. He had come to believe fully. From that day onwards this became his regular route. Now he could bring much more wood into the town and he slowly became a rich man. One day, he invited the *maulvi* for dinner. The *maulvi* accepted and the woodcutter led the way. When they came to the riverside, the *maulvi* looked around and asked, "But where is the boat or the bridge? How are we to cross the river? We cannot walk on the water." The woodcutter looked at the *maulvi* with astonishment and said, "*Maulvi sahib*, don't mock me. You yourself said that if we recite the *kalima* with faith, we will be able to walk on the water." The *maulvi* thought to himself, "This man is surely mad." The woodcutter got impatient and told the *maulvi* to recite the *kalima* and step on the water. He himself recited the *kalima*, stepped on the water and began to walk home. The *maulvi* could only look on.

The *pir* is that man who has put his faith into practice. If one has real faith, Allah will make sure that whatever one wants to do will be successful. The *pir*, who has this faith and regularly practises it, can show the *murid* how he too must believe. The *maulvi*, only preaches. The *maulvi's* work is to set people apart. The *pir's* work is to accept people of every faith and to bring them on to the right path. The *pir* also knows every religion. That is why he can tell them how to follow their religion properly.

The *pir* can guide the *murid* because he is believed to be "spiritually more pure and perfect by the standards of the Quran." And his role as guide is effective because he has knowledge.

A *pir* knows all the secrets of God, even what the prophets, except Mohammed *sahib*, do not know. God has given to the *pir* knowledge of five things: when it will rain, whether a pregnant woman is carrying a male or a female child, when, where and why a person will die, what a person is thinking, and what will happen tomorrow. This knowledge is not given to anyone but the *pir*.

The stars influence human destiny. The *pir* has the knowledge and the power to interpret the stars. He knows what a man will do the next day. He can tell a man what he will eat and wear the next day. Life is completely predestined. Hence, we cannot do what we like. All of us move on our appointed paths. This is because the stars are moving in a particular way and determining all that we do. The *pir* changes all that. He can change the course of the stars. When my *pir* lies down at night his eyes are open. What is he looking at? He is looking at the stars and learning how they determine the destiny of his *murids*. And during the day, he sits with his eyes closed. What is he doing? He is changing the course of the stars and, therefore, the destiny of his *murids*. This is how my *pir* changes my life for the better. Another thing, the *pir* is sacred. His actions may not look holy or sensible. But they are holy and sensible and cannot be questioned by our intelligence. He has a secret purpose that we cannot know and which makes his actions right and moral.

The *pir* can guide also because he is the one who loves, the one who relies only on God, and the one who sees God in all things.

The *pir* loves. Hence, people come to him. The world does not give this love. This love cannot be obtained by payment. This world does not give this kind of love. When the world loves, it loves with a hidden motive. The men of this world say to themselves, "I will love him because he is rich. Then I will be able to take his watch, his clothes, and his camera. May be, he will also give me expensive gifts. And I will be able to stay in his house for long stertches for free." The love of a *pir* has none of these hidden motives. The *pir* loves one for one's own sake and he is constantly thinking of how much more he

can do for his *murids*. This kind of love is called *amal*. That is
why people come to a *pir*, sit with him, love to hear him talk to
them, and obey him.

My grandfather *pir*, the *pir* of my *pir*, was a saint and a very
famous man. His name used to come in the newspapers. Once,
when he was standing at the Ajmer railway station, he saw a
married English couple. The woman was very beautiful. He
went and kissed her. The woman's husband got very angry. He
demanded to know the meaning of this. "Why are you kissing
her? How dare you kiss her?" My grandfather *pir* replied, "I saw
the light of God in her face. That is why I kissed her". The
husband was a very hard man. There was a charcoal fire burning
on a hawker's cart close by. He said to my grandfather *pir*, "If
that is so, then why can't you see the light of God in that charcoal
fire and go and kiss it also?" My grandfather *pir* went to the fire
and put his mouth on the red hot coals and kept it there for a few
minutes. Then he lifted his head and turned to the man. The
Englishman saw that his mouth was not burnt. Then my
grandfather *pir* said, "You were correct, the light of God is in this
charcoal fire also." The charcoal fire became cool while his
mouth was on the coals. The *pir* sees the light of God in all things.

As guide, the *pir* changes the life of the *murid*, in four ways. The
first is by verifying the *murid's* faith.

The *pir* verifies my faith. This means that all my shortcomings
and faults disappear. The *pir* has the third eye, the *qalb*, which
he uses to look into each of his *murids*. He talks to us about the
faults which he sees in us. He teaches us how to overcome them.
He may tell us our faults indirectly. Once, I was sitting with my
pir together with some others. The *pir* was telling another man
that Sayyids should not behave like ruffians. Their work is not
to fight, kill, loot, rob, etc. I immediately realized that the
message was for me because I am a Sayyid and my work was to
beat, cut, hurt, rob, etc. If one sits with a *pir* one's faults begin
to disappear. He knows all my faults without my having to tell

him about them. And when I remember any of my faults while in his presence, he will call me to him and in private give me a method by which I can correct them.

Second, the *pir* changes the life of his *murid* by setting a good example.

My *pir* does not introduce me into this world of living a life devoted to Allah through formal instruction. He introduces me to it by his deeds, which make him a model for me. His life shows me what I should do. My *pir* does not tell me to do this or that. He influences me through his example. His life has not been easy. His father died when he was very young, and he was brought up by his grandmother. He tells me that in all the ups and downs of his life God has stood by him. He shows me that wherever God is and whatever God does, does not matter very much. What matters is whether I am attuned to Him. I have been taught to believe that when I remember the saints, they remember me. The Quran also says, "You call me and I will answer. You remember me and I will remember you." This is true of God and of the *pir*. It may be true of other people also, but it is not true of them in a way that is very effective for my life. It is better to go to those who are effective and can get my prayers answered—my *pir*. Rational categories do not help here. It would appear at times that the *pir* is greater than God, for he does what God does not do. He appears to be more merciful than God. But we must remember that God alone is merciful. The moment we start talking of anything outside God, everything becomes foolishness. Everything is God's, not outside God. My *pir* inspires me through his example. He lost his beloved wife. But he has no resentment towards God. Nowadays, if anything happens, people blame God. According to my *pir*, whatever may happen, one has to bear it with patience and thankfulness. He believes that this world is not everything. If there is no compensation for our good deeds here on earth, there will be compensation in the hereafter.

Third, the *pir* changes the life of his *murid* by making him believe, and by removing all the obstacles that make belief difficult.

The *pir* does not do anything. It is the faith of the *murid* that does everything. Faith means to believe that the *pir* will answer one's questions, to believe that the *pir* will attend to one, and to go to him. When one sits with the *pir,* one finds that he behaves in such a way that one's faith in him increases. A time comes when one learns to believe him absolutely. Then, if I am sick and he tells me that I am cured, I will believe that I am all right. The *pir* is the place where we learn to believe, the place where we learn to have faith. This faith increases our will power. When the will power is strong, one can do anything. One can even tell death to go away and it will go. Everything depends on the will power of the mind. The *pir* strengthens this will power by increasing faith. He is like the man who removes the stone that prevents a stream of water from flowing freely. And he also teaches his *murids* how to remove these obstacles to faith. Hence, the *murid* learns how to believe. And it is through believing that one gets the will power that leads to power. The *pir* also increases our faith by helping us to give the right meaning to things. Each particular thing can have hundreds of meanings, but only some of them are right. The *pir* teaches me which meanings are right and which are wrong. The *pir* also teaches me to talk to the God that is within each of me. And he shows me ways by which the tensions that arise from the troubles of daily life can be reduced. Consequently, I become free to solve the real problems.

Fourth, the *pir* changes the life of the *murid* by training him.

The *pir* destroys the *nafs* of the *murid*. The *pir* trains the *murid* in the same way as the police force or the army is trained. He makes the *murid* cry. Hence, the *murid* begins to think, "Where have I landed?" The *pir* washes the *murid* mentally and to such an extent that the *murid* can think of nothing but the *pir*. If the *pir* is a perfect *pir* then he will tell his visiting *murid* the purpose of his visit.

The *pir* is also closely associated with the Prophet, Mohammed.

The *pir* is the assistant prophet. There is no difference between the Prophet and God. This is because God brought forth the Prophet from His own light. The Prophet and God are one. They are different only in the eyes of the world. The *pir* is the vice-prophet. The assistant takes full charge when the person in whose name he acts is not present. For instance, when the President of India is out of the country on some important work, the Vice-President takes over until the President returns. The *pir* is like that. He is the vice-prophet. The Vice-President has the same powers as the President when the latter is absent, and the same work. In the absence of Mohammed, Ali did the work of Mohammed, and after him the *pirs* do Mohammed's work. They all act in the name of the Prophet. They are all vice-prophets, or acting prophets.

   The relationship between the *pir* and Mohammed is like the relationship between a king and his slave. Mohammed is the king and the one who carries on his mission will call himself his slave. He will not say that he is his father: he will call himself his slave. The *pir* is a teacher and gives the lesson of Mohammed to all others. Mohammed is his head. Mohammed is headmaster; Mohammed is the president. And the *pir* will always remain the vice-president. According to history, the *pir* is the acting prophet because the hand of Mohammed is on his head. The hand of Mohammed is on the head of the *pir* in this way: The hand of Mohammed is on the head of Ali. Ali's hand is on the head of the founder of the *silsilah*, and so on till the hand of my *pir's pir* is on his head. Hence, the hand of Mohammed is on the head of the *pir*.

Consequently, the *pir* is

the one who makes his *murid* sit on his shoulders in order to take him to Mohammed *sahib*. Mohammed himself went to heaven on the shoulders of a *pir*. The *pir* was the flying horse on which Mohammed rode. That is why it is important to have one's own *pir*. The world comes and asks from the *pir*. The *pir* has great work to do. On his shoulders rest the feet of Mohammed.

If one does one's work in the name of the *pir*, one will not have any difficulty. All one's troubles will be taken away. He is not a sinner and has power. How can a *pir* be a sinner? He has recited the Quran eighteen times before being born. Who are the *maulvis* before him! They will become his *murids*. They will realize that he knows everything. They will ask themselves, "Should we teach him or should we learn from him?"

A *pir* can be of any age. He may be a twelve-year-old boy. One is born a *pir*. One is not made a *pir*. And he has recited the Quran eighteen times while in his mother's womb. That is why he is called a *pir*.

The *pir* has also a very close and intimate relationship with Allah.

My *pir* is my God. He is my Allah. Because my *pir* is my God, he knows what I am and the condition I am in. He knows where I am and what I am doing now. He knows everything about me. Allah is in everyone. And one who has recognized his *pir* has recognized Allah. For the *murid*, the *pir* is Allah.

The *pir's* work is to worship. The *pir* and God are together in the same way as you and your bag are together. You cannot leave your bag because it contains the tools of your work. In the same way the *pir* cannot leave God, and God cannot leave the *pir*. The *pir* worships God so much that he cannot leave God; and God cannot leave him because He loves him, and he loves God. The relationship between God and the *pir* may be understood better if we recall the relationship between God and Mohammed. A *qawwali* (song) says, "When the last day and the time for the final judgment comes, it will be difficult to distinguish between Allah and Mohammed." This is because the

faces of both will look alike. But one will be able to distinguish
between them when they sit down, because the throne of Allah
will be slightly higher than the throne of Mohammed. The *pir*
occupies the place of Mohammed in this world. He is very
special and far above other people.

The *pir* has this special and intimate relationship with God
because

he walks on the path of God. Consequently, he becomes God's.
He becomes God's hearing, seeing, etc. So what is the distance
between the *pir* and God? The *pir* has become light. He is no
longer a man though he looks like a man and has all the needs
of ordinary men. If he is merely a man why do people come to
him and touch their foreheads to his feet? He *was* a man; but
now he has become the beloved of God. He has become the
beloved of God because he has killed his *nafs*.

The *pir* has destroyed his *nafs*. If a person eats his fill and
then goes to pray the *namaz*, he will not be able to worship
properly. He will feel sleepy. The *pir* has destroyed his *nafs*
through constant fasting, giving away what he receives, not
caring what clothes he wears, and by worshipping constantly.
He remembers Allah constantly, even in his sleep. People here
have heard *pirs* say in their sleep, "Allah, Allah, *hu, hu,...*"
Remembering God with every breath, he has become Allah's.
And Allah has said, "When he becomes mine, I will become his
eyes, nose, ears, hands, feet, etc." Allah is everything, but Allah
says, "When a man attains connection with me, I will become
his hands, eyes, mouth and everything. He will see, hear, talk,
etc. through Me and know everything just as I know it."

A barren woman once approached the prophet Moses, and
asked him to ask God to give her a child. Moses told her that
he would look up the book of predestination. If the word
"children" was written under her name, he would pray to Allah
to give her a child. But when Moses looked up the book of
predestination, he found "no children" written under her name.

So he told the woman that nothing could be done for her. A few months later, a *faqir* began to shout outside her house, "One *chapati* (unleavened bread) one child, two *chapatis* two children, three *chapatis* three children..." On hearing this the woman took all the *chapatis* that she had prepared and gave them to the *faqir*. And she told him to remember what he had said. A year later she bore a son, and in the years that followed five more sons. One day, many years later, Moses happened to walk by her house. He saw the children playing, and remembering that this was the house of the woman whose fate was to be barren, he called out to her and asked her whose children these were. She told him they were hers and about the *faqir* who had made it possible to have them. On hearing this, Moses went straight to Allah and began to complain, "You have given this *faqir* the power to change what is written in the book of predestination; but not to me even though I am a prophet. What is the meaning of this" Allah replied, "I will explain that later. But first, I want you to go and fill this dish with human flesh." Moses asked, bewildered, "But how will I fill it with human flesh?" "Go and ask people to give me their flesh," Allah replied. Moses went about all day trying to get people to contribute their flesh to Allah, but they only laughed at him. Finally, when he was about to give up, he came across a beggar sitting at the corner of a house. The beggar asked him what was wrong. Moses told him of Allah's command and of how he had failed to fulfil it. The beggar said, "Oh, so Allah wants human flesh. Take mine." And he took the knife from Moses' hand, cut off huge pieces from his body and filled Moses' dish. Moses gave the dish to Allah and told him of that one generous man. Then Allah said, "Have you begun to understand why I gave that *faqir* the power to change what is written in the book of predestination? He is willing to give me anything, even his own flesh. When the other people refused to give their flesh, you, Moses, could have filled the dish with your flesh. But you did not. What will I not do for that one who loves me so much! And how can you complain when I give to him what I do not give to you?"

Consequently, the "real *pir* is all knówing and all seeing"

The *pir* has the light of God. He is lost in God and spends his
whole life doing God's work. Hence, whatever the *pir* says is
said through the light of God. There is a *hadith* that says, "The
true believers see with the light of Allah, speak about what they
have seen with the aid of this light, and not about that which they
have thought about through their own intelligence."

He is also the mediator between God and man.

God will not come to you directly. When you ask of God, ask
indirectly. Do not ask directly. Ask from God, but ask through
someone. There are millions of people before God. Why will
He care for you in a special way? But if you ask through His
friend it is different. For example, you are my friend. If you send
someone to me, and the man tells me that you have sent him, I
will leave all my work and attend to him. I will do this because
I will say to myself, "My friend has sent him to me." Will I not
say that? And then I will tell this man that I will help him because
you have sent him to me. But if he comes to me and does not
tell me that you have sent him, I will not even look at him. He
will sit here and then go away without getting anything. But if
my friend sends him, not only will I help him, but I will *have* to
help him.

This is the meaning of *pir*. It is necessary to have someone's
recommendation in every place, even when one wants to get a
job. The *pir* recommends people to God. Why do so many
people come here? There is no doctor here. But they come here
when the doctor tells them that they will not get children. They
come here when their business is failing, and for other things.
The *pir* will tell them, "Go and recite this, go remember this
name." He will tell them to recite something for ten days. And
they get what they want. They get it through the *pir*. Why do
people come here in such great numbers? Why do they give so

much money to the *pirs*? Why do they put so many thousands
of rupees worth of flowers on Nizamuddin Aulia's tomb? Are
they mad? No, they are not. They come because God is not
listening to them. They come here and say, "I come to you
because God is not listening to me." And they will tell the *pir*
their problem. They bring fruit for the *pir* to eat. The *pir* eats
and feels happy. Then he asks, "Why have you brought this fruit
for me?" The person replies, "No, no, I brought it just like that."
If the person has no money, then he brings a flower and gives it
to the *pir*. It is said, never go to the *pir* empty-handed; always
take something for him. If you have no money, take a flower
and say, "I give you a present." Then the *pir* will become happy
and give him something or the other. He will not allow him to
leave empty-handed. He will pray so that his visitor receives
what he wants. That is why so many people come to the *pir*. The
pir troubles God and gets the *murid's* prayer heard. But before
the *pir* can do this, the person has to become the *pir's* friend, or
he has to be sent by a friend of the *pir*. Only then will the *pir*
recommend the person's case to God.

But then, the *pir's* great influence with God can also be a threat
to the *murid* and, hence, something that is greatly feared. Thus, the
pirs (as far as some *murids* are concerned) must be treated with
reverence and care and, perhaps avoided, whenever possible.

The *pir* through his prayers can change what is written in the
book of fate. He can tell God to rub out the bad things written
about one in the book of fate. He can tell God to write that a
certain person should be rich and to rub out what was previously
written, that he should be poor. But then, he can also make the
strong and rich weak and poor in this way. Suddenly, all their
money will be lost or a thief will come and steal it. Then the rich
will have to walk about naked and beg with bowed heads. The
pir has never told lies. He has always prayed the *namaz* and God
has made him His own. That is why the angels and all the people
come and fan him from all four sides. He is already in heaven.

We must obey the *pir*, whatever the command. If the *pir* orders, "Do not pray the *namaz*", and if we disobey him by praying the *namaz*, he will punish us. The *pir* will throw out his *murid* and also pray to God, "Give him even more trouble. He is a sinner. Make him commit even more sin." The *pir* is a very dangerous man. It is better to remain far from him. He does everything through his prayers. We must approach him with gifts to make him happy. If we obey him, he will pray to God, "Make this *murid* pure." And God will make you pure. You will also become a great man and receive everything that your heart desires. God does everything; but the *pir* tells Him what to do. God does what the *pir* asks Him to do. God alone can change one's fate. But it is the *pir* who tells Him to change one's fate, and He changes it.

To recapitulate: The *pir's* external appearance is typical of a traditional Muslim gentleman. But he is much more than a gentleman. This hidden aspect of the *pir* is indicated by the rings with stones of different colours that adorn all the fingers of his right hand, the place where he sits (usually the precincts of a *dargah*), the instruments of his trade (*tawiz* paper, inks and pens, books on astrology and *tawiz*, etc.) and by the reverence displayed by the persons who visit him. The *pir* himself, and the more advanced *murids* invite the *murid* to discover this hidden aspect of the *pir* by telling him to consider the *pir* as a short examination question that requires a lengthy answer. That the *murid* usually does not have access to any written tradition that explains what the *pir* is, is no impediment, however, as the *pir* and more advanced *murids* discourage the *murid* from using the written word as a means of understanding the *pir* (or answering the question). They advise him to come to an understanding of the *pir* by attending to his own personal experience of him; and they explain how he should use this experience to gain the required understanding of the *pir*, he has to use this experience in the same way as he uses his experience when solving riddles. The *murid* contrasts and compares his experience of the *pir* with his other every day social experiences in order to arrive at definitions of the *pir,* which he constantly revises as his familiarity with his *pir* and his acquaintance with the beliefs and practices (*adab*) surrounding the *pir* increases. These definitions are expressed in stories and statements of belief.

The *pir* is compared and contrasted with the *murid's* experience of his own father. The *pir* is father in the sense that he commands respect and obedience, is ever watchful in order to save the *murid* from troubles and difficulties, constantly cares for, helps and educates him. But he is more than a father because his responsibility over the *murid* extends even after death until the last judgment on the last day. The *pir* is also compared to a *maulvi* who teaches the faith; but unlike the *maulvi,* he practises his faith. Hence, he knows the difficulties involved in putting that faith into practice and the ways of overcoming them. Thus, he has power, not possessed by the *maulvi,* that comes from this constant practice of the faith. Since the experience of the *maulvi* as guide and teacher is not adequate to understand the *pir,* the *pir* is further compared to Mohammed, the Prophet, who gave the revelation, the Quran, and showed the revealed way of putting it into practice, the *sunnah.* The *pir* is, however, subservient to the Prophet because far from bringing any new revelation and practice, he is restricted by the Quran and by the *sunnah* (practice) of the Prophet. Hence, he is compared to the flying horse, Buraq, that took Mohammed into the presence of God (the *miraj*). Just as that flying horse took the Prophet into the presence of God, the *pir* takes the *murid* to the Prophet, and also into the presence of God.

Finally, the *pir* is called the hands, feet, eyes and ears of God (i.e. the concrete manifestation of God) and even Allah, because he is a friend of God. As a friend of God he is in constant contact with God and does only what He wills (i.e. he has no ego and, thus, mediates God to the *murid*). Hence, he can also take the *murid's* needs and requests to God and have them granted: he is an intercessor and is compared to the secretary who takes a visitor's request to Rajiv Gandhi, (the late prime minister of India). The power that comes from this intimate relationship is, however, also frightening for some *murids* because it can also destroy the good fortune they enjoy. Hence, the *pir* has to be kept at a distance and, when necessary, approached with gifts and great respect.

CHARACTERISTICS OF THE *PIR*

Many *murids* pointed out that the *pir* has only two characteristics.

> A *pir* does only two things: he worships and serves humanity.
> Islam is his religion; and Islam means that he worships God and
> does good by serving people. In this way he makes them holy.
>   The *pir* has no occupation. He is busy with his prayers and
> serves whoever comes to him without asking for any thing. That
> is why the *murids* give him money and other gifts and look after
> his family. In this way the *pir* can continue with his prayers
> without having to worry about his family and his daily bread.

Worshipping God would consist in doing many things: depending on God alone, seeing God in all things and loving God, as given
above in the definitions of the *pir*. Further,

> A true *pir* is one who knows and practises the law, especially the
> five pillars, and follows the Sufi path. It is very important for the
> *pir* to pray the *namaz*.
>   *Pir* is a title given to a great man. He can understand very
> much and he can bear every difficulty that God chooses to send
> down upon him. The world is nothing in his eyes. Only such
> a man is called a *pir*. The *pirs* that we see today are not *pirs*. The
> real *pir* is one who does not care for his life and is, satisfied with
> God, whatever be his situation. His wealth consists in eating one
> onion a day. He eats dry crust of bread, not *biryani*. People who
> live such lives truly worship and are called *pirs*. *Pir* is not a career
> or a means to become rich. One has to destroy one's *nafs*. The
> world should mean nothing to you. One must die to oneself for
> the end. Only then is one a true *pir*.

Hence,

> This *pir* sitting here [said in the presence of his *pir*] is also
> searching for Allah. But he is not searching for Him by roaming
> about like you and me. He is searching by sitting in one place.

His searching is worship.

Because the *pir* worships in this way, it is said that he possesses and is possessed by Allah.

If you immerse yourself in worship like the *pirs*, like them you will become a possession of God. It is said, "Become the possession of Allah and Allah will become yours." I am a Muslim: my religion is Islam. And Islam has taught me to perform the five pillars. But no one practises Islam today. If one practises it, one will be set all right. Wheat is ground in the mill. In the same way, men are ground by worshipping, especially by following the five pillars. The *pirs* have undergone this grinding. That is why they are Allah's and Allah is theirs.

Consequently,

The true *pir* has no faults. He has the mercy of God within himself, and he loves other people as God loves. To him the religion of those who come to him does not matter. All are friends of God because they are His creatures. We are all one when it comes to our difficulties, sorrows, and even our joys.

Even when the *pir* appears to be idle (idleness is considered as the workshop of Satan), he is actually worshipping. And through this worship he is serving people (i.e. manifesting God as the all-merciful to people who are not physically present before him).

The *pir* may appear to be a nonentity. But do not think he is nothing. He sits quietly in one place, as if doing nothing. But in actual fact, all the time he is collecting and spending lakhs of rupees. In this way he is doing a lot of good work. Because he sits quietly in one place people cannot see all the good work that he does. If he so desires he can go and earn lakhs of rupees and enjoy himself. But he does not. He sits here quietly doing God's work. He does not exchange his power for money. If he does that, what was the use of leaving the world? He is constantly making life easier for people through his prayers. In this way he is constantly collecting and spending lakhs of rupees. For instance, my *pir*-brother, who is the *khilafa* of my *pir*, has a *murid* in Hyderabad. This *murid* fell seriously ill and had to be operated upon. During the operation the doctor made a mistake. The *murid's* wife was informed that he was very close to death. One night an old man said to her in a dream, "Do not worry. Your husband will get well again." From that day onwards his health began to improve. A few months later she came here with her husband and their *pir* for the *urs* of Hazrat Nizamuddin. The *pir* brought them to their grandfather *pir*, my *pir*. When the woman saw my *pir*, she exclaimed that he was the one who had appeared in her dream. Then at the bidding of her *pir*, she stepped forward and fell at the feet of my *pir*. These things are common but not talked about openly.

The *pir's* service to the people is not limited to prayers. As would be obvious from the definitions of the *pir* given above, he also serves them by forgiving, by resolving their problems, by helping them to find ways and means to solve the problems themselves, by correcting faults, suggesting methods for giving up bad habits, and by helping them to give new and more helpful meanings to the situations they find themselves in. Further, he serves by making himself available to those who need him.

The *pir* attracts others by his good qualities. He does not catch your hand and pull you towards him. You yourself will be drawn to him. He has that spiritual power. He attracts people through his goodness, his honesty, and by the fact that this world means nothing to him. The *pir* forgets the wrongs we do. He will say,"It does not matter", and forgive. But he will also tell us not to repeat that sin.

Sometimes, the *pir* may appear to be a crook or wicked. Even so, he attracts people to himself because of his power, which he always uses to give something to other people. You may have heard of Panagh Sharif. It is a *dargah*. The *pir* who is buried there was a very handsome man. He liked to wear expensive and flashy clothes. He enjoyed playing chess. People said that he was a crook and not a *pir* because he used to chew tobacco, and ogled at girls. If a girl attracted him, he would tell her to cry before him; watching her made her more attractive to him. He had three wives.

A Pathan lived opposite his house. He was childless. Once the Pathan said, "I am the *murid* of your father and, hence, your *murid*. I am childless even though I have great wealth. What use is all this wealth without children!" The *pir* told him that he would get a child. The Pathan asked him to pray for him. A few days later, the *pir* was playing chess in the Pathan's house. The Pathan's household was watching their play. The *pir* called the Pathan's wife to sit next to him. When she drew near, he slapped her shoulder and said, "Go. You will bear a son. Call him Afzal Ghani. Two months from now you will know that you are with child." Nine months later, when the child was born, the parents found the imprint of four fingers on one of his shoulders. Hi, to whom Allah gives, he gives. It is the pleasure of Allah. What can I say about this! And his *dargah* earns crores of rupees today. Even Indira Gandhi went to him. While he was alive no one could claim to be a greater *pir*.

It is important to go to a *pir*, whatever people may say or think about him. He it is who gives. One must go and serve him and give him gifts. That I will never become a *pir* does not dismay me. My *pir's* good pleasure and blessing is enough for me.

This ceaseless giving seems to be the main visible characteristic of the *pir*. This giving is independent of the gifts that he receives from people.

The *pir* gives. He has no need to take from anyone. His work is to give and to bless. The work of all others is to receive. Everyone else is begging, "Please give me something. Sir, I am hungry since yesterday. Sir, I have so many problems." Their hands are stretched out to receive. But the *pir*, like God, has his hands stretched out to give. If he receives a gift from you then his right hand will cover what his left hand receives. He will just not take, like other people.

The *pir* gives ceaselessly because he loves everyone, whatever their religion and their social and religious status. He loves in the same way as a mother loves her child.

The *pir* is interested in human beings, not in religion or caste. He knows that we are one because we are human beings, and not because we belong to a particular religion or caste. He asks the one who comes to him, "How can I help you?"—not "What is your religion?" And he treats all who come to him well.

The *pir* is like a mother with her unlimited love. The mother does not think, "This child of mine will serve me one day. It will look after me one day. Hence, I must be careful how I treat it now." She does not think of all these things when she feeds it with her milk. She does not think of the future benefits that she will get by serving the child now. She does everything for the child and brings it up. If the child wets the mattress at night, she will lift the child and put it in her place and she herself will lie in the wet place. If there is very little food, she gives the food to the child and goes hungry. That is why a mother's prayer are the most powerful prayers on earth. If one wants to keep Allah happy, progress materially and spiritually, and attain paradise on the last day, one must make one's mother happy. The *pir* loves other men like a mother. That is why his prayers are so powerful. It is said that he can draw gold from the *murid*.

But like a father, the *pir* is also a man of responsibility. He will not only be punished for the sins of his *murids* but also will be punished more severely than others for his own personal sins.

Greater responsibility is expected from the more educated than from the illiterate in Sufism and Islam. Education makes one an

alim. If the educated does wrong, he will be punished for seven
sins; if an illiterate person does wrong, he is punished only for
that one sin. He can tell Allah, "I did not know." But not the
pir. Allah will say to him, "You reached such a high station that
fifty men were your *murids,* and still you dared to commit this sin.
You did wrong knowingly. Hence, you will get seven times the
punishment." Even the *pirs* are answerable to God and will be
punished or rewarded by Him.

Finally, a *pir* has material wealth. The *pirs* themselves say so. Also
certain *pirs* are criticised, not for their wealth, but for not displaying
the other qualities of a *pir.*

Seven months ago, the President of Pakistan came here. After
praying to Nizamuddin, he met me. He asked me what work
I was doing in the *dargah.* I told him that I am the servant of
Nizamuddin, and that I spend my time kissing his feet. "So you
are a *khadim,*" he said. "How much do you earn every month?"
he asked. Not a single paisa, I answered. "What is your monthly
household expenditure?" Ten thousand rupees, I replied. I do
not earn anything, yet this amount comes to me every month.
Nizamuddin gives me what I need. I have no need to beg from
anyone; Nizamuddin looks after me. On hearing this, he bent
down and touched my feet and asked to become my *murid.*
    Wearing expensive and flashy clothes, eating expensive
food, roaming about in cars and taxis does not make one a *pir.*
One must also kill the *nafs.* One must have the power to guide
the *murid.* One must have the knowledge.

To recapitulate: The *pir* is described as having two major
characteristics—worship and service. Worship seems to mean the
process of becoming the possession of God. This process involves a
number of other characteristics like following the *sharia* (law), being
satisfied with God even in the midst of great adversity, fasting, and
service. Service is an aspect of worship and involves attracting people
so that he can lead them to God. He accepts everyone, irrespective

of caste and religious affiliation; displays an understanding, helpful, forgiving and merciful attitude; gives something (material things and also spiritual things like blessing, spiritual advice, *tawiz*, etc.) to all visitors, clients and *murids*; and displays a sense of responsibility for all those who come and visit him.

The *murids* understand the characteristic of worship (the process of becoming a possession of God) to be like being ground in a mill into flour. They explain their own experience of the *pir's* attitude of service in terms of a mother's selfless devotion to her child.

DUTIES OF THE *PIR*

The main duty of the *pir* is to lead the *murid* to God.

> The *pir's* duty is to see that the *murid* becomes one with him.
> When the *pir* makes the *murid* one with himself, the *murid* begins
> to possess all that belongs to the *pir*. Then the *pir* takes the *murid*
> to his *pir*, who in turn takes him to his *pir* until the *murid* reaches
> Mohammed. And Mohammed takes the *murid* to God. When
> the *murid* is taken to the grandfather *pir*, he has to lose himself in
> him, and do the same thing with all the other *pirs* and with
> Mohammed. And when Mohammed takes him to God, he must
> lose himself in God also. Then he becomes God. He becomes
> God because what belongs to God becomes his.

> Once, a poor man came in and sat down in one corner of a *pir's*
> office. "What can I do for you?" asked the *pir* after attending to all
> his other clients. The man replied, "I am in search of Allah. What
> else is there to desire!" "What do you want?" asked the *pir*. The man
> said, "I want to become your *murid*. I want to learn to love Allah.
> I want your prayers." "If God wills, if God wills," exclaimed the *pir*.
> Then he said, "Come day after tomorrow. Now go and pray the
> *namaz*. And after that recite Allah, Allah." This main duty of leading
> the *murid* to God (whatever be the way in which it is described)
> involves many other lesser duties on the part of the *pir*. The *pir* has
> to impart knowledge to the *murid*.

No one respects a man for himself. They respect his knowledge. If one dresses a sweeper in a three-piece suit and takes him to a five-star hotel, he will still behave like a sweeper because he does not have the knowledge that will enable him to behave like one who is used to that suit. The *pir* has to give that all-important knowledge to people so that they can behave in the right way and, thus, earn respect.

The *pir* tells the *murid* good things. He teaches him the meaning of the Quran and the holy words written in other books. We have to be taught this if we are to be good. That is why we need a *pir*.

We have to pray the *namaz*. But usually we do not pray it properly. We pray very quickly and then go away, as if we are doing some exercise. The *pir* taught me to keep Allah before me, to believe that He is before me, and that I am bowing to Him. He taught me to concentrate on Allah while reciting the prayers. The *pir* has to convince the *murid* that his worship has to be of the highest quality.

Suppose someone yawns during *namaz*. The correct etiquette is to cover our mouth with our hand when we are with other people. The same thing we must do when we are before Allah. Also, when we love and respect someone, we always sit facing him, and not with our backs towards him. In the same way, whenever we sit in the mosque or in the *pir's* office, we must never sit with our backs towards the *qibla* or the *pir's gaddi* (the cushion on which he sits). The *pir* tells us that if we want to love Allah we must love His friends; and we must not do to them what we would not do to Allah. If one is doing something wrong, one must not do it facing their direction. Also, if one is having intercourse with one's wife one must make sure that one is not facing the direction of the *pir's* house. We must do all this if we love Allah. This is the *adab* the *pir* teaches his *murid*.

The *pir* gives the *murid* spiritual instructions like, how to pray, what to pray, and how to get the securities of life. The *pir* will also tell him what to believe. He makes the *murid* radically different from the official Muslim—the Muslim who is merely included in the statistics.

The *pir* teaches humanness. He teaches one not to tell lies, not to steal, etc. He teaches us to depend on God. He does this by making the *murid* walk on the path; and the path consists in denying oneself. Then one will find God, and one's life will be changed easily.

The *pir* shows us how we should talk to the inner *pir*. He will tell us what prayers to say. He will make our faith in this inner *pir* grow. This inner *pir* is the God within us. We have to learn to concentrate on it. The *pir* teaches us how to concentrate on it and how to get to know it.

The *pir* is a trainer, a teacher, and a coach. He finds out how much the *murid* is capable of and helps him attain that much. He does not overburden the *murid* with duties he cannot fulfil. Hence, he does not discourage the *murid*. To bring the *murid* to the right path, he repeatedly reminds him of his promise to obey him. This work of the *pir* continues even after his death because he has permission to leave his grave and to roam about. The *pirs* come in various forms to different people and continue to instruct them.

The *pir* is necessary to make the *qalb* known to the *murid*. If there was no *qalb* there would be no need for the *pir*. It is the *qalb* that brings the hidden knowledge. It is through the *qalb* that one communicates with the great men of religion.

Finally, the *pir* teaches the *murid* by answering his questions and by giving good advice. This may be done indirectly.

The *pir* answers the *murid's* questions indirectly. He may answer the questions by talking to someone else while the *murid* is listening. It is as if he is talking to that other person, and as if he has not heard the *murid's* questions. But if the *murid* listens carefully, he will find the answers to his questions. The counsel of the *pir* must be heeded because he has a prenomination of future events. For instance, five men once visited Hazrat

Nizamuddin. As they were leaving, he told them to go by the road along the river, and not to go through the jungle. But they did not listen. As they walked through the jungle, a hot wind (*loo*), began to blow, and four of them died from the heat. The fifth managed to reach a well, but while drawing water he fell into the well and drowned. If they had listened to the *pir*, the hot wind would not have bothered them because as it passed over the river it would have cooled. The advice of the *pir* is good. One may not understand why it is being given but one must listen.

The *pir* must look after the material welfare of the *murid*.

The *pir* is like a father. He looks after all aspects of the *murid's* life, both his spiritual welfare and physical welfare. The *pir* will take away the worldly difficulties of the *murid* through his prayers. If he wants success, wealth, etc., the *pir* will give it to him.

The *pir* has been given the spirit. Light shines from his face and God has given him the power. So he must solve the problems of ordinary people. If we tell him that someone is ill, the crop is not good, etc., then he must do something to cure, or to correct the matter. He also has to teach, give answers to all our questions and clear all our doubts.

The *pir* also has to

keep the mind and heart of the *murid* clean. He does this through his power. To reach God and Mohammed, a clean heart is a must. The *pir* will make the heart and mind of the *murid* clean by making him confess all his sins. Then he will give him good advice. After that the *pir* will prevent him from telling lies, since lies are the key to all sins.

The *pir* has to protect one when Satan or anything else attacks. He has to protect us when we recite the name of Allah, or a verse of the Quran, because then the emotions rise so high that one can go mad. Many indeed have. But then, they did not have a *pir* to protect them.

The *pir* has to make the *murid* beautiful, just as a bride is made beautiful before her wedding.

Finally, the *pir* has to protect the *murid* in the after life.

When I die, my *pir* will come to my grave and drive away the angels who come to torment me for my sins. He will tell them, "Go away. This is my *murid*." This is his duty. [The *murid* began to weep here and then continued.] The grave is full of peril. To be saved from its torments is a very great thing. In the grave the angels will come and ask, "What have you brought for us?" If I take nothing what will I give them? And what will they give me? They will punish me. But if I take something—if I have recited the *kalima*, done the *namaz* and good works—then the parts that have done these things will become full of light and drive the angels away.

The *pir* helps in the grave. He will come and answer the questions put to one. If he cannot come because he is still alive, then his *pir* will come instead. That is why it is important for the *murids* to recite the names of all the *pirs* in the *silsilah*.

At the final judgment, each person's character and all his deeds will be brought before him. The book in which all these things are recorded will be opened, and one will have to answer for everything. The *pir* will help the *murid* even there. He will tell him what to say.

On the last day, a court will be set up. There, all will look alike. And no one will help anyone else: neither one's brothers, sisters, wife, children, parents nor friends. All will stand in the same uniform and in the same place. Then the account books will be brought forward and opened. Everyone will then remember all his sins. And everyone will look for support from someone else, but only those who are *murids* will find such support. They will go to their *pirs*. The *pirs* will have to take them along as they go to their own *pirs*. And their *pirs* will take

them all to the heads of their respective *silsilahs*, who will take
them to the head of all the *silsilahs*, Hazrat Ali. And Ali will take
them to Mohammed who will be sitting in the court of Allah.
Salvation will depend on knowing the right approach—and the
right approach is the approach of Mohammed. Those who do
not know this approach will go to their prophets, but they will
disown them. They too will be forced to go to Mohammed. But
will Mohammed recognize them!

To recapitulate: The main duty of the *pir* is to lead his *murid* to God.
This involves many lesser duties like finding out the capabilities and
talents of the *murid* and training him according to his aptitude;
looking after his material and spiritual welfare through correction,
advice, *tawiz*, and prayer; helping him overcome the dangers of the
path; saving him after death from the torments and dangers of the
grave by answering the questions put to him by the angels and driving
them away when they torment him; and finally, by ensuring that the
murid attains paradise at the final judgment.

This duty of leading the *murid* to God is likened to the training
of a sweeper in the etiquette and ways of higher society. It is not
enough to give him a three-piece suit and have him sit at table in a
five-star hotel. It is more necessary to train him in the appropriate
ways of behaving in that society. The *murid* sees in the *pir* someone
like his father who sought to ensure his spiritual and material welfare
while he was under his care. Finally, when the task of leading the
murid to God is seen to nearing completion, the *pir* is likened to the
women who dress, adorn and beautify a bride on her wedding day.

ADAB FOR THE *PIR*

The *pir* has to love his *murids*.

For the *murid*, the *pir* is Allah. So the *pir* has to look after his *murid*.
If the *pir* has a son and a *murid*, and if both fall ill at the same time,
the *pir* has to attend to his *murid* first, and only then his son.

The *pir* cannot exult in his spiritual power.

The *pir* cannot say, "I have spiritual power." It is wrong for him to say so. Allah will not be pleased and He will take away his power. Also, if the *pir* makes his power known, he may be punished in another way. Crowds will flock to his door and he will have no peace, day or night.

A *pir* cannot abuse the saints just because he has spiritual power. Forty years ago there was a *pir* here. He used to drink liquor and had many European *murids*. Whatever he said came true. Also he could read the minds of those who came to him. He would tell them what they wanted before they opened their mouth. One day he became very proud and shouted at the people, "Why are you going to Nizamuddin? He is dead. What can he do for you? Come to me. See my power." As he spoke his power began to disappear; and by the time he finished speaking all his power had left him. When he realized what had happend he repented. He went to Nizamuddin's tomb and begged for forgiveness. But he never got back his power. And all his *murids* left him.

The *pir* cannot scandalize anyone or behave unconventionally.

Having power does not mean that the *pir* can set a bad example. Once, a man was sleeping in the mosque in the *dargah*. When the call for prayer was sounded the servant of the mosque began to sweep the place for *namaz*. He woke the sleeping man and told him to go and prepare for *namaz*. The man answered that he did not have to pray the *namaz*. At this, the servant was very angry and started a quarrel with him over the matter. The man said, "I will show you why I do not have to pray the *namaz* so that you stop troubling me." He took him to a meeting at which Mohammed, the other prophets, and all the saints were present. After some time, Mohammed asked the servant why he had come. He told Mohammed that he had been brought there by the other man and then complained, "This man says that there is no need for him to pray the *namaz*. I do not agree. And I want you to pass judgment." The Prophet said, "You are right. He must pray the *namaz*." Then he sent them away. And the man who had this power found that his power had disappeared. One cannot abuse the power. It can be taken away at any time.

A *pir* cannot do whatever he likes. There was a *pir* in this *dargah*, who used to say he loved God in all things. And he used to kiss every good-looking girl that visited the *dargah*. No one could say anything to him. But one day when he visited the Maike Dargah (the *dargah* of Nizamuddin's mother) on the occasion of her *urs*, as he was climbing the steps to the shrine, a huge black cobra reared its head before him. He stopped. Then he heard the words, "So you see God in all things! Come, see God in me also. Come, kiss me on the lips." But the *pir* did not move. The snake again urged, "What! Do you fail to see God in me? Come, kiss me on my lips. Come, see God in me also." Then the *pir* caught his ears and begged for forgiveness, "I am sorry. Please forgive me. I kiss only those I am attracted to. I do not see God in them." And the snake went away. Now, only he heard the voice speaking to him. Those who were standing around heard only what he said. When they asked him what had happened, he told them what he had seen.

The *pir* has to give without desiring a reward. But if he still wants one, he has to follow certain rules: He cannot demand a fixed amount of money. He can only ask the client to decide and tell him what he or she wishes to give him once the job is done. A portion of this amount he has to give to the poor. Also, the *pir* cannot reject a gift.

If someone does not give a gift to the *pir*, he cannot think, "This person has not given me a gift. I will not help him." If a *pir* does this he sins; and God will punish him. God will say, "You have taken up this work of a *pir*. It means that you educate your *murids*, set them on the right path, stop them from sining, etc. But you have been thinking, if I get five rupees from each *murid*

I will get five lakh rupees from one lakh *murids*. You have failed in your responsibility as *pir*. Now take your punishment. You must suffer, not only for your sins, but also for all the sins of all your *murids*."

The *pir* cannot ask monetary payment for his services, because he serves through his prayers. If he demands money in return, he is exchanging prayers for money. If I exchange prayers for money then the prayers will become ineffective. But if people give money to the *pir* of their own accord, he must accept it, be it one rupee or lakhs of rupees. We cannot ask for money in exchange for prayers. We can ask the client, "What will you give me, if I do this work for you?" But we cannot demand that he give, neither can we demand that he give a certain amount. The *pirs* who demand money in exchange for their prayers are ineffective. People have to go to them repeatedly, and their work is never done.

There is another thing. If I had the time I would have shown you where it is given in the *hadith*. Once a holy man was passing through a village. He saw a big crowd gathered outside one house. They told him that inside a man was dying of an incurable illness as punishment for his sins. The holy man went to the relatives of the man and asked them what they would give him if he cured the sick man. They promised him four goats. He prayed to Allah, read a verse of the Quran over some water and gave it to the dying man to drink. The dying man was cured, and the holy man received the four goats. He went to Mohammed with them. Mohammed said, "One part of your reward is mine." Hence, a *pir* has to keep aside a part of what he receives as Allah's share. And with it he has to feed the poor once a month.

The *pir* must accept the offered gift. Otherwise the heart of the giver will break. The *pir* can give away the gift to someone else even in the presence of the giver, but he has to accept it. If he refuses he loses the blessing that he enjoys. This reminds me what happened here in the *dargah*. Once someone came here— man or woman I cannot tell, but it was a human being. It asked

me, "How many people are in the *dargah*?" I gave the figure. It
called out to them and began to give them money. One worker
did not come to receive the gift, so I sent for him. When he
arrived, this person stretched out its closed fist to give him
something, but the man refused to accept. And he refused so
insultingly that everyone present felt bad, and said to the giver,
"Please ignore his behaviour. He is mad." When the person left,
I asked the servant why he had behaved so. And he uttered an
expletive. He revealed what was in his heart. Some old men,
there also upbraided him. They said, "This person is giving
something to you. You cannot possibly know what he is and
what he is not. Why did you refuse his gift? Who knows what
he is! Who knows what is giving you what, and in what form?
If you did not want it, you should have accepted and given it
away. Why did you kick what was coming to you?" The man
replied, "I do not know whether it was a man or a woman. How
can I take anything from it?" They asked him, "Have you seen
Allah? Has anyone told you what He looks like? Has anyone
told you that He is a man or a woman? You can make love to
a woman. So I see Allah as a woman. He is a mother, a woman,
a sister, and a daughter. I have not seen Him but I can say this.
You can make love only to a woman. You can give Allah
another sex." The servant did not remain in the *dargah* even
one second after that. We did not tell him to go away. But his
health was ruined. His heart got frightened. He took his
belongings and ran away. Who knows where he went! He had
kicked the hand that had been stretched out to give. That was
why he was driven out of the *dargah*.

A *pir* may not, under normal circumstances, bring down evil on
anyone. But he may, under certain conditions.

A *pir* may not do evil to anyone. But he may give someone
trouble if that person is giving too much trouble to someone else.
Mohammed said, "If anyone beats you, you can bring down evil
on that person." And if someone wants to kill you, you may kill

him before he kills you. But this is the last stage. Before that, it is written, one must suffer.

Once a woman, who had been divorced and thrown out of the house at midnight, came to a *pir* demanding that he do something to kill her former husband. The *pir* listened to her for two hours, allowed her to make a number of phone calls, and tried to pacify her. But when she refused to be pacified and continued to demand that he kill the man, the *pir* got angry and said, "I am a *pir*. My work is to show mercy, not to kill. How can you demand that I kill him." The woman persisted, "I have suffered so much. He must die." Then the *pir* left the office. She continued to sit there till evening. When the *pir* returned they worked out a plan to get her belongings from her former husband. Finally, the *pir* phoned her family and asked them to come and take her home.

Another woman once walked into the *pir's* office on another occasion. The *pir* gave her a *tawiz* that he had prepared beforehand, which he told her to bury in a grave yard. She had to bang it while reciting the name of her husband, who was living with another woman and giving her endless trouble. He said, "If you want, I can bring about his death. I do not generally do this kind of work for anyone. But for you I would. Give the order and it will be done. The decision is yours. I am your servant." "No, no," the woman said, "I don't want him to die. Only I don't want to see him again." The *pir* replied, "Then do what I have told you, and make sure that you do not lose this *tawiz*. It must not fall into anyone else's hands."

The *pir* cannot give *tawiz* in the day time during Ramzan. But this and the other rules cited below do not generally seem to be followed.

After 7.00 p.m., when fasting is over for the day, I will begin giving away *tawizes*. Not before. This is His order. We are sitting and doing this work in the name of our *pirs* in the *silsilah* of

Nizamuddin, Moinuddin, etc. And they are also fasting in the name of Him who has created us. *Pirs* do not eat during the day. They eat at midnight when all their work is over. During the day they drink only tea, or they chew only the betel leaf.

I do not call people on Saturday. Saturday is a day of prayer. I must set aside one day for myself. My *pir* told me never to call anyone on a Saturday. It is like this. Saturday is a very difficult day for people. They keep their goodness and respect in the safe keeping of the *pir*. Saturday is the day of the *pir*. We do not do any work for people on that day. On that day we have to recite our *vazifa*. If anyone comes to us with his problem on that day, we will only say, "Yes, yes" to him. Then we call him on the next day. No *pir* will ever work on a Saturday. Sunday is completely free for all kinds of work. On Saturday we pray for ourselves. We prepare ourselves so that we can continue to give to the people. By doing this we are not over-strained.

Finally, the *pir* must be gracious to and help all who come to him, be they poor or rich.

A *pir* cannot throw out anyone who comes to him, even one dressed in rags. Who knows what form Allah assumes when He comes to us!

To recapitulate: The *pir* has to show greater care and concern for the *murid* than for his own children. He cannot scandalize people by glorying in his power, insulting the saints, refusing to pray the *namaz*, running after women or by using his power in acts of revenge. He can use his power to destroy someone only if that person is troubling someone else. Also, he cannot demand money in payment for his services or refuse to serve those who will not give him anything. He can only ask them what they intend giving him. Others may see it as a subtle demand for payment but most *pirs* and *murids* refuse to see it as such. The few who concede the point legitimize it as a concession made to the material necessities of the *pirs* and their families. Finally, the *pir* has to welcome and attend to all who come to his door.

The *murids* believe that a *pir* follows this code of behaviour even when he publicly seems to break it. They believe that if indeed he broke the code, he would lose his power and could no longer function as a *pir*. The fact that great numbers of people continue to visit the *pir* with their difficulties is seen as proof that he has not lost his power. His apparent breaking of the code is seen as a riddle beyond comprehension of the *murid*, or as a hidden service to someone at the command of God Himself.

THE *PIR'S* POWER

Hardly anyone speaks of the *pir* without some comment on his power. To the *murid*, this power is of utmost importance, not only within the *piri-muridi* relationship but also when he is in the process of choosing a *pir*, as we shall see later. For many *murids,* it is also an important personal goal. The *pirs* and *murids* describe this power in different ways.

There is something called *karamat*. What is *karamat*? It is like one's knack of cooking. There are many books on how to cook. If someone who has never cooked before tries to cook guided by these books, the meal he prepares will not be the best because he lacks experience. But his wife, who works in the kitchen daily, does not need the help of the books to prepare a very good meal. Exeperience gives her the power in cooking.

We have the Quran, the *hadith*, the *sharia*, etc. They tell us what to believe and what beliefs to practise. But nothing happens only by reading them. One has to think of ways of believing in what they say, and find ways to practise these beliefs. In the effort to believe and in the process of practising the beliefs, one gets practical experience. The *pir* has this practical experience. This gives him his power. He knows how to believe in what the books say, and how to practise these beliefs. Hence, he is successful while the ordinary people are not. The *pir* has gained this experience by submitting to guidance. When one goes to college one has to think about what is taught. One has to take it apart and put it together again. And one must allow oneself to be corrected because one may not have put it together in the right way. In this way alone can we learn anything properly. There is a particular method of getting experience. The method is *piri-muridi*. The *pir* has gone through this process. He who has used this method and gained experience is the one who has power. He is the *pir*.

The power of the *pir* is only this: His prayer is heard more quicker than other people's. God listens to everyone, but to the *pir* He listens more quickly. Others will cry out to Him for one month, and may still not be heard. But the *pir* has to pray only once and he is heard.

Sometimes, by the grace of Allah, whatever I say happens immediately. At other times it takes time. I should not be proud. I cannot tell you that everything I say comes about. Sometimes, even work that is lawful takes a long time to take effect. If someone asks me for a *tawiz* for someone to fall ill, for an enemy to get robbed, or for a husband to divorce his wife, I cannot help him. Such work is possible but not allowed. I can do only good work like bringing about love between an estranged couple.

I visited someone this morning. He had come to me earlier. His daughter's first marriage was unhappy because her in-laws ill treated her. Hence, she returned to his house. The second marriage was equally unhappy because her in-laws made her the house servant, and worried the life out of her if she wore nice clothes or ate something tasty. She returned home for the second time. Now he wanted her to be married into a house where she would be happy. He wanted my help. I told him to send his daughter to me. When she came, I made her sit here and recited something for a long time and then recited the same thing along with her. What we recited I cannot tell. I told her to come again the next day. I told her that we would have to recite the same thing together for seven days. My heart told me to give her this instruction. But she did not come on the fifth day. On the sixth day her marriage was arranged. And on the seventh day she got married. Her new in-laws are really good people. Her parents tell me that everything they could wish for her has been fulfilled with this marriage. She is treated like a daughter in that house.

The *pir's* power concerns knowing the special way in which the spirits and *jinn* can be controlled. This special method has to be learnt. It is learnt from heart to heart. Besides this, one has to accept certain restrictions. One must not eat meat, fish, eggs, onions, spices, etc. One must follow the *sharia* and spend one's life in doing good works. ‑

Learning "from heart to heart" is another way of saying that the *murid* learns by observing the *pir* in the course of living with him and keeping him company. In this way the *murid* accumulates ways of understanding and doing things without any deliberate or conscious effort. He is socialized into a particular way of life.

When you come here and meet me, I may say nothing. You also may say nothing. But our eyes meet. We sit before each other. Heart to heart contact is taking place. You may not realize this, but all the same it is taking place. Then when I talk to someone, you listen. Then we drink tea together. When it is time to leave, you take my permission. Heart to heart contact has taken place but you do not know this.

The *pir's* power, it is commonly believed is gifted, never achieved.

One can get this power only by becoming a *murid* of an authentic *pir*. A *pir* who does not have this power is not a true *pir*. One does not have to do special studies to attain it. The *pir* does not give it by teaching the *murid*. He knows when he will die. When the moment comes, he will call his *murid* and embrace him. At that moment, his power will flow from his chest to the *murid's*. That power coming from above, will be transferred to the *murid* in all its fulness. The Prophet Mohammed transferred his power to Ali. Ali did it to the heads of the various *silsilahs*, who did the same thing with the other *pirs*. In this way that power has travelled down from Mohammed to today's *pirs*.

To receive this gift may call for great effort. The *murid* may have to undergo great asceticism or serve the *pir* in an extraordinary way.

A *pir* worshipped for twelve years. He did not eat anything in those twelve years. But that was not enough. Even then his worship was not over. He tied a stone to his stomach. He even tied a cooking vessel to his stomach and did many spiritual exercises for those twelve years. Even so he did not attain the knowledge. So, what did he do? He hung himself upside down in a well for another twelve years. During this time a crow used to come and perch on his body. And he used to tell the crow, "Eat whatever part of my body you find tasty, but do not touch my eyes. These eyes are reserved for the Beloved." When the twelve years were over, he came out of the well. He saw birds flying about. He said, "Die." And they all fell dead. Then he said, "Fly." And all the birds came to life again and flew away. He then said to himself, "I have received some knowledge."

As he walked away, he felt thirsty. He went towards a well. There he saw a woman drawing water and throwing it on the ground. When he asked her for a drink she did not hear him. The *pir* repeated his request. She then told him that she would quench his thirst after putting out the fire in her mother's grave. The eyes of the *pir* followed the course of water. It led to a grave out of which huge flames were leaping up. He also saw that the water was putting out the flames. When the fire was put out, the woman called to him and offered him water. But he said, "I will drink only after you tell me how you knew that there was fire in that grave." She replied, "I have the power. My husband who was a *pir* gave it to me. One night he asked me for a glass of water. But when I returned with the water, I found him asleep. So I stood by his side all night with the glass of water in my hands, waiting for him to awake. When he opened his eyes in the

morning he asked me why I had not kept the water by his side
and gone to sleep. I told him that I had brought the water
because he had asked for it. But since I found him asleep on my
return and did not want to disturb him I waited by his side. Then
he looked at me and opened my eyes and my heart." Then Baba
Farid recalled all the efforts he had made to attain the same
amount of power for the last twenty-four years and marvelled at
this woman who, with just one night's service, had received all
that he himself had.

Asceticism and service in itself may not be enough to attain this
power. The *murid* has to be given a special kind of knowledge to
attain it.

This power is obtained by doing *chilla*. *Chilla* is reciting a
particular divine name—any name—for forty days at certain
fixed times. One must also pray all the five *namazes*. Then one
must give alms, do good deeds and fast. One must not take salt,
spices, fish, meat, etc. Of all the allowed foods only one kind is
allowed. For instance, if you drink tea on the first day, you have
to survive only on tea for all the forty days. Water is allowed.
Then one will begin to experience the effects of *vazifa*. You will
get power. But this is a very difficult thing to do and very few
people do it. ["Why are you telling him all these things?"
shouted another *murid*. "Let him take the *bai'a*, and then all these
things will be told to him."] Yes, this one has to take the *bai'a*
also because without the *pir* nothing happens. The power comes
only through a *pir*.
    The power comes with learning the way of reciting *vazifa*
and writing *tawiz*. My *pir* taught me. How else would I know!
Besides, whenever I see a *faqir* I go to him. It does not matter
whether people go to him or not. What matters is that he is
sitting there and reciting a name of Allah. Naturally, he has
gained some knowledge. Who knows, he may have spent thirty
or forty years reciting a name. And with this constant roaming
about, he has seen and heard much. Hence, I go and serve him.

I give him money and anything else that he may need. Then, if he tells me to recite a particular formula, I begin reciting. One has to recite ten lakh times, sometimes a thousand lakh times. My *pir* sometimes calls me and gives me a new *vazifa* and *tawiz*, and he makes me recite and write it out in front of him. He then tells me how many thousands of times I have to continue writing and reciting it. In this way my knowledge and power increases.

It may well be that the service, which involves dying to oneself and becoming aware of one's servantness, convinces the *pir* that one is capable of and responsible enough to handle the power.

If the *murid* serves the *pir*, he will give him the power. The *murid* has to do all the work that the *pir* gives him. He has to make the place where the *pir* sits comfortable, attend to his guests, and look after his every need, like taking his children to school, doing the shopping for his wife, picking up his lunch and serving it to him in the office, looking after the old and sick members of his family, running errands for his important guests, etc. Only then will the *pir* give him this power.

The power can be attained if one is able to forget one's rights and only think of one's duties. Take Nizamuddin. He fasted all his life. When he forgot to fast and sat down to eat, he used to think of all the friends of God who were poor and hungry—and he used to vomit out all that he had eaten. He remained hungry all his life. But he used to give food to all those who went to him. The most important thing is to kill one's *nafs*. Then one will get that direct connection that is the power of the *pir*.

The spiritual power does not come to one just like that. It requires many years of practice. The *murid* has to pass spiritual tests. When he passes the tests he receives the power—and more power as he passes further tests. He does not receive power just like that. No one gives a gun to a child of five. He would kill three or four people with it. He is not responsible and mature enough to have a gun. In the same way, spiritual powers are not given to one who is not fit to have them. He who receives power

must be capable of handling it responsibly. Someone irrespon-
sible would use such power to trouble someone. One's sense of
responsibility is examined through tests. This power is meant to
help people, not to give them trouble.

A good number of *pirs* and *murids* also accept that the *pir's* power
depends only on his experience, personal holiness, influence with
God and ability to write *tawizes*. The attitude of the *murid* or the one
who will experience this power is extremely important if the power
is to be effective and demonstrable.

The power of a *pir* cannot be understood by talking about it. It
can only be demonstrated in action. It happens just like that.
When the eyes meet, love is born. The eyes meet without
planning. But after the eyes meet, the heart begins to do its
work. If the eyes do not meet, the heart cannot do its work.
There will be no love. In the same way, first, the *murid* has to
surrender himself completely to the *pir*. Only then will the
power of the *pir* manifest itself to the *murid*. It manifests itself
automatically. If the *murid* does not surrender himself, the power
will not manifest itself. I can show you this power if you
surrender yourself to me.

  The power works of itself. The *pirs* themselves do not know
that they have brought about a certain thing through their
power. When someone is in trouble we may just say, "Go,
everything will be all right." And everything does become all
right. The power has worked by itself. The *pir* is not even aware
of it. Often I am surprised when someone tells me what has
happened to him. But I cannot show my surprise. If I do, my
murids will lose faith in me.

It would seem that the faith of the *murid* to his *pir* is very
important, if not the most important factor in the demonstration of
the *pir's* power.

As far as the *murid* is concerned, the *pir* is a *pir*. Whatever the *pir* does is his own affair. It does not concern the *murid*. In the eyes of the *murid*, his *pir* cannot do wrong. Otherwise, the *pir's* power will disappear.

If the *murid* does not believe in the *tawiz* I give him it will be ineffective. It is of utmost importance that he believe in what I give him.

Sometimes we have to make a big *tamasha* [demonstration] to convenience the client. We may surround him with lighted joss sticks. Then we call out the *jinn*. The *jinn* has to leave him because of what we are reciting. Suppose people have brought me a woman troubled by a *jinn*. If I just tell them that the *jinn* has left her, they will not believe me. So, we light a lamp, act as if we are catching the *jinn* with our hands and flinging him into the fire. Then we tell them that the *jinn* has been burnt and will not trouble her again. It is most important that they are convinced. If they doubt, nothing can be done to help them. The work is done without all this *tamasha*—but the *tamasha* is necessary to convince people.

This dependence on the faith of the *murid* is explained as resulting from the freedom of man.

Allah has not written that we should do evil. But we do evil. And when there is a lot of evil in the world Allah begins to give us trouble. We do the evil and bring down the trouble on ourselves. Allah has written good works. He has decreed that we should not rob, not kill, not commit adultery, etc. If Allah wanted He could have made us do good works. But He has also written "freedom". He has written, "Do what you want to do." We will be rewarded according to what we do. If Allah wants, He can destroy us in one minute. So all that Allah has done is to make man free. It depends on us to decide whether to walk on the right or the wrong path. He will not prevent you from doing evil. He never stops anyone from doing anything.

Since the faith of the *murid* in the power of the *pir* is of utmost

importance, a great deal of effort is exerted to convince him, through
stories, the sharing of experiences of this power, by predictions and
magical tricks, and by making him experience the effects of *vazifa*.
Stories and the experiences of power are shared by the *pirs*, the more
advanced *murids*, visiting Sufis and clients.

A man does evil because God has written so in His book. If God
writes that he will do good, it will be so. If God has written that
he will be rich, he will be rich. But the reward is for the good
things. If you give one paisa to someone you will receive seventy
paise in return. And if you give the *pir* anything, the *pir* will say
in your grave, "He gave me such and such a thing. So don't
trouble him." But if you have not given him anything, he will
say in your grave, "This man has given me nothing. So burn
him." And the fire will consume one in the grave.

Look at this *trishul* [trident]. It was once used to trouble the
dead in the grave. Once the angel of death was troubling a *murid*
with it. The *pir* got very angry. He went to the tomb of this *murid*
and snatched the *trishul* from the hand of the angel. Then he
went to all the graves and snatched away the *trishuls* from all the
angels and distributed them to the *faqirs*. And, this instrument
of torture became a plaything. This weapon contains the power
of that *pir*. That is why the *faqir* can plunge it into his abdomen,
his throat, his tongue and nothing happens to him.

The founder of the Bahamani sultanate was a landless
labourer. He did not even have enough to eat. His mother once
told him that she had heard of Nizamuddin, who made people's
lives easier through his power and prayers. When the king of
Delhi was leaving the presence of Nizamuddin, this man arrived
at the door of his *khanqah*. His clothes were dirty and muddy.
Nizamuddin said, "One king is dead and another has come."
Everyone there began to wonder what he was talking about. It
was true that a king had just left. But where was the next king?
So Nizamuddin called to the poor man standing at the door. The
people said, "His clothes are dirty and torn. And you say that he
is a king!" Nizamuddin said, "Let him come to me." Anyone

who went to Nizamuddin, always received something from him. At that moment Nizamuddin had a *chapati* in his hand. He gave the *chapati* to the man saying, "I am giving you the canopy of a king." The poor man thought to himself, "What kind of *pir* is this? What is he talking about? I do not have enough to eat and he says I will become a king." None the less, he took the *chapati* and returned to his mother. He said to her, "I went so far, and what did I get? A dry *chapati*. I still have it with me. When giving it to me he said that I would become a king." She said, "If he said that you will become a king you certainly will become one. Whatever comes from the mouth of a *pir* always comes true. Do not try to find out why he says peculiar things. Just believe." From that day he began to prosper. And he became a king. His dynasty lasted three hundred years. This is the power, and it remains with the *pir* always. God tells the *pir* what to say. The *pir* says everything with full faith. He does not say meaningless things.

When Moinuddin Chisti first went to Ajmer he began living on an open ground meant for the king's animals. The king's men told him to leave, because, they said, the place was reserved for the king's animals. Moinuddin Chisti said, "Allright, let the animals sit. I am going." And ll the animals that sat there refused to get up. The King's men went to Moinuddin Chisti and complained that the animals refused to get up. Moinuddin said, "Very good. You threw me out so that they may sit. Now they are sitting." This is the power of the *pir*.

Thousands of such stories are current, illustrating the power of the *pir*. But this may not be enough to convince a *murid* of the power of his *pir*. To demonstrate his power to him, the *pir* may resort to magical tricks. For instance, he may apply some sticky substance to one end of a clove when the *murid* is looking elsewhere. Then he will draw the attention of the *murid*, mutter something and pick another clove with the clove that is in his hand. This done, he will separate the cloves and shake them up in a tin of cloves. Once, after displaying this trick, the *pir* explained,

This was possible because of my power. When I said something with my mouth, the power travelled from my mouth to my arm, then down my arm to the clove in my hand. The power then travelled from the clove to the next one. That is why the other clove stuck to it and could be picked up.

This over, the *pir* showed him all the *tawizes* he had so far prepared for the different diseases and difficulties people experience and told him how he was always busy writing *tawizes* and reciting *vazifa*. He said,

All the power of the *tawizes* is within myself. Hence, my *tawizes* are immediately effective. If they do not work immediately, it is because their recipient does not have a pure intention.

Another *pir* showed great reluctance to give a *tawiz* to help catch a thief. He said,

Such work is not lawful because it goes against the will of God. God has written that such and such person should be robbed. How can I undo what God has pre-ordained?

The man (a military officer) began to plead for help. The *pir* then lowered his head, took up a pen and a clean sheet of paper and muttering to himself, drew a magic square and began to fill it with numbers. All the while, the man talked about the theft, giving him all the details. After some time the *pir* lifted up his head and asked, "Was the shirt on a hanger?" "Yes" answered the man. "Was there some paper in the pocket along with the money?" "Yes." The *pir* added another figure to his magic square. Again he lifted up his head and said, "Not all the money was taken. Is that not so? One or two rupees were left in the pocket. Is that not so?"

The man agreed and began to say, "There were also two tickets in the pocket. In the other pocket there was a name tag." The *pir* kept his head down all the time and his pen busy, giving the impression that he was indifferent to what the man was saying. Suddenly, he lifted up his head and interrupted him, "See, it is like this. The man who stole your money is living with you. He is tall and fair. And there is only one man involved.

"What is his name?" the man asked. The *pir* replied, "I cannot tell. If you want your work to be done, come on Wednesday." The man protested, "But sir, I have already told you that we are leaving tomorrow at 11.00 a.m. I have to leave with my Commanding Officer." The *pir* replied,

If you leave so soon, I cannot do this work for you. I have to do a lot of things to succeed in this work. I can also give you something to ensure that the thief will accompany you on your journey. I do not wish to get involved in this work. Even so, I have told you so much already. If the man is ill or in the grasp of Satan or some other evil thing, I will do the work immediately. But I am not so sure.

"I am from Bihar," said the man. "I know," replied the *pir*. The man continued telling him about the theft and about the people who were living with him. The *pir* interrupted him again. "It is a man from your own group. He has with him a white shirt of good quality. Have you realized who it is? That is all I will tell you." "But there are many tall men among us, and many of them have white shirts," protested the man. The *pir* replied,

This white shirt is new and made of tericot. It has not been with him for very long. I have told you all the important things. Usually, I do not tell anyone so much. The shirt is white, new and made of tericot. It has long sleeves and glittering buttons. This is all I am allowed to tell you. I know more; but I am not allowed to tell you the rest. The rest you must find out for yourself.

The man went away thanking the *pir*. A *murid* who had been

watching all along said, "You know so much." "No, I have
nothing," replied the *pir*. Then he continued,

> I can even tell you what you have eaten before coming here and
> whether you have eaten or not. I know this through my faith.
> Faith is a great thing. Even marriage takes place because of faith.
> Everything comes about through faith and trust. The weight of
> faith and trust is the same. They will weigh the same when they
> become one. My wife is someone else's daughter. Why is she
> staying in my house? She is staying because of trust. Her name
> was written in my fate. And my name was written in her fate.
> This is the great predestination. See this cotton thread. What
> will I do with it? I will turn it into a wick [He dipped it into oil
> and lit it]. And with it there will be light for the world. The
> world is in darkness. The electric bulb burns. But below the
> bulb there is darkness. There is darkness in man also. There is
> deception and confusion in him. He who does not have this
> confusion and deception is holy. When he is holy, anything he
> desires comes about. Each man is given only as much power as
> he can use properly.

The *pir* also convinces his *murids* that he has power by making
predictions. Once, a number of clients working in the home
ministry came to a *pir* for *tawizes* to ensure that they would not be
transferred. They were talking among themselves to the effect that
Mufti Mohammed Saiyed's kidnapped daughter would be released
soon. When the next client came along, the *pir* in the midst of a
conversation with a *murid* came out with the following prediction:

> He is love. All He wants is love. I have asked Him to protect
> this Mufti *sahib*. I have asked Him to fulfil his desire, his noble
> desire. You have not understood what I am saying. Let me
> explain. When I go to the airport people come to carry my
> luggage. They are Sikhs, Punjabis, Hindus, etc. The Muslim ...
> his condition is very bad nowadays. Mufti! He is not in his
> proper senses. See, this is the problem. If you are not in your

senses, you are my friend. I have seen that if one wants to attain humanness, one has to make a promise. If one wants to recognize God, one must first serve Him in one's own home. I will write to Mufti *sahib* and tell him that his daughter will be released within one week [She was released while he was speaking].

Then the *pir* called a *pirzada* and told him

Write *salaam ale qum*. Address him as Mufti *sahib*.—I cannot bear to see you in the present difficulty. I listen to everyone and I know that you too have prayed. A *faqir* of God does not go to anyone. I am carrying out the order of my father—and my night's earnings! Those who earn in the day time have nothing. I earn at night and distribute what I earn in the morning. I have requested God that your daughter will be released within eight days. I am the servant of Someone. I am the servant of the King.

The *pir* asked for the date of the pervious day. He was informed that it was the 12th of December.

Write—Every night I pray for all men because I was created for the world and the world was created for me. This is my order: that within the period from the night of December 12, 1.00 a.m. to 1.00 a.m. eight days later, your daughter will return to you. She can come at any time within this period because I am working hard towards this end. If God and His Prophet wish, this work will be successful. I do not go to anyone. But seeing that you are in difficulty, I am writing to you. This is also painful for me. It is a kind of difficulty that I too cannot bear. That is why I am praying to my father for you.

The *pirzada* changed and shortened the letter, much to the annoyance of the *pir*. None-the-less, he had it sent by taxi. In April the following year the *pir* said,

Now I am going to remove Pratap Singh. This is the judgment that has been passed in the unseen. The judgment says, "Let him carry on for a few more days." After that, it says, he will be removed. It says that the ground on which he stands will be dug out from under his feet. The one who is inside [pointing to the shrine of Nizamuddin] has said this. This will definitely take place because it has been said here. And with him is the judgment of the whole world.

A *murid* began to say, "Please do not bring Rajiv Gandhi back." The *pir* shouted, "I threw out Rajiv. What makes you think that I will bring him back? I will bring someone else."

A *pir* may also demonstrate his power by making his *murid* recite a verse from the Quran, or a particular divine name, and wait for him to experience the effects.

My *pir* told me to recite a verse from the Quran at the tomb of Nizamuddin Aulia. I was to recite it for forty days. This is called *chilla*. He told me to stay in the *dargah* day and night. I was told to recite that formula from 2.00 a.m. until the morning *namaz*. After I finished this task, I was once standing near the main gate of the *dargah*. Two old men walked up to me, and one of them asked me to show them around the *dargah*. They said that they had come from Bombay, but did not give me their address. I took them to the gate, helped them to deposit their sandals in the proper place and to buy rose petals for the tomb of Nizamuddin. Then one of them gave me a gold coin saying, "Son, do not spend this." That coin is in the safe keeping of my mother. Then they disappeared. That night a man appeared to me in a dream. He said, "I am Nizamuddin Aulia. I met you this morning. And you showed me the way." I said, "Great Sir, I did not recognize you then." "Then recognize me now," said he and disappeared. We are blind. What do we know about what appears to us in human form? One has to stay with and obey the *pir* if one wants to see his power.

Predictions, magical tricks and the effects of *vazifa* serve to
increase the *murids'* faith in their *pirs*. A *murid* says,

> My *pir* has the power to capture your spirit. He can take away
> your spirit. He can lessen your breath. He has such power.
> Whoever has such power is a real *pir*. One who has this spiritual
> knowledge, the ability to control the breath of other men, and
> one to whom Allah has given such power is the true *pir*. It is
> useful and profitable to become his *murid*. Even if I get nothing
> in this world I will one day go to paradise because of my *pir*.

The *murids* not only believe everything the *pir* says, but also obey
him—if not out of love, then out of fear, as will be seen later. The
power of the *pir* also places grave responsibilities on his shoulders.

> A lot of desperate people come here. I have to give them advice
> and confidence. If I do not encourage them and make them
> believe that I can really help them, they may go and commit
> suicide. If I do not help them, tomorrow Allah will say, "That
> man came to you yesterday. Why did you not help him? Did
> you not have the hands to embrace him? Did you not have the
> sense to understand what he needed?" Hence, it is extremely
> important to help the people who come here in every possible
> way. Otherwise I, myself will become a sinner before God.
>
> If the *pirs* did not have this power, the people who rule the
> earth would have destroyed it by now. They would have wiped
> out the poor who have no one else to help and support them.
> The ruling elite are selfish. They care for no one but themselves.
> The *pirs* limit their destructive influence. That is why rulers fear
> them. They fear their power. The *pir* is nothing. He may sit
> naked under a tree. He has no money. And yet, kings feared his
> word. This is a matter of recorded history.

This power cannot be abused.

A boy who had not studied for his approaching exam went to his father's *pir* and asked him for a *tawiz*. The *pir* asked for Rs. 500 for the *tawiz*. The boy got the money from his mother. The *tawiz* he hung around his neck. But the boy failed the exam. In anger he smashed the locket containg the *tawiz*, and when the *tawiz* fell out he opened it and read, "He who does not work is not fit to pass. Only the one who works is fit to pass." The boy thought to himself, "The *tawiz* tells the truth." He was so impressed that he went and became the *murid* of the same *pir*.

To recapitulate: There are different explanations for the power of the *pir*. Some say that, it is the expertise resulting from many years of putting into practice the Quran, *sunna* and *sharia*, and from the constant recitation of *dhikr* and *vazifa* under the instruction of someone (a *pir*) who has himself learnt and practised those things at the hands of another experienced person. To many *murids* who do not understand it, it is a mysterious something (much desired, but greatly feared) that is gifted to the *pir* by his *pir* or a saint. To others it is a gift that is given only after the practice of great asceticism, the giving of much whole-hearted service to a *pir* and in such a way that he notices it, the recitation of many *vazifas*, taking instruction in the way of writing of *tawiz*, and performing *chillas* (forty-day retreats during which a person recites a particular *vazifa* prescribed by his *pir*, abstains from certain foods like meat, fish, onions, etc. which are considered as hot and as leaving a bad smell in the mouth, and fasts). While doing all this, the *murid* has to demonstrate forgetfulness of self, and the negation of his ego to a remarkable degree.

The power itself is described as nothing more remarkable than the ability to have God answer one's prayer for others more quickly than is usual for the ordinary run of men. Or it is described as the ability to give meanings (words of the Quran, or the divine names, roots, supports and realities) and influence existent things to manifest their effects and properties as demonstrated in *tawiz*. Some, however, say that the *pir's* power is an illusion made possible by his close relationship with God. The relationship results in his knowing what God will do at each successive moment and he agrees to do only that which God is going to do. Thus, people believe that the *pir* has power when in actual fact only God has power.

In actual practice, the *pirs* who are believed to have power invariably showed ignorance about the manifestations of their own power. Usually *murids* attributed their psychological, imaginal and chance physical experiences to the intervention of the *pir*. The *pirs* concerned said that they do not as a rule contradict such *murids* because it is important to retain their faith if *piri-muridi* is to function at all. Also, their power is manifest only when someone either surrenders himself to a *pir* (i.e. becomes a *murid*), or when someone believes that a *pir* really has the power to affect his life for better or for worse. Hence, the *pirs* expend much energy to make clients and *murids* believe that they possess the power. They use tricks, so-called predictions and stories about people who have suffered or benefited as a result of this power for this purpose.

Some *pirs* justify these tactics when confronted in private by pointing to desired ends: to frighten a *murid* into giving up a bad habit, to make people believe that their problem can be solved so that they find the courage to do something about it, to make themselves available to people who would rather suffer than go to a psychiatrist or a relative to have a problem solved, and for many other such good ends.

The *pirs* and *murids* also explain this power to *murids* and clients by using different images drawn from the *murids'* and clients' life experience, for instance, the example of cooking: The wife can produce a very good meal with ordinary ingredients, but the husband will produce a meal that no one can eat with the very same ingredients and even with superior ones. This expertise of the wife is like the power of the *pir*. A *pir* and/or a *murid* may also explain this power by using the example of our normal way of looking at things: If we look at a female human being we may see different things, or roles. At one moment she is a woman, at another she is a mother, then a daughter, and finally a wife. Or she may be all these things to different people looking at her at the same moment. But her correct meaning at any particular moment can only be one of these. The *pir* knows her correct meaning at each particular moment.

Hence, he can deal correctly with her at each moment. In this lies his power. Sometimes the power of a *pir* is described as a *tamasha* (a big show) that creates faith in him so that the watchers open themselves to his good influence and go away feeling better.

THE *PIR'S* CONCEPTION OF HIMSELF

All that has been said so far about the *pir* may be called his public image. He has to maintain that image if he is to function as a *pir*.

> When one sees a beautiful thing one loves it. Nobody goes to see what is inside it. They look only at the surface. Men praise you by looking at your outer appearance.

The *pir* also has a private conception of himself which he reveals only very gradually to his *murids*. He knows that he is only a *murid*.

> What did that *murid* tell you about *piri-muridi*, [asked one *pir*]. I told him that he had said that a *pir* has a direct connection with God. This is wrong [said the *pir*]. I do not have a direct connection with God. But the *murid* has to believe that a *pir* has a direct connection with God because it is a belief proper to his station. The *pir*, however, knows differently. He, like the *murid*, is connected with God through someone else. He too is connected with God through his own *pir*. It is like electricity. The current goes through the meter. It does not go directly to the electric bulb. If it goes directly to the bulb, the bulb will burst. The line is direct in the sense that there is only one line. But at the same time it is indirect. The *pir* has not seen God. He has only seen his *pir*. That *pir* has also not seen God. He too has only seen his own *pir*. God has no face. If one connects a line from the power house directly to the electric bulb, the bulb will burst. The direct current gives one thousand watts while the bulb can take only sixty watts. If a man has a direct line with God, he too will break; he will become blind. That is why all men need someone through whom they can be connected to God.

In this way someone looks after me and makes sure that my connection with God does not destroy me. Only if there is this other person between oneself and God can one do some work. Otherwise the person will be destroyed. In every case, the current comes through Mohammed. Current, current . . . connection, switch on and there is light. This is the line. We have the line from Mohammed *sahib*. I, the *pir*, call my *pir* when praying, he calls his *pir*, and his *pir* tells Mohammed. My body is my *pir's* body. And my *pir's* body is the body of his *pir*. This is how it is. I am nothing. My *pir* is everything. He is my professor. He is such that I cannot leave him. I can leave everyone, even my children and my wife, but I cannot leave him. It is necessary that I obey every word of his. When I do anything good, he is also doing that good thing.

Once, when I was having dinner with a *pir*, his *pir*, *pir*-brothers and *murids*, the *pir* said,

I have been doing this work for the last forty years. All I have to do is to serve God and everything will come to me. I have to recite the name of Kali, and do the *pir's* work. I do my work through my *pir*. This is my food, but it has come to me through my *pir*. [Then the *pir's pir* began to speak.] If you come to me directly, I will be polite to you but I will not help you. You have to go to this *pir* for help. He is your way. My work is done by my *pir*. In the same way I will do his work. Come to me if you want to, but remember that he is the one who brings you to me. He is doing my work. He is working in my name. I have roamed the length and breadth of India and I have seen all there is to see. When someone plants a tree I do not go and destroy it. Rather, I go and water it so that it bears fruit.

You must go to this *pir*, and this *pir* will bring your problems to me. Only then will I attend to them. And your *pir* will come to me only if he cannot handle the problems himself. Look at Moinuddin Chisti. He is a very holy man. Once, he pointed to Qutbuddin and said, "This is my representative. You must respect and love him. If you do not respect and love him, and if you do not come to know him, how will you come to know me? When he is happy with you, I too am happy with you." Have you understood? This is the *khilafa* of Nizamuddin. He sits on the throne of Nizamuddin. Have I called you here? I do not even know you. Hence, talk to him and through him you will have come to me also. This is the way. I will not talk to you if you come to me without his permission. He is your guru. He is your way. Do not hide your beloved. Do not hide your line. If you break relations with your beloved, you *pir*, then you have lost the line. And when you have lost the line you are destroyed. This is why I appeal to you, do not destroy the line. The line will be yours only as long as you are connected to your *pir*. And when you come to me, then you must clearly state that you are his *murid*. In this way you will bring him along with you. If you do not come through him, what was the use of my making him a *pir*? By making him a *pir* I have begun a new line. It is true that I am everything to you all, but I am everything to you only through him. Make him happy. Bring every one of your problems to him. And come to me with your problems only if he sends you to me. Who knows how many more such thrones will spring up from the throne of Nizamuddin!

My *pir* does not allow me to leave this place. He tells me that I am his. And again he tells me, "I am yours if you behave properly. I am yours when you manifest me in your behaviour, your politeness, and your gestures. If you are not mine, I will destroy you. And nothing good will come of you. But if you remain my own, the world will become yours." I am in prison. But if I leave this prison, my troubles will start. If I remain in this jail, he says that the world will become mine. I cannot leave this jail. If I do I will be slowly destroyed. I will start begging from door to door.

In this awareness of being a *murid*, the *pir* constantly reminds himself that he is nothing.

If the *pir* gives the *khilafat* to anyone at all, his name will get spoilt. It is true that I am a bad man. But I am not so bad that I will spoil his name. That is why he made me his *khilafa*. I know that I am a bad man. But I also know that I am good enough for people to come to me. I am also bad, I am very bad. I am nothing on my own. My *pir* has given me everything I have. He just said one word and it happened. Even my own self does not belong to me. Hence, I cannot do whatever, I like. If you come, I am yours; if he comes, I am his. I am not my own.

When a client walked into a *pir's* office to thank him for a donation he had received through his prayers, the *pir* replied,

Praise be to Allah that you have received what you wanted. But how often must I tell you that you are not to talk like this. "But it is true" [protested the man]. [The *pir* replied,] In this place, nothing is taken and nothing is given. I am not God. My medicine works through prayer. I pray to God and He gives. That is why if anyone remembers me, he will get what he wants. It is not I but God who gives.

I have nothing in this world. Whether I will get or not get anything in this world, I cannot say. Such is my life. The world thinks that I have everything. It thinks that I have a lot of money and much of everything. In actual fact, I have nothing. When I look at myself, I see that I really have nothing. People come here to observe me carefully, to see what I have. I tell them the truth, that I have nothing. Yet I want for nothing because of my *pir*. If he does not give, I do not eat. That is good. And if I get, I eat. That also is good. But then I also have wants. If I could not fulfil my wants here, I would not be sitting here. I am sitting here because I can fulfil my wants in this place.

An old *pir* who fell and broke a few ribs said,

I am the *murid* of Nizamuddin. No, I am not his *murid*. But I am a *murid* in his *silsilah*. I am not a *pir*. I am still young in spirituality. How can I act as a *pir*? I am a *murid*. Allah is the greatest. What am I? I am just a servant. I am the slave of this *dargah*. I am the slave of Datta *sahib*. I am the slave of Alimuddin Nizami.

The *pir* is also aware of his sinfulness.

It is very difficult to get respect in this world. People talk ill of me and they carry on talking ill of me because they can see my many faults. But I must not add to my faults by talking ill of them. If I myself do not talk ill of them, no evil will befall me, whatever they may say. We must obey the teachings of the *hadith*. The *hadith* forbids cheating and lying, and tells us to invite those who visit us with love in our hearts. The *hadith* also says that we should not talk against anyone behind his back: it is like eating the flesh of one's dead brother. I must not do evil to anyone.

Some time back, a thought came to my heart, "Why keep the fast? What can happen to me if I do not keep the fast?" But when I talked about this with the other *pirs*, one of them said, "When a man falls sick, he is forced to keep the fast. He cannot eat anything. Glucose is injected into his blood to keep him alive. And this goes on for months on end." After hearing him I thought it is better to keep the fast and, thus, live in peace. And I found that all the laziness that I feel when I eat too much goes away.

It is very important for a *pir* to get married. So many beautiful women come to me. If I want, I can easily have sex with them. I am still a young man. I have no physical or mental defects. And I know that no woman will ever say no to me. If my heart wants to have sex with any woman, I am sure that she will say yes. A woman can never say no to sex. And this is specially true today. Hence, it was very important for me to get married as soon as I became a *pir*. Now, when I feel tempted I can go to my wife. Marriage prevents me from looking at other women with lust. It is very difficult to kill the *nafs*.

I sit here from morning till evening. I have to see that no

evil comes out of my mouth. If I sit idle when I have no visitors, Satan will come into my heart and then evil will come out of my mouth. Hence, I must never be idle. I must constantly recite some *vazifa*.

Some time back I realized that I had become a chain smoker. This happened because I used to buy a full packet of cigarettes. There is nothing wrong with smoking. But then one needs money to buy many packets of cigarettes. And the easiest way of earning money is by telling lies to people who come here. I can tell them that an impossible task is possible and then take a lot of money from them. But once I start telling lies, I will have to tell more lies to cover up the previous lies. I will be on to the path of lies and all my good qualities will leave me. All that will be left with me will be lies and only lies. Hence, I decided that it is better to destroy the reason for telling lies. Now I smoke only if someone offers me a cigarette.

The *pir* is only a man like other men. He has to work.

I am only a man. And I have to work like other men. But my work is different from that of other men. When I am working very hard, it may look as if I am idle. I have to recite many things to make sure that the *tawizes* I give really work. Or else people will make fun of me. And then the status of a *pir* will be lowered in the eyes of the world. My whole being is concentrating on this work. This makes me very tired. A lot of heat emanates from my body and I have to bathe four times a day.

He does not know what is in the hearts of people and can, thus, get fooled.

I am also a *qazi*. I can marry people. But I do not know what is in their hearts. I do not know whether the people who come to me in order to get married have love in their hearts.

A woman came and complained to a *pir* that her husband had left

her for another woman. She wanted him back, for which she needed
a suitable *tawiz*. When she gave the name of the other woman, the
pir said,

> I know two women of that name. Which one are you talking
> about? One of them is involved in the export business; the other
> is staying in Gandhi Nagar. [The woman replied,] "She is
> staying in Gandhi Nagar." What is her father's name?" That I
> do not know, [replied the *pir*]. I know very little about her. She
> is tall, slim, fair and has big eyes. "Yes, yes," [responded the
> woman]. See, it is like this, [said the *pir*]. What has happened
> has happened. The woman came here and said that this man was
> running after other women. She said that he is her husband; And
> now you say that he is your husband. How am I to know whose
> husband he is? I made sure that he would remain with her. If
> you come here with a man and tell me that he is your husband,
> I have to believe you. "I am not criticizing you. I just want you
> to deal with that woman and make my husband come back to
> me," [said the woman]. All right, [said the *pir*]. You must remain
> close to me. Meet me regularly and remember me when you do
> not come to visit me. Hang this *tawiz* on a wall in your house
> and bring me his clothes. I will recite something over them and
> return them to you. If he really is your husband he will return
> to you. Keep my photo with you. You must remember me.
> If you remember me you will profit. But if you forget me what
> can I do, and what do I lose? You will lose, and I will not be able
> to help you. Keep coming to me. When you cannot visit,
> telephone.

The *pir* loses things.

> I am sorry I have lost your photograph. It must have fallen out
> of my bag when I was showing your documents to the official.
> I will need another one. Please do not be angry. You must
> remember that I too am an ordinary man. Like others, I can also
> lose things and make mistakes. I am not God.

He believes in God because, like other men, he has been taught
to believe.

I have not seen Allah. I have only heard about Him and believe
what others have told me. Allah can come to me in any form.
I must be able to recognize Him when he comes. If I had seen
Allah, I would have been able to make a statue or a drawing of
Him.

The *pir* also can be led astray and needs protection as much as his
murids. Once, a *murid* brought an astrologer to his *pir*. The astrologer
had been designating this *pir* and had somehow convinced that *murid*
that he was greater than his *pir*. The *murid* wanted to watch the test
of strength between the astrologer and the *pir*. The discussion
revolved around the *pir's* fate. The astrologer examined the *pir's*
palm and then calculated his destiny by changing a combination of
the *pir's* and his mother's name into a number. He made a number
of mistakes, which the *pir* pointed out. The astrologer, however,
refused to admit defeat and insisted that his predictions about the *pir's*
terrible future were true. When the astrologer and the *murid* left
three hours later, the *pir* said to the other *murids*,

I could say that his calculations were wrong because I too know
those calculations. I am not a fool. But he would not listen. He
did not even understand what I was saying. I do not believe in
astrology. I believe in Allah. He has created us. I watched this
man calculate and saw his mistakes and pointed them out to him.
It was then that my *murid* who brought him here put his head
down in shame. I allowed that man to behave in this fashion
because his *pir* used to come here to pray to Nizamuddin. That
was why I showed this man respect. But he wanted to misguide
me. Nizamuddin protects me from the snares set by men.
Nizamuddin can change the fate of people by changing what is
written in the book of predestination. He is the feet of Allah.
When he was living he never ate meat or eggs. He fasted and

worshipped God. He did not beg for a single paisa from anyone. He can change the fate of people. From his grave he feeds thousands of people in this *dargah*. I believe in Nizamuddin, not in astrology. This astrology is against the will of God. Just as I am your friend and love you and you love me, Nizamuddin is the the friend of God. God will give him whatever he asks for. People come to me for *tawiz*. Why do I give them *tawiz*? Because I believe in Nizamuddin. I am the child of Nizamuddin. I have the line with Nizamuddin. And I work through this line. I give *tawiz* in his name. He is the one who makes the *tawiz* work. I am the representative of Nizamuddin. This astrologer was trying to make a fool of me. He was Satan in disguise and I have overcome Satan. He is making friends with my enemies. He is earning at my expense and he came to give me trouble. But I defeated him.

As man, the *pir* has also economic problems.

I have helped so many. But they have not given me even one paisa. One fellow kept coming here for six months. Then he asked to become my *murid*. After the *bai'a* he invited me to his house, but he did not give me even fare money. If people do not give me any money how am I to live and support my family? I give all my time to this work. If they do not give me anything, how will I live? Still I carry on doing the work of a *pir*. I carry on serving those who come to me. I must remember that I am at the mercy of God. What people do or don't should not matter to me. I must serve them. It is good that their difficulties disappear. They may do what they like. Allah sees everything. I must continue to do good as I am doing now. I have blessed them and given them a good future and they repay me by giving me nothing, not even fare money when I visit their houses. Whatever they may be, God is one to all. He has given me the gift of a perfect faith.

People have been coming to me since morning. They have not given me anything, and I did not ask for anything. One *murid* asked me after the guests had gone why I did not ask them for some money. After all, I too have to eat and clothe myself. All I could say was, "If I asked for money, what great thing would I have done? These people have come to take something from me. How can I ask them to give me something in return?" If I need to ask I must ask from Allah. If I take money from my visitors, instead of giving them something, I am taking something from them. If they reward me of their own accord it is a different matter. When they reward me they are not bound to me in any way. If not, they are indebted to me. I have expenses. I have to travel. I have to give my guests something to eat. If they realize that I am a man like them and, therefore, also need money to live, they give something.

The *pir* may be under great pressure to ask his clients for money.

My mother complains very often. She says, "So many people come to meet you and you do not ask for anything from them. How are you going to make a living when you devote all your time to this work?" All I can tell her is, "What shall I take from them? What can they give me? They come to me because they are in trouble. They are full of grief. Poor people—that is why they come to me. They tell me their difficulties. I listen to them and give them solace and advice. They listen to me and when they get some peace, they go away. If they give me anything, it is because they want to give. But I cannot ask them for anything." Then she says, "But son, how will you make a living?" I tell her, "If I do not get anything today, Allah will give something tomorrow. If he does not give, nothing bad will happen. I have to live by my convictions. I have still to become a close friend of Allah. When the line is established, everything will come by itself. You don't have any problems if I don't earn just now. Father is still earning. Ask him, if you need anything. You have only to give me two *chapatis* daily. It is the wish of my *pir*, not only that a flame burn in my heart, but that it get bigger with each passing day. If that flame dies out now, all is finished.

I will not be able to light it again."

This morning, just as I was leaving, my wife said that she needs Rs.300 to buy clothes for the children. I told her the money would come but would take time, may be a month.

I have a rich friend. He sees how little I earn. And he constantly urges me to give up this work of a *pir* and to go into business like himself. He earns Rs.3,000 daily. He also tells me that he will set me up in business. But then, everyone in this village knows me and my work. They come to me. Through them other people hear of me. And they too start coming to me. If I left this work and start selling goods in the marketplace, I would spoil my name. I would not be able to show my face to anyone. I would be finished. People would stop believing in me. And when they lose their faith and confidence in me, they would lose their faith and confidence in Allah because I am His representative. They would make fun of me and say, "Look at him. There used to be a time when he sat in one corner reciting the names of Allah. Light used to shine out of his face. Now he has given up Allah and has started selling goods." If I greeted them they would reply, "Who are you?" Would I be able to tell them that I was a *pir*? If I did, they would look me up and down and say, "I see! And what are you today?" I have thought very deeply about all these things and find it better to continue with this work. I will continue to recite the names of Allah even if I am bankrupt. Even if I forget God, I will still belong to Him. I cannot run away from Him. More than the wealth of this world, I need the wealth of religion. If I waste my time amassing the wealth of this world, what will I do with it? I will spend it. It will get over. What will I do then? It is better to remain in the way of religion. I have no pleasure in the wealth of this world. The wealth of religion will always remain with me, even to the last day.

But the combined pressure of family, peer group and the need to live reasonably well forces the *pir* to ask people for money, specially when he has no other source of income. And the *pir's* family and *pir* may help him to take this step. A *pir's* mother said,

> Yes, it is true that God gives everything. He gives us our daily
> food. But we ourselves have to use our hands to put the food
> into our mouths. God will not put the food into our mouth. Do
> not test God. Take what He gives you.

Further, the *pir's pir* who is fully aware of his *khilafa's* zeal, may
force him to ask for money from his clients.

> Look at this fool. He does not take money for the *tawizes* he
> gives. Son of a dog [and other expletives], have you no shame?
> When you are asked for a *tawiz* you promptly write out one and
> give him. But what has he given you? Not one paisa. Why did
> you give him a *tawiz*? When you give a *tawiz*, you fool, you must
> take the *hadiya*, the reward of the *tawiz*. It is your duty to give
> the *tawiz*, and his to reward you for it. It is also your duty to tell
> him how much he should give you and to tell him that if he does
> not give the gift, the *tawiz* will be ineffective. It will be
> ineffective because you will not do all that needs to be done to
> make it effective. Your time and energy has to be paid for. If
> the *tawiz* is ineffective after he has given the gift, you have to tell
> him that he is not paying for the *tawiz*. He is paying for your time
> and effort. Whether the *tawiz* is effective is in the hands of God.

Consequently, the *pirs* demand money for their services.

> Once, when a rich man came here for a *tawiz*, I told him that I
> needed Rs.2,000. He gave me the money after two days and I
> gave him the *tawiz*. As he was leaving, I asked him if he had
> anything against giving me the money. If he had, he could have
> the *tawiz* free of charge. But he caught my feet and said, "Why
> are you asking me this question? I have nothing against giving
> you the money." And his work was done very quickly.
>
> Yesterday a man came here and took me to his shop. He had
> a lot of customers. After an hour of attending, when there were

fewer customers, he left the work to an assistant and took me outside. He pointed to another shop across the road and told me to do something to destroy it so that he would have more custom. I told him that I cannot do that. I can only increase his custom, but without destroying the other shop. I also told him that he would have to set aside Rs.10 from every hundred rupees that he earned. He would have to come and give me that money every month. What I did with that money was my concern entirely. I also told him that I would pray that the other shop might prosper. If he did not honestly set aside my share, that would not be to his advantage.

We have to earn our living somehow, while doing good work. If the client appears stingy, the *pir* has more aggressive ways of forcing the client to part with his money. If the person appears stingy, the *pir* subjects him to many rude questions to find out how much he really earns and how much he can afford to pay. He also demands advance payment, which may vary from a few rupees to more that Rs.10,000.

On occasion, the *pir* also experiences his powerlessness.

The villagers attacked my home and beat up my wife who was alone at home. What could I do? I went to the police. The police said, "You are supposed to be people who do the work of God and here you are fighting among yourselves." I told them that I had no hand in the fight. I am a *faqir*. People are trying to take advantage of my goodness. Yesterday the police went and questioned those people. Now they are frightened of me. I went to the police because before they attacked me they had threatened to shoot me. I did not tell anyone that I was going to the police, not even my brother. When I went home in the evening, my family members told me, "The police have surrounded the place." I told them, "I do not know anything." Now I have filed a court case against the people who attacked us. I have made sure that they will not be successful. They take everything from the *dargah*. Yet I say nothing. I am not interfering with them. I am doing my own work. Why do they have to give me trouble? After I had spoken to the police, those people called me, and when I went to them, one of them pointed a pistol at me. I asked him, "What is this?" "Do you not fear death?" the man asked. I replied, "I am dead and yet alive." Then I asked them to give me that pistol so that I could examine it and see how it works. They went away in frustration. What can they do to me? When someone takes a small piece of land away from them, they fight. And here they want to rob a very big piece of land from me. Will I not fight for my land?

When I go to the *dargah*, my uncle who sits there showers abuse on me and my family members. His words are so filthy that all who hear him hang down their heads. I just turn my head and look the other way. I do not reply to him. I remain calm. In this way I am free to carry on my good work. My grandmother—his mother—cursed him once saying that he would never be happy. From the time she was seventy-six years old he forced her to cook in his kitchen. And when she was eighty years old, he threw her out of his house late one night. She came to my house and we took her in. He came to my house and tried to force us also to throw her out. But we refused. When she was dying he came to visit her, but she said, "You, your wife, and your children will never know peace and happiness." He is mad. Even after hearing that curse he goes on giving trouble to other people.

All the four hundred and fifty people of love who live here, went to my house on a Sunday morning at half past nine and beat up my wife and son. Both of them ran away. But these men with long beards ran after them, caught them and took them to the police station and insulted them. When my wife and son told the police that they belong to the family of a *pir*, to my family, these *pirzade* began to say, "We do not know who he is." I was not involved in the fighting. I removed myself from the 'war front'. If the general is captured, the army cannot fight. Hitler did not go to the war front. He directed the war. He told other people how they should fight. I have power. But I am a *pir*. And

as a *pir* I have to remain far from fights. I have promised never
to shed blood. Those people, who said they do not know me,
greeted me before going to beat up and humiliate my wife and
son. They even called down blessing upon my son. And now,
after having done all this they come and greet me as if nothing
has happened. The inspector also came here and called all of us,
them and me, for a meeting. He asked me to explain the
problem. I said, "Look, a *pir faqir* does not fight. I feel ashamed
that these people stooped to fight in a holy place where so many
people touch their foreheads to the ground." They said, "We
did not do anything. Your son and wife beat us up." I replied,
"In that case you should feel ashamed of yourselves. One
woman and one thin boy beat up four hundred and fifty fully
grown men!" The inspector was listening while they were
hissing like cobras. He was impartial. He realized that I was in
the right and gave me his love. I still have his love. I told the
inspector, "If these people are willing to lay their hands on the
Quran and say that they did not beat up my wife and son and for
no reason, I will believe what they say." But when he asked
them to do this they turned their heads and looked away. After
that they could not look anyone in the eye for four months.
Their faces were blackened for four months. They continue to
spit in my face. I bear all this. And I sit here and do my work
as if everything is normal. I am waiting to see whether the day
will come when they will be able to look me in the eye. I go
to the saint and ask for justice. I say, "Tell me my fault. What
wrong have I done to deserve such punishment? I am doing
good works. Then why did this happen? I also am yours. I may
be bad. I may be a *gunda*, a *badmash*, anything! But I am yours.
Every man does some wrong in his youth. Show me one man
who has not done any wrong. But as he grows older he begins
to understand. Everyone commits sin. But is my sin so great that
I must be rejected wherever I go?" People come and ask me
what happened. I tell them, "I am not fit to talk about it. I am
a bad man. Remain far from me. Remain far from the bad one.
I am spoilt. I am bad." What I mean is exactly the opposite. I

am actually saying that they are not fit to talk to me. Now they have lost their courage. The police have visited them six times already. I can also give them trouble. I will give them thousands of worries. Now I can roam about without fear of being attacked.

How can I myself tell anyone that my *tawiz* is useless? If I do, people will stop believing in me. I alone know how much power is in my *tawiz*. If I write a *tawiz* with a holy intention, what power on earth can stop it from being effective? I take the permission and good pleasure of Allah into consideration when writing a *tawiz*. I do not know of anything in this world that can come in the way of the will of God. A *tawiz* will not work if God does not want it to work. But if it is His will that it should succeed, it will find some way or other of fulfilling its purpose. Truth is on my side. Obstacles come because Allah is not on my side alone; He is also on the side of other people. If I ask for something good and someone else asks for something evil, both will be heard because Allah's court is like this.

The *pir* does not know everything. He is constantly learning.

A woman who comes to me who is troubled by a *jinn*. I will call you when she comes again. As long as you do not hear her speak you will not understand what I am saying. I, who have already seen so much, get confused when I listen to her. This is a genuine case. There are also false cases. I have made great efforts to force this *jinn* to manifest itself. But it refuses. She has a good husband. But at night she finds her husband sleeping on one side of her while this filthy thing lies down on her other side. Further, this dirty thing has sexual intercourse with her. It shows itself to her. But when it appears to her, it looks like her father, and sometimes like her brother, both of whom have died.

She cannot be lying. Why would she lie? Everyone has self-respect. No one wants other people to think ill of him or her. They come here with this type of problem only when the problem becomes unbearable. When such a stage is reached, they have chosen between committing suicide or solving the problem permanently. We believe that those who die are kept in a special place. They cannot leave that place and go roaming about. Hence, this thing that troubles her cannot be her father or her brother. It has to be something else. It could be a *jinn*, a *prit*, a *pari*, a *jogiyan* or a *chabissan*. These things roam about in this world and trouble people. Our books say that these are the companions of Satan. These evil spirits walk about with other women also. And the women are usually defeated by them. They appear like men in every case.

Another woman says that the spirit of Moinuddin Chisti comes to her. She is a widow. Her husband was a military officer. He died in one of the wars with Pakistan. She is a Hindu, and quite young. She lived in London for a number of years and is now living in Delhi. I asked her how she knew that the spirit was Moinuddin Chisti. All she said was, "I just know." She said that she had sexual intercourse with that spirit. I told her that a holy spirit does not have sexual intercourse with women. This spirit is a dirty one. Then I gave her something. I told her that as long as she kept it with her, the spirit would not come to her. But this woman enjoyed the sexual relationship. She threw away the thing I gave her, and the spirit began to visit her again.

The *jinn* belongs to a community just like us. They receive an education just like us. And like us they work on the basis of knowledge. Sometimes these *jinns* capture human beings and make them their slaves just as we capture *jinns* and make them our slaves. If we want to make a *jinn* leave a person, we have to give the *jinn* something. If he wants food, we give him food. And he eats the food. We know this because the food given to him dies. Now suppose you are possessed by a *jinn*, I will take a cock and revolve it around your head and say, "In exchange for this life, I give you another life." I will not kill the cock. The *jinn* will kill the cock.

A woman used to come here. She has stopped coming now. She too has sexual relations with an evil thing. And milk of different colours comes out of her breasts even though she has no baby. Sometimes it is red and sometimes green. If she comes again I will first tell her what I know about this kind of phenomenon. After that I will call out the *jinn*, and ask, "Who are you? Why are you troubling her?" Then I will tell him to leave her. He may leave her just like that, or he may ask for something. I will give him everything he asks for. If he still refuses to leave her, I will kill him. I will burn him. You will not be able to see this. I will keep a burning lamp and throw him into the flame. As he gets burnt, you will smell an evil odour coming out of the flame. I am a *pir*. When I think that something is in the flame and burning, it is really burning.

These things do not show themselves when many people are around. They show themselves only to one person at a time. For instance, the place on which the Oberoi hotel now stands used to be a forest. It was used as a toilet by the people of this *dargah*. There are reports that men who went there alone were found dead because a female *jinn* used to come as a very beautiful woman, attract them to her, and then bite them on the neck and suck out their life. If a man wanted to be safe from her, he had to lower his eyes to the ground and strip himself naked as soon as he saw her. Only then was he safe. That *jinn* never appeared when there was more than one man.

That first woman I was talking about is a confusing case because the *jinn* possessing her does not speak and identify itself. Once it does that, the work begins. I still do not understand what these things are and why they possess women. I have not yet come across a man possessed by a *jinn*. I am still searching for knowledge of these things.

Despite everything—his humanness, sinfulness, ignorance, powerlessness, etc.—the *pir* has the responsibility of showing mercy to all who come to him, even in the face of stiff opposition.

I just celebrated a marriage. Everyone in this *dargah* is against me for celebrating it. A Muslim boy from this *dargah* got married to a Sikh girl. The couple had gone to other *qazis* in this *dargah*, but

all of them refused to marry them. Finally, they came to me.
Both the boy and the girl had run away from their homes. I knew
that everyone would turn against me if I conducted the marriage.
But then, day before yesterday, both the boy and the girl came
to me and sat here. An hour later, the girl's uncle came. "What
is the matter?" I asked him. He did not reply. I said, "The girl
has run away from her home. Will she be respected if she goes
back home without marrying this boy? She is pregnant. If you
do not care for your niece, think of the child. Is it good to make
the child illegitimate? Accept their holy desire to marry. If you
accept, there will be no problem. Problems come when we do
not accept the existing situation." Then I phoned the girl's
mother, told her that I was going to celebrate the marriage, and
asked her to give her consent. She replied, "I have already given
my consent. I gave my consent long ago." I told her to attend
the marriage. It would be better for the couple. If I did not
celebrate the marriage, they could always go to someone else,
and one day they would find someone willing to marry them. I
did not celebrate the marriage of some Sardarji, as the *pirzade* are
saying. I celebrated a marriage between two human beings.
When the father of the girl came here I said, "Your daughter is
pregnant. If the child is born outside marriage, it will be
illegitimate. Does the child know the face of Guru Nanak? Does
it know the face of Mohammed? The child is a child. It has no
religion. You are so old and still you do not know what happens
when two people have sex. If you knew you would have
married off your daughter long ago, and more so, when she is
earning and financially independent." Before the marriage, the
girl's parents and relatives came here and accompanied me to the
marriage ceremony. Both the boy and the girl are fit to marry.
He is twenty-four years old and she is twenty-three. Most of the
boy's family are not against the marriage. They say the boy is old
enough to decide for himself. It is only his eldest brother and his
friends who are making trouble. If the *pirzade* are against me on
this count, so what! It is Allah who looks after me. What can
they give me and what can they take away from me? They

cannot give me my daily bread. That is in the hands of Allah.
Even to the worms in the ground God gives food to eat. The
girl is pregnant, what could I do! I had to celebrate the marriage.
And the girl was even willing to become a Muslim in order to
get married. "This is a very good thing," [said a man who had
been listening all along]. "It is very good because the girl became
a Muslim." [The *pir* replied,] Forget that. Being a Muslim has
no meaning. We Muslims do a lot of evil. What does one get
by being a Muslim, except blows and insults from one's fellow
Muslims? And if anyone becomes a Muslim, then Muslims
come and insult him. I have seen this happen with my own eyes.
It is more important to become a human being.

The *pir* despite his weakness, considers himself as someone
special.

I am a very special man. I belong to a special category. It means
that I am alone. I am separated from everyone else. I am different
from other people. I am surely with people, but not of them. I
am different. My eating, sleeping, walking, and loving is
different from that of others. Oh my God, come into my heart.
God, please reserve my heart for yourself. God has reserved my
heart for Himself. My heart is the heart of God. Now, do you
understand how I am different? One has to call to God and keep
Him in one's heart. And if he keeps God in his heart, he cannot
do anything wrong. He cannot kill or beat anyone. He will
recite the Quran. He will love and constantly give others what
they need.

   Look at Hazrat Nizamuddin. Even though he has drawn a
veil between himself and the world, he still remembers the
world. That is why the people of this world still come to him.
He is alive. What, if he is buried! What, if there are just bones
in his grave! What if his flesh and muscles have become mud.
His bones are intact. They are alive. It is these living bones that
attract people to him. It is to these living bones that people
address their difficulties. Like Nizamuddin I too have power. I

have the power to overcome and even overthrow the government. My *pir* knows what good I do and what sins I commit.
And he prays for me in the place where he now lives [His *pir* is
dead]. I have lakhs of enemies. But I am not afraid of them. I
also have a wife and children. How do you think I look after
them when I have no job? I may look poor. But I have a lot of
money. When I sleep, people come to ask me to remember
them in my prayers. Who is the Prime Minister in front of me?
He sits on his throne. What does he know about what is
happening in Delhi? I know what is happening in Delhi, what
he is doing, what he is not doing, and what he should do. My
pir told me to destroy my desire for wealth. That is why I have
given up everything. Who is the Prime Minister? He is my
servant. I am the true King. I tell him what to do. And if he
does not obey what I order him to do, he will remain a servant.

   I became a *murid* because it is necessary for every Muslim to
become a *murid*. My *pir* told me to do good works. Now I am
a *pir*. I never beg even though I sit with beggars, and go about
as if I am poor. It is true that I have nothing. But I have one thing
that money does not and cannot buy. I have respect. Both the
rich and the poor come and greet me. They come and give me
money, sometimes a fifty rupee note, sometimes more, just like
that, whenever I am in need. And the other beggars stare at me
and wonder why the person is giving money only to me and not
to anyone else. They wonder why only I am singled out for this
honour. They do not know who I am. Even the Prime Minister
came to me before he got that post. He wanted the power to
become Prime Minister. And he promised me that he would
take away all the poverty that is plainly visible. He agreed to
open many factories and, thus, create employment for the
people. Hence, I gave him the power. I wrote out something
on a piece of paper and gave it to him. I told him to keep that
piece of paper with him always. See, he has become Prime
Minister and escaped many attempts on his life.

   A *pir* is a great man. Do you know why? It is because he
has complete confidence and faith in what he says. Even if he

is telling a lie, it will profit at least a hundred other men because he tells it with complete confidence.

As someone special, the *pir* has certain rights. Most *pirs* do not pray the *namaz* during the day time. Many people consider this a failing and say,

> Look at the *pirs* in this *dargah*. Most of them do not pray the *namaz*. I know *pirs* who have not prayed the *namaz* for years on end. They are all false *pirs*. Mohammed *sahib* himself prayed the *namaz*. The *pir*, who is the representative of the Prophet, must also pray the *namaz*.

Most of these critics, however, do not pray the *namaz* themselves. Most *pirs* pray the *namaz* on Fridays, perhaps because Nizamuddin is supposed to have said that those who do not pray the *namaz* on one Friday get one black stain on their hearts, two stains if they do not pray two Friday namazes, and automatically excommunicated from the Muslim community if they do not pray three Friday namazes. All the *pirs* I have met maintain that it is essential to pray the *namaz* five times a day. They also justify their own failure to pray the *namaz* daily.

> I do not pray the *namaz*. But I live as one should live if one prays the *namaz* regularly. My life is meaningful. What use praying the *namaz*, then cheating, forgetting God, and doing all manner of evil, and then again going to pray the *namaz* without any intention of changing one's life? That kind of *namaz* is useless. It is making a big show of one's holiness without gaining anything. If one wants to pray the *namaz*, one's faith has to be pure. I do not do evil to anyone. But when anyone comes to me, I do not think that he is a Hindu, a Muslim or a Christian. I think that another human being is before me.
>
> I spend the whole day writing *tawizes*. Sometimes, when I am engrossed in this work something says to me, "When you become mine, I will take your life. If you are not mine ..." Son,

there was a time when I was hungry for the love of men. And
I found that all they cared for was wealth. That is why I do not
pray the *namaz*. If you look at anyone, you will find that he has
robbed someone else, he may have robbed someone's land.
These mosques that have been built, have been built for
worship. But the person who builds a mosque should be pure.
Only then can other people go and worship in it. Today we have
forgotten the mosque that God has built. We ourselves are the
mosques of God. And we go and call these other houses that we
have built the houses of God. Usually, the one who worships
in the mosque has forgotten the real house of worship. What did
I say? "You are saying that our bodies are the real mosques,"
[replied a *murid*]. [The *pir* continued to say] Am I telling you
anything wrong? Look at the *maulvis*. When they are invited
to someone's house they will always ask, "What will you cook
for me?" There is no respect for truth. [This particular *pir* does
the same thing.] It is not the *faqir's* job to eat chicken and liver.
The *faqir* must fill his stomach by worshipping and remembering
God. He considers his life fulfilled if he can constantly look at
his Beloved. Son, the world has spoilt the name of God in every
place.

Now you are sitting with me. You are my guest. It is also
time for the *namaz*. I can tell you to go away so that I can go and
pray the *namaz*. But that is not the *adab*. The *adab* is to attend
to you, to treat you with great love, to give up everything else
while attending to you and, thus, make you happy, When you
are happy, God is happy. Many people come to me everyday.
They come weeping under the burden of their lives. How can
I leave them or send them away because I want to pray the
namaz? What is the value of that *namaz*? It is true that if I pray
the *namaz* at the proper times, I will get a hundred per cent profit,
and if I pray the *namaz* at the wrong time, I will get less profit.
I may get eighty per cent profit. But it is better to get the eighty
per cent profit.

It is absolutely essential to pray the *namaz*. Anyone who tells
you that there is no need to pray the *namaz*, is not a Muslim. You

will not see us, *pirs*, praying the *namaz*. We have a special *namaz* at midnight. Then we pray the *namaz* while hanging upside down. During the day we are very busy attending to people's troubles and have no time to pray the *namaz*. There is also another reason for praying the *namaz* at midnight. One who has wealth, does not proclaim it from the rooftops. One hides the fact. Otherwise someone will come and rob everything. One does not make love with one's wife in the marketplace in broad day light. If one does this, the police will come and arrest one. But one can make love to one's wife behind closed doors. In the same way, one who loves God, will not display it openly. One must hide the fact. That is why we, Sufis, pray the *namaz* at the dead of night when no one is looking.

To recapitulate: The *pirs* remind themselves that they are *murids* by constantly praising and remembering their *pirs*. Believing that these *pirs* can see everything they do, they also manifest the fear of being punished by them for their sins. Consequently, they try to practise the *adab* for *murids*, and also the *adab* for *pirs*.

As *murids* who have received the *khilafat* from *pirs* or as having received the mandate to function as *pirs* from a dead saint, they are aware of representing their *pirs* (and/or a saint) and continuing their work: They have been entrusted with the mission of making the mercy of God manifest to all those who come to them. Hence the keen awareness of being persons set apart, which gives them the courage to defy the vested interests of social groups and powerful individuals whenever required, in order to help people and, thus, make the mercy of God present in their lives. The loss of the privileges they enjoyed at the hands of those social groups and individuals does not seem to matter at these moments.

But *pirs* also know themselves to be ordinary men in that they feel hurt, vulnerable and powerless in the face of slights, insults, slander and physical attacks on themselves and members of their immediate family. They also find that they have expenses and need money, lose things, get fooled by clients, *murids* and acquaintances, are misled by enemies, and are in constant need of increasing their knowledge in order to solve the confusing problems people bring to them. Further, they know of their own sinful desires and how easily these desires could lead them to betray the responsibility entrusted to them. Hence, they constantly express their need of guidance from their own *pirs* and/or a saint, and devote all free time towards the recitation of *dhikr* and *vazifa* and imaginal interaction with their *pirs* and the saints.

The *pirs* present this relationship with their own *pirs* to themselves, and to their more advanced and trustworthy *murids*, by comparing themselves with electric bulbs that cannot take the high voltage coming "from the power house" (or coming on the overhead high tension wires). If they do receive that voltage and current they will "burst" because they are still impure and weak human beings. But they still do receive voltage and current because of their relationship with their *pirs*. He is the "meter" (the step-down transformer) that reduces the current and adapts it to their individual capacities so that they can still give light, or manifest the mercy of God to those around them, whatever their personal weaknesses. In their function of manifesting the effects and properties of the names of mercy they compare themselves to a gardener who, rather than let the plants planted by someone else die, waters and cares for them so that they may grow and one day bear fruit. And they remind themselves of their responsibility to manifest mercy by comparing themselves to the saint, Nizamuddin, who continues to care for and shower blessings on the thousands who continue to flock to his shrine.

KINDS OF *PIRS*

There are two kinds of *pirs* in the Nizamuddin Dargah. The first kind consists of those who were once *murids* and have received the *khilafa* from their *pirs*. There are only four such *pirs* in this *dargah*. These *pirs* have made many of their *murids pirs*. They operate outside the *dargah*, in Delhi and other parts of India. The other type of *pir* consists of those who have never been *murids*. They claim the right to be *pirs* through their close blood relationship with Nizamuddin. They say,

All *pirzade* are the blood relatives of Nizamuddin. Hence, we are automatically his *murids*. He looks after us. Also, any one of us can do the work of a *pir*.

Nevertheless,

The age of forty is the best time to begin this work because by then all one's passions are spent. One has had some years of married life, and time enough to enjoy life. Hence, one's greed becomes less.

Most *pirs* in the *dargah* are *khandani pirs*. Besides their posited blood relationship with Nizamuddin and the ubiquitous economic reasons, there may be other reasons for taking up the work of the *pir*.

One night a holy man appeared to me in a dream. He said to me, "Give me the wine of love. I am thirsty. Give me that wine of love in which my Beloved lives". I said, "Tell me where that love can be found. And I will go and fetch it." He replied, "Jump into the sea and you will find it. I will show you how." Then he jumped into the sea and began to swim. After that he ordered, "Lay your hands on those who come to you." He really said this. Then he continued, "If anyone comes to your house give him something to eat, and if you have nothing to offer him, at least give him water to drink. And when you give him food or water, bow before him. If anyone dies, bury him and if you have money, support his dependants. If you have money and do not obey me, whatever you eat will be impure and destroy you. All your wealth will be *haram*. You must deny yourself. You must bury your body, which is made of mud. You must make yourself fit to take the people who come to you to paradise. You must remember that all your wealth is the wealth of God and on the last day that wealth will give an account of you." That is why I began doing this work.

When my father died, I refused to take up this work. He was

a very great *pir* and people from all over the world used to come
to him and become his *murids*. I do not have much education.
I have studied only up to the third standard. I did not study much
because my father kept me here with him in the office and I spent
most of my time observing him, and listening to him. Now, if
I never wanted to become a *pir*, you may ask, why do I do this
work now? It is like this. Two female relatives came to me with
their difficulties soon after my father's death. I told them that I
did not do the work of a *pir*. So, they had to go elsewhere. Also
a number of my father's *murids* came to me with their difficulties,
asking me to act as their *pir*. I refused. But I noticed that those
two relatives continued to come regularly to the *dargah* even
eight months later. I asked them what was wrong. They told
me that a *pir* had taken Rs.10,000 from them and had not yet
done their work. When I heard this, I felt sorry for them. I went
and told my eldest brother and all the other members of my
family about the predicament of these two relatives. We had a
meeting and my eldest brother ordered me to take up my father's
work. That is why I am here. I am not interested in money. I
only want to help those who are in trouble.

Whether a *pir* has been a *murid* or not, does not really matter to
the *murid*. What does matter to him is whether the *pir* is true or false.
Different methods are employed to distinguish between a true and
false *pir*, as we shall see later.

To recapitulate: There are two kinds of *pirs*: The *khilafa pirs* who
have undergone training at the hands of a *pir* and have been given the
permission and the task of making and training *murids*. Such *pirs*
consider themselves better and more qualified than the other kind of
pir, the *khandani pir*. The *khandani pirs* claim the ability to guide by
virtue of their close blood relationship with a saint. Monetary
considerations do play a role in the making of such *khandani pirs*. But
in their own consciousness a profound spiritual experience that calls
them to do the work of a *pir*, and/or the plight of troubled, exploited
and overburdened people who have nowhere to go assumes greater
importance and significance. Finally, the *murids* are more interested

in a *pir* who can guide and help, than in the distinction between a *khilafat* and a *khandani pir*.

SUMMARY

The *pir* is the official locus of the self-manifestation of God as far as the *murid* is concerned. This awareness may be expressed in different ways, as seen above. As the official locus of the self-manifestation of God, the *pir* is supposed to manifest the effects and properties of the divine names of mercy in his own life and in the lives of his *murids*. If he manifests the effects and properties of the divine names of wrath, he must be able to help himself and his *murids* to understand how that particular manifestation of wrath leads to mercy. The *pir* is keenly aware of his responsibility to manifest the effects and properties of the divine names of mercy and he strives to make this a reality in his own life and in the lives of his *murids* by giving them *tawizes*, encouragement, advice, etc., and by doing good works. He is keenly aware of himself as a sinner and, hence, like his *murids* needs an official locus of the self-manifestation of God. He finds this locus in his *pir* and/ or a saint. Finally, all those who are involved in the *piri-muridi* relationship recognize that the locus of the self-manifestation of God is the only way by which they can come to know Him.

THE *MURID* IN THE NIZAMUDDIN DARGAH

Murid, as seen earlier, is one who desires. He desires to achieve union with God by attaining union with his *pir*. This basic definition is expressed in different ways by the *pirs* and the *murids*.

DEFINITION OF THE *MURID*

Unlike the definition of the *pir*, all those interviewed gave me similar definitions of the *murid*. He is one who becomes the slave of the *pir*.

> The *murid* is a slave bought without money. The *pir* has bought him. Hence, the *murid* can only do what the *pir* tells him to do. He cannot talk in the presence of the *pir* without his permission. He cannot eat, sleep, or do anything without the consent of his *pir*. The *murid* has surrendered himself to the *pir*. Hence, it is meaningless for the *murid* to criticize or judge his *pir*. He has sold himself to his *pir*.
> The *murid* is one who ties a rope around his neck and gives the other end to a holy man, the *pir*.

But the *murid* has to display the following attitudes in some measure if the *pir* is to accept him: He must be ready to love the *pir*.

> The *murid* must love his *pir* completely. He must love his *pir* with faith in his heart. He has to lose himself in his *pir*. In this way he becomes the possession of his *pir*. He becomes one with his *pir*. Consequently, all that belongs to the *pir* will also belong to the *murid*.

He must trust his *pir*.

The *murid* is like a vessel. The *pir* has to put something precious in that vessel. Hence, the vessel has first to belong to the *pir*. But before buying that vessel, he will examine it to see whether it can contain the precious thing. If it is faulty, why should he put anything into it? The *murid* will have first to correct the fault. Only then will the *pir* buy it and put the precious thing in it. The fault in the vessel is the *murid's* lack of faith. The *murid* has to trust the *pir* completely. Only then can the *pir* do something for him.

The person must be ready to undergo training.

The *murid* has to be changed. He has to be trained. Hence, he has to obey the *pir*. If he gets angry with his *pir* in the course of the training, he cannot show his anger. His *pir* is the *pir*. If the *pir* orders him to stand up, he has to stand up, however insulted he may feel. After all, he has surrendered himself. Even if he is very sick, and the *pir* tells him to do some hard manual work, he has to do it and carry on doing it until the *pir* tells him to stop. He has to obey the *pir* completely. This is the *murid*.

Then, he must be ready to die to himself.

The *murid* is one who seeks to die to himself. He is one who obeys the *pir*. The *pir* may order his *murid* to do anything. The *murid* has no right to say that he will not obey.

Finally, the *murid* must be ready to lose himself in his *pir*.

Nizamuddin said about his favourite *murid*, "I and Amir Khusrau are one." Amir Khusrau said, "I am the body of my *pir* and my *pir* is my soul. If the soul is taken away from the body, the body is dead." A person remains alive only when the body and soul are together. Hence, you cannot make out the difference between Nizamuddin and Amir Khusrau. They are copies of each other. The *murid* is one who tries to lose himself in his *pir* in this way.

Losing oneself in one's *pir* and thus having all that belongs   to him may be understood in the words of another *murid*.

I want my *pir* to sit in my heart. And when he sits in my heart, I will be able to control him. When this happens, wherever I go, people will come to me. At first a few men will come and then more. Slowly, so many will come to me that it will be necessary for them to build a town around the place where I live. This is not yet true in my case. I only know that when my *pir* begins to sit in my heart, and when I begin to control him, a town will spring up around me.

I was the *murid* of another *pir*. He made me a *pir*. And he showed me what I must do when I take *murids*. But he did not sit in my heart. Hence, no one comes to me and I can do nothing. So I became a *murid* of this *pir*. I hope that this *pir* will sit in my heart. I know a lot about *piri-muridi*, but what is the use of that? If the *pir* sits in my heart, wherever I go, even to a forest people will follow me and build up a town around me. I have tried so hard to achieve this. But I have not yet been successful. If God wills, I will make it one day. At this moment, I do not even know who is my *pir*.

When I am able to answer any question to the questioner's satisfaction, I will know that my *pir* has begun to sit in my heart. I will know this because I will not answer after reflection. I will just utter the words that come into my heart at the particular moment, and they will be the right ones. Consequently, I will be able to tell people the right way of doing things. Only then will people come to me. They will come because those who have experienced my power will talk about me. Slowly people will come to me from all four directions. And then I will become a great human being, such a great human being that people will worry me all the time. That, however, will carry on only for some time, because soon after I reach that stage, I will be taken away. I will leave this empty body on earth. My spirit and my *pir* will disappear from this body. People will bury me and build a *dargah* around me and light camphor sticks at my grave.

To recapitulate: The *murid* knows very clearly that he is a slave who has sold himself to the *pir* but without getting or wanting any money in return. He is very well aware that this slavery involves the giving up of all rights over himself, including the right to have private property, enjoy social relationships and make contracts with people of his own choice, etc. These rights have been handed over to the *pir,* who now decides his fate. Further, as a person who has sold himself into slavery, his only immediate aim in life can be to please the *pir,* and make great efforts to love him and attain union with him through service, following the *adab,* etc.—irrespective of whether the *pir* treats him with kindness or as a doormat—with the hope that he will be rewarded with union with God.

Since, the *murid* has no prior experience of slavery, he tries to present this relationship with the *pir* in terms of the experience of buying and possessing animals and things: He is like a cow or goat that is being led away by its purchaser. One end of the rope is around its neck and the other end is in the hands of the new owner. The *murid* himself has tied one end of the rope around his own neck and given the other end to the *pir.* The *murid* also compares himself to a pot that is bought after much examination so that it can fulfil the purposes of the buyer, the *pir.* The *murid* has sold himself to the *pir* and hopes that the *pir* will put some precious thing (esoteric knowledge) into him [it may be worthwhile to recall here the pots of gold and precious stones in the story of Ali Baba and the forty thieves]. And he compares his efforts to please the *pir* with the efforts made by an ideal *murid,* Amir Khusrau to please an ideal *pir,* Nizamuddin Aulia. Amir Khusrau, a courtier, stooped to disguise himself as a dancing girl, and danced and beat a drum in front of his *pir,* in order to appease his anger, make him laugh, forgive him, and feel pleased with him again.

TYPES OF *MURIDS*

Many *pirs* and *murids* said that there are basically two types of *murids*.

Some become *murids* to get some worldly gain. They are not interested in the secret knowledge. They only want the protection, help and blessing of a *pir* to solve their worldly difficulties, and make their worldly life easier. The other kind of *murids* are those who want to meet God. They seek after the secret knowledge.

This distinction, however, is not strictly true. Only two *murids* said that they wanted worldly gain alone.

We became *murids* to solve our problems. Why else should we become *murids*? Suppose you murder someone, you too will find that you need a *pir*. You will come to the *pir* and say, "Beloved of God, have mercy on me, forgive me." And if Allah wills it will be done. Someone else may come and say, Please give me a child, and he gets one. Another may say, "There is sickness in my house, please bring health." The *pir* is able to fulfil all these wishes because of the power within him. That is why it is important to become a *murid*. If anyone asks the *pir* for one rupee he will give him lakhs of rupees. But one must believe that the *pir* can do all these things. Otherwise, nothing happens.

I became a *murid* to learn to have confidence in myself. If you believe in someone who can make all you do successful, and let his memory remain in your mind all the time, you will definitely be successful. You will be able to see all the difficulties even when they are far off, and you will see them going away. They go away because you believe in your heart that you can overcome them and will find some way of solving them. This is possible because you have confidence. And confidence comes only by taking a *pir*.

All the other *murids* I interviewed combined the characteristics of both types of *murids*.

I became a *murid* because it is good to be connected with a *pir*. These people pray for us and give us their love. Then, being a *murid* is good for my business. My *pir* prays for my business, my children, and my home. He prays that I may have no difficulties, and that those I do have may go away. This is a very great thing. What greater thing can there be than having children, wealth, a good home and happiness? Is it not for these very things that men pray? Of course, there is also something else to being a *murid*. I have come closer to God. One has to work hard to make that possible. One has to recite many things with complete concentration for long hours, day and night. And one must devote oneself to the service of one's *pir*. But I have a family to look after, and children to bring up and educate. So, I have worked out a compromise. I recite the divine name, Allah, the names of all the saints in my *silsilah*, and come here on Thursday evening. Also, I try not to commit any sin; and if I do, I ask my *pir* and Allah to forgive me.

The coexistence of the qualities of both types of *murids* becomes even more clear when we examine their reasons for becoming *murids*.

To recapitulate: Even though respondents in the field divided *murids* into two types those who want only earthly rewards—and those who want union with God—I found most *murids* displaying the characteristics of both kinds. Most felt that worldly advancement is necessary in order to look after their families and to be free from the worldly cares that would distract them from advancing on the spiritual path.

Murids can also be divided into male and female *murids*. The latter sometimes seem to outnumber the male *murids*. I was, however, not allowed to interact with the female *murids*. A female researcher could provide valuable information here.

REASONS FOR BECOMING A *MURID*

People become *murids* for different reasons. They need a helper.

Allah Himself needed someone to help Him. Hence, He made Mohammed. How can we say we do not need a helper? It is true that Allah is everything. But He was alone and needed someone to keep Him company. He needed a beloved. This beloved was Mohammed *sahib*. There are very many prophets, but we believe in Mohammed. Mohammed is the only beloved. He belongs to Allah. Hence, you will not find the tenderness of Mohammed with anyone else. The *pirs* are also the beloved of Allah. They are the beloved of Allah because they want for nothing. Yet, they need to make *murids*. This is their duty. We also need a beloved in the same way as Allah needs His beloved Mohammed. The *pirs* are our beloved and our helpers. A *pir* is like a walking stick. Just as a walking stick prevents an old man from falling, the *pir* will prevent his *murids* from falling. Satan will not be able to put obstacles in their way. If anyone does not have this helper, Satan can put obstacles in one's way. The *pir* is the sign board that tells Satan to keep far away from a particular person because he is protected. Some dogs have collars around their necks; others don't. The dog without a collar is beaten, kicked about and even killed. But the dog with the collar is treated with respect because that collar tells people that it belong to someone. The *pir* is like that collar. He tells Satan that I am protected, that he should keep a respectful distance from me. Without a *pir* the journey ahead is dangerous because one can be attacked at any time. If Allah Himself needed help, then we too need help. Allah is the master of everything and yet He needed a helper. Will we also not need such a helper?

They need to learn the *adab* that destroys *nafs*.

The *pir* alone can teach me the *adab*. Without *adab* there is nothing. Hence, I had to become a *murid*. While learning to practise the *adab* I will be polished. *Adab* is the first thing to be learnt. In learning *adab*, the ego disappears. This ego is a very dangerous thing. It destroys the lakhs of good works that we might do. It is the most deceitful. We can destroy it only with the help of a *pir*. Look at Aurangzeb. He was an honest man and a true Muslim. But he had no *pir* and his ego led him astray. It made him do evil. He used to shout out a greeting whenever he passed by a *dargah*. If he received a greeting in reply, he used to carry on with his journey. But if there was no reply, he used to have the *dargah* destroyed. If Aurangzeb had a *pir,* he would not have done any evil. He would not have done evil because a *murid* fears his *pir*. It is only through the *pir* that one gets the line.

People need to make sure that they are under the influence of guidance and not misguidance.

This world is full of misguiders. Mohammed gave the right guidance. A man with a shining beard, beautiful clothes and face may come before me. And I may think he is a very good person and do whatever he tells me to do. But how do I know that he is giving me good advice? He may be Satan in the guise of a holy man. The *pir* is the one who protects me from misguidance. He can tell me whether someone's advice is true or false. Then, the *pir* gives me something to recite. If the thing to be attained or captured is very powerful and does not want to be subject to me, it will try to overpower me and make me subject to itself. At that moment only the *pir* can help his *murid*. He can help the *murid* because he knows the thing to be attained. Further, he has ordered his *murid* to recite something in order to attain it. Hence, while the *murid* is in the process of reciting, he concentrates on him and adds his own strength to that of the *murid*. Consequently, the *murid* is successful.

Some want to avoid the punishment of the grave.

I became a *murid* so that I would have no difficulty in this world
and in the next. After death the punishment will begin, the
punishment of the camel, the punishment of Hashra [The *murid*
began to weep here and then continued]. After death, the way
will be full of difficulties. But it is written in the Quran, "Your
beloved is your way. If you want to attain Me take someone
through whom you can come to Me." The *pir* is the way.
Hence, I will not have to bear all those punishments.

Others want to remember God constantly.

I just want the power to carry on reciting the names of Allah, and
the power to write His names. My *pir* gives me this power. I
do not know whether I will get anything from my *pir*. If I get
nothing from him, I consider that to be the will of Allah for me.
I must be busy with my work, the work the *pir* gives me, and
with the recitation of the divine names. I only want my journey
to paradise to be easy and peaceful. What will I do with cars and
horses? I do not want cars and houses, gold and silver. All I want
is the power to recite the name of Allah so that I can reach His
place.

A good number of *murids* want to reach Allah.

The *pir* is the way to Allah in the same way as the Prophet is the
way to Allah. Besides the *pirs*, the saints also are a way to Allah.
A good man is another way to Allah. The *pirs*, the saints, and
the prophets are all men. Yet they are the way to Allah. They
are the way to Allah because they are good men. We look for
those good men who are still alive. Then we choose the best
among them to take us to Allah. Any good man can take us to
Allah. But in order to enable him to take us to Allah, we have
to serve him, listen to what he says, obey his orders and practise
what he teaches. In this way, he will take us to Allah. This
guidance is necessary for all men because Satan appears in the
form of guidance and then misleads us. He takes people away

from Allah. By following the *pir* we will be protected from misguidance. Thus, we will get paradise.

A few *murids* want to become *pirs*.

I have become *murid* because the *pir* knows everything and so can, help me. I also want to become a *pir*. But I can become a *pir* only if I become like my *pir*. And I will become like my *pir* only if I serve him, obey his commands, and put his teaching into practice. Then I too will be able to do all that he does. I will get the power. This power can only come through someone else, through the *pir*. It is like wearing spectacles. Without them, one cannot see properly. In the same way, if one does not take a *pir* one will not get the power. The *pir* will give me his power by teaching me how to worship Allah. To get what we want, we have to work. If not, who will give us our food? Without the cooking fuel, there will be no cooked food. Similarly, if one does not become a *murid* and work to become one with the *pir*, one will get nothing from him.

People become *murids* also to acquire the good pleasure of Allah.

Everyone has an aim in life. If I do some work, I do it to obtain something. I work because I have an aim. It may be to get money so that I can feed and educate my children. Spiritual work also has an aim. I may become a *murid* in order to learn something about my life and to solve my worldly problems. I believe that if I pray like the *pir* and learn to serve like him, I will be something before God. I have become a *murid* in order to acquire the good pleasure of Allah. And when I have gained His good pleasure, the power will come to me automatically. I have not become a *murid* in order to acquire this power, but all the same it will come as I walk on the path pointed out by my *pir*. This power is not a great thing. It does not bring joy and happiness. It only brings responsibility.

My main objective is to make Allah happy, and when I have

made Allah happy, I will have achieved my objective. Then I
will not want for anything in this world. I will have all that I can
wish for. I try to make Allah happy by trying to make my *pir*
happy. And I try to make him happy by obeying and serving
him, and by putting all that he teaches into practice. My *pir* can
do with me whatever he likes. My service does not mean that
he has to reward me. I ask my *pir* to solve my worldly troubles
so that my mind may be completely free from all worries. Thus,
I can concentrate on the formula that I have to recite. If I do not
have food to eat, I will be constantly thinking of food. If my wife
is sick, I will be worried about her health. Such worries and
difficulties only serve to distract me from the tasks given to me
by my *pir*. Hence, when I ask him to take them away I actually
ask him for the strength to concentrate fully on the tasks he sets
me. Only if I learn to concentrate like him, will I be able to make
Allah as happy as he makes Him.

One person wanted to be dependent only on Allah.

I became a *murid* because I wanted to be dependent only on Him
who made the world. I do not want to continue depending on
men. One has to think. Without thinking one will not get the
light. Man is not in need of man or anything made by man. Man
is in need of only God. And God is in His holy friends. We know
this because they have the power. When you ask them for
something you will get it.

   I say this because I have seen all kinds of things happen with
my own eyes. There was a man standing in the *dargah* at Ajmer
and saying that he would take only from the hand of Moinuddin
Chisti. Many people tried to give him money, even gold, but
he refused. Then suddenly, an old man came along and said,
"This is what you wanted. Take it and go." And the man took
it and walked away. Who was that old man? He was Moinuddin
Chisti. He himself came and gave that man what he desired,
because that man believed that Moinuddin Chisti would himself
come and give it to him. The point is that we have to instil in

ourselves faith that gets results. When I am able to believe like this I will become something. What is the use of depending on men? Men cannot forgive our sins. If you depend on men you will have to listen to ten insults, even from your own brother.

Do you think that I do not commit any sins? I commit sins but my *pir* forgives me. If he were merely a man, he would not be able to forgive me. However many sins I may commit, the *pir* will go on forgiving me. This is the difference between depending on God and man. What is the use of depending on men? God gives everything. Men give only after receiving an application, and even when they give, they donate only half of what one asked for. But if you ask the *pir* for something, he will give you everything you ask for in some way or other. You will get exactly what you ask for, and instead of giving you just that one thing he will give you ten such things. You will not be able to understand how you are getting.

There are many other reasons for becoming a *murid*. But as one *murid* told me,

If you set out to collect all the reasons for becoming a *murid*, you will fill many volumes and still find more reasons to record.

To recapitulate: There are as many reasons for becoming a *murid* as there are *murids*. All these various reasons, however, besides showing the material and spiritual aspirations of the *murids*, demonstrate that they feel the need for a *pir*.

This need for a *pir*, or for living in the *piri-muridi* relationship may be expressed by the *murids* in terms of the relationship between God and Mohammed: God too was in need of a companion, and hence, He made Mohammed from His own light. The *murid* is, however, not God and needs the *pir* also for guidance and support. His need for a *pir* may be expressed by comparing the *pir* with the collar on the neck of a dog: Those dogs that have collars are left alone because the collar tells people that they belong to someone. Dogs without collars, on the other hand, are beaten, kicked, and even killed.

Similarly, being associated with a *pir* keeps away Satan, misguidance and the misfortune he is associated with because the *pir* is a sign that one belongs to a special group that has to be treated with respect. Finally, the *murid* may explain his need for the association with his *pir* by comparing him to a walking stick that prevents an old and frail man (the *murid*) from falling and hurting himself—the *pir* prevents the weak *murid* from falling into misguidance and into the clutches of Satan.

CHARACTERISTICS OF THE *MURID*

A *murid* may be extremely poor or wealthy, illiterate or educated, well groomed or in rags. It is only their common beliefs, the *adab*, the practices, problems and, most important, their relationship with the *pir* that brings them together under the single category of the *murid*. Besides the beliefs already given above, the *murid* has to hold certain beliefs about his *pir*. The *murid* has to believe that the *pir* changes his life by mere contact with him.

> Everything happens because of my *pir*. I am completely changed because of this association with my *pir*. My thinking has changed, my behaviour has changed. I cannot explain this change to you. But I can demonstrate it through an example.
> There is always communal tension in Delhi. Hindus and Muslims hate each other and are constantly killing each other. Curfew is regularly imposed upon the walled city and on the areas surrounding Jama Masjid. About two years ago, when there was curfew in these areas, and when anti-Hindu and anti-Muslim feelings were explosively high, the *urs* of Nizamuddin was being celebrated at this *dargah*. While Hindus and Muslims were killing each other in other parts of this city, Hindus, Muslims and Sikhs were sitting with each other and praying together in this *dargah*. It was as if there was no communal tension in Delhi. What a great difference between the walled city and this *dargah*! The government has used all its resources to bring about communal harmony, but it has failed. But here

communal harmony is achieved just like that. Visitors also remarked, "Outside this *dargah* Hindus are killing Muslims, and here they are sitting together like brothers." This kind of change has taken place in me also. I cannot explain it to you. That is why I have given you this example.

Even if the *pir* says nothing to the *murid*, and they sit before each other in silence, the *murid* has to believe that the *pir* is teaching him. He is changing his heart even though he may not understand how. The *murid* may understand what teaching has been given only when he sees the effects of that teaching. This type of teaching cannot be described. The *pir* is teaching the *murid* through his power. Together with this teaching comes the power to understand. There is an invisible current moving from the *pir* to his *murid*. Its effect is seen when the *murid* begins to love his *pir*. The *murid* will find it difficult to tell anyone what teaching he has received. But everyone can see its effects. His life, words, and acts change. No *murid* can explain what takes place between himself and his *pir* because it takes place without the *murid's* knowledge.

If the *murid* does not accept the *pir*, he does not have faith. Without faith, how can the *pir* help the *murid*? And how will the *murid* know that the *pir* is helping him? He will not understand anything. Faith is most important—to believe that what the *pir* is saying will come true. Otherwise, it is useless to become a *murid*. We have to believe that the *pir* is the symbol of Allah. If we say he is just a man, he will no longer stand as a symbol for Allah. Only if the *murid* believes in his *pir* can he become something. Hence, the most important thing for a *murid* is to learn how to believe in his *pir*. You must believe the *pir* in the same way as you believe your parents. There is no proof that they are your parents; but you believe that they are. If you do not believe that they are your parents what can they do for you? Only if the *murid* believes that the *pir* can do everything for him, will the *pir* be able to do something with him.

One who has recognized his *pir* has recognized Allah. By the act of becoming a *murid*, I have recognized God. For the *murid*,

the *pir* is Allah. One who has become a *murid* has no father,
mother, brothers, sisters, etc. The world thinks he is mad, but
he is not actually mad. My mind works properly, yet people call
me mad. They call me mad because I no longer fear anyone. If
someone pointed a gun at me and told me that he would shoot,
I would pull the gun out of his hand and then slap him. That is
why I am called mad. I have received so many things from my
pir that I no longer care for the things of this world. I receive
from my *pir* and, sometimes, I receive directly from God in a
dream. The *pir* is a means, a way, to God. I do not care whether
or not I have anything. I do not care whether I am here or there.
I am a very daring man. I do not need anyone. My *pir* is my
advocate. When one has engaged this advocate, one has found
God.

The *murid* cannot say that the *pir* is useless even if others say
so. For me he stands in the place of Allah. His conduct and his
sins do not concern me. What does concern me is my behaviour
towards Allah as represented in him. If I forget that he is Allah's
representative for me, I am wasting my time. I will not find God.
So many people come to this *dargah*. If I begin to dislike or hate
someone because of what he does, he will also begin to hate me.
And neither of us will find God. If I want to find God, I must
remember that God has made not only me , but also the other,
that He looks after not only me but also that other person. True,
God has made all of us different. He has made you a Christian,
me a Muslim, and someone else a Hindu. Why did he have to
make us different? He is the Maker, and He alone knows why
He has made these differences. He alone knows the measure of
each person, whether a Sikh, a Hindu, a Christian, or a Muslim.
He has worked to make each of us and, so He looks after us. He
looks after us as a shepherd looks after his sheep. That is why the
prophets looked after their people. That is also why the *pirs* look
after their *murids*. Allah has said, "Take one step towards me and
I will take ten steps towards you." I have taken that one step by
becoming a *murid*. Will He not take the ten steps towards me?
If I do not believe in my *pir*, whatever he may be, then I know

that I have not really taken that one step. God looks after me when I believe that He is present to me in my *pir*. And He also looks after my *pir*.

True worship consists in keeping God before oneself. One has to be able to say, "Only you Allah, are everything to me. You have created me. Have mercy on me. Father, mother, brother, sister and profit mean nothing to me." This is real worship. Only if one worships like this will everything one says come true. Only then will Allah's mercy be revealed to oneself. And when God's mercy is revealed to anyone, he can understand the difficulties and sufferings of other people. If I make myself a *pir* and you my *murid*, you will come to me with your problems, but I will not be able to solve them. Only a real *pir* can solve your problems. He can do this because he has a direct connection with Allah and can speak directly with Allah. He will pray, "Allah, this is my *murid*. He has asked me to do this work for him. You alone can do it. Please do it." When the prayer is answered the *murid* learns that the *pir* has a direct connection with God.

I was a bad man. But I surrendered myself to my *pir*. If one surrenders one gets everything. My *pir* has his own son. But he loves me more than his son. That is why he made me his *khilafa* and, thus, gave me everything. I worked very hard to please him. I worked in the same way as you are working. This is a question of love, of attachment to the *pir*. If one makes an effort one will get what one wants. If not, one will get nothing. One gets only in the measure that one works.

The *murid* has to believe and act as if his *pir* is ever present before him.

My *pir* is with me all the time. He sees every action of mine. My *pir* is with me. He is attached to my body. He is with me because I think of him all the time. And when I am not consciously thinking of him, he is there at the back of my mind. He sees everything I do. Thus, he can help me.

Finally, the *murid* has to believe that the *pir* will not mislead him.

The *pir* does not show me the wrong path. He only tells me what
is right. If the *pir* cannot give, God will give.

The *pir* is one who gives the right guidance. Even if he is
on the wrong path himself, he will not allow his *murid* to walk
on that wrong path. And the words of a *pir* have an effect on the
murid only if he has faith in his *pir*. It is this faith that leads the
murid to ask the *pir* for a solution to his problems, and then think
that the *pir's* advice is correct. The *pir* will never tell his *murid*
to do wrong. We believe that God is in the *pir*. But how is he
in the *pir*? I do not know. Just now it is enough for me to believe
that God is in the *pir*. If I do not believe that God is in the *pir*,
He is not in him. More important is my faith, my belief.

The only guarantee for the *murid* that his *pir* will not misguide
him is the belief that the *pir* knows and accepts that he will have to
suffer for all the *murid's* sins if he misguides him.

Adab, or the special code of behaviour towards the *pir* is an
extremely important characteristic of the *murid*. As one *murid* said,

If you have *adab*, you will get everything. However learned you
are, you must know and practise *adab*. If you have *adab*, people
will refuse to see the wrongs you do. This refusal to see the
wrongs is itself *adab*. When the wrong is forgotten, only the
good is talked about and, hence, only the good spreads from one
to the other, and the bad thing disappears.

A *murid* can have only one *pir*.

A person can become the *murid* of only one *pir*. He remains his
murid even after the *pir* dies. It is possible to remarry, but not to
take another *pir* even if he dies. One remains his *murid* even
during the final judgment on the last day.

The Quran says, "If you surrender yourself to someone, or
if you take the *bai'a* with someone, you are permanently attached

to that person." He may be a ruffian, a crook or anything else.
Whatever he may be, he remains one's *pir*. If the *murid* leaves the
pir and takes another one he commits a sin. That sin can never
be forgiven. It may be true that the *pir* is bad, but that does not
make the *murid* bad. The *pir* cannot make the *murid* bad,
whatever he may be.

The *murid* remains under the same *pir* even after his death
because his power remains in his grave.

When a *pir* dies and is buried, he continues to remain alive. His
spiritual power remains in the grave. Hence, the *murid* has to
keep him as his *pir*. I will give you an example. In Haryana, there
is an isolated grave close to a village. The villagers gather at that
grave every Thursday evening and sometimes put a green *chaddar*
on it. They are not Muslims. They are Hindus. But they have
accepted this friend of God, and all their prayers at the grave are
answered. A *pir* from the Qalandar *silsilah* is buried there. His
name is Mohammed Taranzuri. Those people have tried to
build a structure over the grave. But every time they build
something it collapses. Hence, the grave is indistinguishable
from the surrounding land. I have seen a structure built over the
grave collapse overnight. Some years ago the government took
over this land and contracted an agency to level it. When the
bulldozer reached the site of the grave, all the villagers gathered
together and stood in front of the grave. They told the driver
of the bulldozer to leave the grave alone. The driver refused to
listen. They defied him to drive over them first. The supervisor
was called, and later the police. A case was filed in the court.
Finally, the site of the grave was left untouched. Those people
would not have risked their lives for that grave if they had not
experienced the power of that *pir* in their daily lives. It means that
the power of a dead *pir* remains in his grave.

Nevertheless, *murids* do take other *pirs* when their *pirs* die or
when they themselves migrate to distant places. Also, when a *pir* dies

it is not uncommon for his *murids* to go to his son, or successor and tell him that he has taken the place of their *pir*. One person, who had taken another *pir* because he could no longer contact his first *pir* who lives in Bangladesh, said,

> I have not taken another *pir*. My first *pir* remains my real *pir*. But I serve and obey this *pir* as I would my real *pir* because I see my *pir* in him. And whatever I do for him, I am actually doing for my first *pir*.

The rule to keep one *pir* forces the *murid* to retain the relationship with his *pir* even if the *pir* is so angry that he drives him away.

If a *pir* displays anger when a *murid* greets him, the *murid* cannot even utter one word in self-defence. And then, if his *pir* sends him away, he will have to leave immediately. The *pir* may even say, "Do not come to me again." Even then the *murid* is not allowed to say anything. He cannot even ask the *pir*, "What has happened? What wrong have I done? Why do you not want to meet me again?" He will have to leave in silence. But this does not mean that he should keep far from his *pir*. It is his duty to return to his *pir* after two or three days and sit silently before him. Neither the *pir* nor the *murid* will speak. And this will carry on for a few days. Then one day, the *murid* will have to say, "You have given birth to me. You have looked after me. How have I offended you?" He will have to ask this question. He has to behave as a child behaves before its father. The child will worry and think, "Why has he refused to see me?" If the *murid* does not return to ask this question, he becomes a non-believer, a man without a religion. In front of his *pir* he has to be acutely aware that he has no power and no rights. When a *pir* rejects his *murid*, the *murid* may like to say that his *pir* is an evil and bad man. But if he realizes that three other fingers are pointing towards himself, and telling him that he is three times more sinful than his *pir*, he will not say anything to anyone. He will not talk about his *pir* even if people come to console him. He will only say, "He is my *pir*." The *murid* has to keep every defect of his *pir* secret. And by maintaining secrecy he keeps far away from the *pir's* sins. If he does not keep the *pir's* defects secret he takes upon himself the punishment due to the *pir* for his sins.

Once, Nizamuddin was very angry with Amir Khusrau, and sent him away. Khusrau began to wonder what he should do to appease his *pir*. He dressed up like a dancing girl and covered his face with a veil. Then he went to Nizamuddin's door beating a drum. Khusrau the courtier did this. Nizamuddin asked his *murids* to find out who was at the door. They told him that a woman was beating a drum and asking for permission to meet him. Nizamuddin gave his permission. Hence, Khusrau danced into Nizamuddin's presence and when he was very close to Nizamuddin, he lifted the veil and revealed his face. Nizamuddin recognized Khusrau and began to laugh. Then he asked Khusrau how he came to be dressed as a dancing girl. Khusrau replied, "I have done something to anger you. I do not know my sin. Yet I am still yours. You are my *pir*."

The *murid* has to consider all his possessions as the belongings of his *pir*.

When you become a *murid* you cannot say that this bag which you are carrying is yours. You will have to believe that everything you have belongs to your *pir*. And if the *pir* asks you whose bag it is, you will have to tell him that it belongs to him. You will have to tell him that everything you own belongs to him. This is how you will have to speak before your *pir*. If you do not tell him that it is his, he will make you believe that it all belongs to him, and not to you. He will take control over your soul and force you to say that everything you possess belongs to him.

The *murid* has to learn to treasure poverty even though this may prove difficult.

What is the use of money? One can get everything with money. But what is the need for money? What can one not get with money? But what is the use of money? I am the lover of my *pir*. To become a lover one has to give up money because when one has money, one begins to think that one cannot share a meal with someone because he is very poor, or because he is a Hindu, or a Christian. Also, when one has money one becomes proud and begins to judge other people. One begins to say, "He is a non-believer, he eats pork. I will have nothing to do with him." One forgets to love. So, it is better to have no money and, continue to love everyone who comes to me. Only so will I continue to lose my senses every time I hear the name of Allah.

Poverty is a wonderful thing. One does not have to worry about being robbed. Look at these rich people. They are rich because they have robbed the poor. They enjoy what is ours by right. But what can we do? They have all the power. The poor are the best kind of people. They are the greatest in the eyes of God. Why do you ask about *piri-muridi*? You do not need a *pir*. You have everything. It is only we, the poor, who need a *pir*. It is good to be poor because poverty brings about hunger, and hunger forces one to remember one's *pir*. And when I remember my *pir*, my *pir* begins to remember me and pray for me. The *pir* is constantly praying for me. But what can the *pir* do if God does not wish to give. Look at my ankles. They are twisted. Also, I am nearly blind. My *pir* prayed for me, he did a lot for me, but nothing happened.

He has to visit his *pir* regularly.

Only the *pir* blesses. And Allah blesses only through the *pir*. Ten minutes in the company of the *pir* are more profitable than a whole year spent in earning money. God has said that He has become the eyes, hands, feet and ears of the *pir*. Hence, we must visit the *pir* regularly.

Once, a *murid* who had not visited his *pir* for many months received a scolding, first from his *pir*-brothers, and then from his *pir*. He told his *pir*-brothers that he had not come because he had not received the order to come. But when his *pir* scolded him and told him that he would throw him out if he persisted with such long absences he could only apologize.

The *murid* must also take along a gift for the *pir* whenever he visits him.

> When one visits one's *pir* one must bring him a gift. By this one shows to the *pir* one's respect and love for him. If you do not respect your *pir*, no one will respect you. What you do to your *pir* will be done to you also. If you are very poor and have no money, at least bring along a handful of mud from the place where you live and throw it in front of the *pir's* office saying, "I offer all I can afford. I bring this mud as a token of my respect and love for you." Only then will the *murid* get everything from his *pir*. One must strive to make the *pir* happy.

He has to take the permission of his *pir* before leaving him or his office.

> Once, a person left his *pir* without taking his leave. And he could not reach home. He went roaming about all night until he found himself at the *pir's* office the next morning. He did not believe in his *pir* earlier. But after this experience he began to believe in his *pir*. How did this happen? It is like this. You have both the positive and negative aspects of Allah within yourself, but you do not know this. The *pir* knows this. That is why he has a *maukil* with him. When this man left the *pir* without taking his permission the *pir* concentrated on him. Hence, the man had to return to him. This is the work of the *pir's maukil*. The *pir* did not allow him to go home. He made him walk in circles until he returned to him.

> If a *pir* is not in his office when we come to visit him, and we want to leave, then we face the cushion on which he sits and ask for permission to go. Then we leave.

The *murid* has to invite the *pir* to his house.

The *murid* has to invite his *pir* to his house from time to time, and when the *pir* visits him, he has to treat him with great respect, and attend to all his needs.

He has to protect the *pir* in case he is attacked.

The *murid* makes a person a *pir* by becoming his *murid*. Through this one *murid* the *pir* gets many more *murids*. I do many important things for my *pir*. I do not allow him to get frightened. When he is frightened because someone has threatened him, I urge him to keep calm, and then I give him advice. These *pirzade* are against us. They came to attack us. But I did not get frightened. I said to them, "Do what you will and then suffer the consequences. Remember, you are about to attack a *pir*. And you are going to attack a *pir* who has done no wrong, who is busy doing the work of Nizamuddin. Does he sin by doing the work of Nizamuddin? He is my *pir* and I will not hand him over to you. He is different from all of you. He is not interested in making money." They all got frightened and went away. It was my duty to protect my *pir*. Now I have to do another duty. I have to go and lead his father to the mosque for the *namaz*.

The *murid* has to respect his *pir*.

The authority of one's *pir* is greater than that of one's parents. Parents beget children unknowingly. And they do not consider themselves responsible for their children when they are grown up. With the *pir*, it is different. On the last day, every *murid* will stand with his *pir* because it is his *pir's* duty to save him. He who has no *pir* will stand alone. With a *pir*, the last day will pass easily because the *pir* will intercede for the *murid*. Only those who have a direct connection with God can make effective intercession. Hence, one has to respect the *pir*. One must respect him as much as one respects one's own father. To respect one's *pir* means that one talks to him in a soft voice, and that one obeys him. Even if the son becomes greater than the father, he remains the son. He can never call his father his son. Nor can he ever be equal to his father. In the same way the *murid* can never be equal to his *pir*, even if he attains higher knowledge than his *pir*.

One must not smoke in front of the *pir*. One must not say or do anything evil before the *pir*. Now I smoke. Sometimes my *pir* takes me along with him. Then I cannot smoke. But my *pir* knows that I smoke. After every hour he tells me to go and take a stroll. In this way he allows me to smoke.

He must obey the *pir*.

A *murid* has to obey the *pir* unquestioningly. He has to obey believing that whatever the *pir* orders is right. He must never feel that what the *pir* is saying is wrong. Even if the *pir* says something wrong, the *murid* has to accept it immediately as true.

The *pir* may not like the *murid* to do certain things. These may not be wrong in themselves. But if the *murid* does those things after the *pir* forbids them, he becomes a non-believer. He becomes a non-believer because he has disobeyed his *pir*. In these acts of disobedience he displays a lack of respect and love for the *pir*. He has lost his *pir*. When one loses one's *pir* one loses one's path to God. One loses one's path to God because God speaks to the *murid* only through the *pir*. What God has said through the Prophet reaches the *murid* in a profitable way only through the *pir*. Hence, a disobedient *murid* has also lost his faith and paradise.

Did you hear that bell ring? My *pir* is calling me. I have to go. I cannot continue to talk to you. Whatever I have told you, whatever service I have rendered you, was given in the service of my *pir*. Worship, for me, consists in serving my *pir*. If I continue to worship like this, he will pray to Allah for me and Allah will forgive me. God will forgive me because I worship my *pir*. Allah has said, "If you are lost in the worship of men I

will not forgive you. I will insult you." I am telling you
something very important.

When one becomes a *murid*, one has to give up everything.
One has to give up one's parents, home, etc. One has to be fully
attached to one's *pir*. If my *pir* orders me to give up my job, I
will have to give it up. If he tells me that I must get married, or
to go about in torn and tattered clothes, then too I have to obey.

The *murid* cannot judge the *pir*.

The *pir* is a road on which the *murid* walks. The *murid* has to study
the *pir* because the *pir* is the lesson. The *murid* does what the *pir*
tells him to do, not what he does. And if the *murid* sees the *pir*
doing something wrong, he must remember that the *pir* does that
so that the *murid* may learn not to judge him. It is done to remind
him that he does not know the intention of the *pir*. The *murid*
has to believe that the actions of the *pir* are only apparently
wrong.

Even if the *pir* is drinking liquor, the *murid* has no right to
say anything. He cannot ask, "Why are you drinking?" He
cannot even get up and walk away. He has to continue sitting
in front of his *pir* and with his head bowed. He cannot judge his
pir.

Murids cannot test their *pirs*.

Sometimes people ask the *pir* to do certain things to test him.
This is wrong. If he tests his *pir*, his *pir* will never help him. So
there is a way of asking. If one asks the *pir* for something with
a pure heart, and with full faith, the *pir* will help. It is important
to believe that what one is asking for will definitely be given. If
this faith is not there, the *pir* will not even listen to the *murid*.

The *murid* must not look at the faults of other people.

A *maulvi* lived opposite the house of a prostitute. He spent many

hours in worship each day. He was a good man. But he had one
fault. Whenever the prostitute received clients, he used to peep
out of his house to watch the goings-on in her house.

One day the prostitute died. She was buried with much
pomp by the townspeople. A few days later the *maulvi* also died.
No one knew about it. But when the stench of his rotting body
disclosed his death, they came and buried him.

At his burial, a strange thing happened. The mound of earth
over his grave would not remain in place, whatever the people
did. All wondered at this strange happening. One night they all
had a dream. They saw the prostitute in paradise and the *maulvi*
in hell. They asked him how he came to be in hell after all his
worship when the prostitute was in paradise. The *maulvi* replied,
"The only wrong I did was to keep a secret watch on the goings-
on in the prostitute's house. I made a small hole in the wall and
used to peep into her house through that hole."

Till today, I have never watched anyone in secret. I do not
look at the faults of others because when I was a child I was told
that the person who talks against anyone behind his back has
eaten the flesh of his dead brother. Why should I eat the flesh
of my dead brother? I may do thousands of bad things, but I also
do good things. And the more trouble people give me, the purer
I become. My *pir* told me, "When you leave someone, always
leave him with a blessing on your lips. When you visit someone,
respect him by sitting with him, and when it is time to leave,
pronounce a blessing. Even if the host has not behaved properly,
and if he has not even given you a glass of water to drink,
pronounce the blessing when leaving. If you do not do this, your
life has no meaning. If you have wealth, do not show it. If you
have children, do not put them on display. If you do, people
will wait for an opportunity to cut off their heads."

I will tell you one more thing. My *pir* told me, "It is true
that it is dangerous to trust anyone. But then you must
remember that the All-merciful is also here. God's name is taken
by everyone, by the maid servant, by the eyesore and the vile.
Everything is contained in the name of Allah." I am His. Even

if I do evil I am His. I am His, because I trust in His name. That I belong to Him is enough for me. Whether people like me or not, whether they listen to me or not does not depend on me. I, for my part, should continue chanting the names of God. I will continue to follow the mother of tenderness (the mother of Nizamuddin). And I will continue to commit myself to a life of tenderness. Whether people like me or not, I will continue to chant the sacred verses. Amir Khusrau received the highest position by kissing the feet of his *pir*, Nizamuddin. People do not understand this gesture. They criticize it because they think that the *murid* is prostrating before his *pir* [or adoring his *pir*].

Mohammed has called suffering the place of rest and leisure. Even Allah is suffering. He says to the angel Gabriel, "My forms are sleeping. They do not remember me. But do not awaken them." I am dried up, I am feeble. Hence, I must do what Amir Khusrau told me to do. I must put the soles of my *pir's* feet into my heart, into my understanding. Only then will the coldness leave me. Only then will I begin to love. Khusrau used to kiss the feet of Nizamuddin. He used to rub his eyes on the feet of Nizamuddin. Only after doing this would he sit down. Today they call this prostration [adoration]. Angels do the same thing before the *pir*. One must go to one's *pir* with respect. And when one does this, who knows what will be given to one! One may receive Medina, wealth, authority, etc. The *pir* is the gate to God. Gabriel used to stand at that gate. Now men have become the guardians of that gate. When we sit together, my whole attention is upon you. We are communicating from heart to heart. If you stand up and walk away, then I will not care for you. The love that comes to me goes to you.

Finally, the person has to take the permission of his parents before becoming a *murid*.

He who becomes a *murid* without taking the permission of his parents commits a sin. For men there is a paradise and a hell. For the *jinn* there is no paradise. For woman there is no paradise and no hell. She herself is paradise for me. My mother is paradise for me. I have come from that paradise. If I respect and look after her, I will go to paradise. But if I do not respect her, if I do not feed her and look after her, I will go to hell. It is extremely important to have the permission of one's parents before becoming a *murid*. If one does not respect one's parents, what is the use of becoming a *murid*? What is the use of earning lakhs of rupees and giving them to the *pir*, and celebrating the *urs* of the saint with much pomp if one does not feed one's parents? The *pir* will tell the man who does not respect his parents that he cannot become his *murid*.

To recapitulate: The only characteristics that unite the *murids*, who come from different economic, educational and cultural backgrounds, are their desire for union with God, their special relationship with their *pirs* and the *adab*. The *adab* tells the *murid* what thoughts and attitudes he should entertain with respect to the *pir*, fellow *murids*, other people, and himself. It also gives him a set of rules to follow when interacting with his *pir*, fellow *murids* and others. Inasmuch as it is enforced, it makes the *murid* treat the *pir* as the locus of the self-manifestation of God, the social actor. Forcing the *murid* to treat the *pir* as the locus of the self-manifestation of God before he knows how the *pir*, a man, can represent and present God to him, seems to rest on the famous Sufi principle: External practice leads to internal transformation and knowledge.

PRACTICES

A man who wanted to become a *murid* asked the *pir* if there was anything special he had to do. The *pir* told him that he had only to remember him and visit him often. If he could not visit him, he had to at least write to him regularly, irrespective of whether he replied or not. The man asked if he had to do anything special, for instance, special ablutions. The *pir* replied in the negative. He just had to remember him as often as possible and visit him regularly. *Murids*, however, follow a number of practices in addition.

Just before going to sleep, I lie down and cover my eyes and ears with my fingers. After remaining like this for a few minutes, I recall the faces of my parents, through whom I came into this world. I remember them and ask them to forgive me. I also ask them to pray for me. Then I go to sleep. When I awake in the morning, I again cover my eyes and ears with my fingers and see their faces. Then I ask them to pray for me. After that I begin doing the work my *pir* has given me. My real *pirs* are my parents. I have come into this world through them. If I forget them I am lost. They are my chief *pirs*. And I can look at the face of my *pir* only if I have looked at their faces first thing in the morning. What is the use of looking at the face of my *pir* if I do not look at their faces? When I look at their faces, the face of my *pir* automatically comes before me. If I forget my real *pir*, what is the use of being the *murid* of this *pir*?

Before beginning a particular work, I remember my *pir*. I remember him with faith. Then I say to myself that I am working through him, and that the fruits of the work are his doing. But before doing all this one must remember one's parents. Otherwise, one gets nothing.

Without the *pir* there is nothing. The *pir* is between myself and Allah. I have not seen Allah, but I have seen the face of Allah in the face of my *pir*. This happens specially when we remember the *pir* in a special way. We imagine the full body of the *pir*. We see his feet, his torso, his beard, his forehead and his cap in our mind.

When a *murid* visits his *pir*, he must kiss his hand. He may even kiss the feet of his *pir*. In this way he reminds himself that he belongs to the *pir*. (Once I observed a *pir* stretch out his right hand to a female *murid*. She was sitting beside him along with another woman. Then he told her to kiss his hand. She obeyed with much hesitation. He told her to do it again. Then he told her to rub her eyes on the rings on his fingers. This carried on for quite some time until all her hesitation disappeared.)

The *murid* loves the *pir* and this love makes him imitate his *pir* in every possible way. He even imitates the way in which the *pir* dresses. He does not wish to maintain any difference between himself and his *pir*.

We must have only one master and study only one thing. Only then can we concentrate fully and become experts. When I hear my *pir* say something I reflect on it for three days. In this way I get insight. After the three days, I have to tell my *pir* what I have understood. The *pir* is my master. He tells me what I should study and he will lead me on the right path.

My *pir* instructs me at night. If there are others with me, they also listen and learn along with me. But if the *pir* instructs me alone, the instruction is only for me. I cannot tell you or anyone else what I have learnt. That girl who just left was told to recite something by my *pir*. He also told her not to tell anyone what he had given her to recite. She did not tell even me. When she refused to tell me, I said to myself, "What is concealed must remain hidden." I asked her to tell me so that I could help her to recite and, thus, help her to gain the benefit she seeks quickly. Still she refused.

My *pir* told me to do three things: rob, sleep with my mother, and to eat what is forbidden. You may feel bad to hear this. But there is no need to feel bad. The words are one thing. But the meaning is quite different. "To rob" means to worship. Just as a thief steals in the dead of night with fear in his heart, so too must we pray in the dead of night and fear everything that is not God. We must love God alone. "Eat what is forbidden" means that our faith should be as strong as our desire for forbidden things. For example, anger is forbidden. But when we get angry we get the strength to do things we cannot normally do. When we get angry we forget ourselves. Our faith must be like this anger. We must forget ourselves completely when we act with faith. It is not I but my *pir* who is doing the good works. "Sleep with your mother" has to be understood in this way: When you were a baby you slept with your mother.

But when you grew older it became sinful to continue sleeping with her. But look at a mother's nature. When you were a baby, she fed you with her own milk. She loved you and looked after all your needs. The earth is also a mother. Like our mother, she provides for all our needs. We get our food from her, even our clothes from the fibers of the plants that grow on her. And when we die, we will have to go back to her. The earth looks after us like a mother. So we should respect her like a mother. We should always keep in close touch with her. We should keep in contact with her just as we kept in touch with our mothers when we were babies. We should walk barefooted, sleep on the floor, and respect all creatures of the earth. If we respect the earth in this way, the earth will look after us.

There are people who pray the *namaz* and keep the fast. But they do not give anything to the poor and the widows. What is the use of all their prayers? It is very important to worship at night. What is the use of worshipping in the day time to show people how holy one is? The question is, what does one do at night? Does one sleep at night? One must pray at night when no one can see one. Also, one must not kick and insult the poor and the widows. One finds them wherever one goes. One must remember that the saints protect them. He who treats them badly, will be punished. Ever since my *pir* told me this, I began to get frightened. I began to say to myself, "May be I have hurt them unintentionally." If one does not want to give them anything. one must ask their forgiveness for not giving anything. Then one has to protect and help one's neighbours to the extent one is capable. One has to serve them also.

The *murids* of a *pir* and a few guests gather together to recite the *dhikr* at night after 9 p.m. The *dhikr* begins with the recitation of the name of Allah, followed by the recitation of the name of Mohammed, Ali, and all the saints in the *silsilah*. The *dhikr* ends with a prayer for each of those present. If there is a newcomer, then the prayer stops till the *pir* gets his name. The recitation of names begins very slowly and proceeds at an increasingly faster pace. But before the recitation reaches an emotional peak, it is cut short and the recitation of another name begins. This is possible because the congregation follows the pace set by the *pir*. Besides the *dhikr*, *vazifa* is common. The *vazifa*, however, is usually recited in private and is not audible. A *pir* may also recite it along with a *murid* or a client, inaudibly. Each recites privately, sitting together and reciting the same name, sentence, or verse. Meditation does not seem to be practised. A *khalifa* said,

> I cannot tell you anything about meditation because I have never done meditation till now. I have not received the permission to do it. But I have recited a lot of *dhikr* and *vazifa* and written a lot of *naqsh* (*tawiz*).

The most important practice is the service of the *pir*. The poorer *murids* may have to take the *pir's* children to school, lead his father to the mosque, attend to the invalid members of his household in every possible way, look after the guests, clean the office, do the shopping for his wife, run errands for him, his guests and family members, etc. The rich and educated *murids* must be ready to render the same service. But they are usually expected to donate money and give gifts to the *pir*, and to use their influence to help the *pir* and those he sends to them.

To recapitulate: Besides the *adab*, the constant remembrance of the *pir*, and visiting him as often as possible, there seems to be no set of practices prescribed by *pirs* for all their *murids*. Nevertheless, the *murids* have a number of practices like remembering their *pirs* and parents before going to sleep and on awakening, reflecting on what the *pir* says for three days and then asking him to correct the resulting interpretations, keeping secret the instruction of the *pir*, performing *dhikr* in community, etc.

SUMMARY

Whatever be the private motives for becoming a *murid*, the *murids* seem to be aware that the *pir* is the official locus of the self-manifestation of God. They also know that they have to learn to treat him as the self-manifestation of God the social actor.

PIRI-MURIDI IN THE NIZAMUDDIN DARGAH

We saw earlier that *piri-muridi* is a social institution in which the *murid* is socialized to consider himself as a servant or a slave, and the *pir* as the official locus of the self-manifestation of God. Once the *murid* learns to interact with the *pir* as the locus of the self-manifestation of God, he also learns to treat all things as the effects and properties of the divine names, or as divine self-revelation. Consequently, he constantly interacts with God the social actor.

DEFINITIONS OF *PIRI-MURIDI*

For some *pirs* and *murids* there can be no definition of *piri-muridi* because it has to do with the spirit or the heart. The heart, as seen earlier, is the ability to look at oneself and at the outside world in a particular way. Hence, as far as these *pirs* and *murids* are concerned, *piri-muridi* cannot be explained. It can only be experienced.

Piri-muridi is not a question of knowledge. It concerns the spirit. If a man is not spiritual he will not be able to understand *piri-muridi*. This is a basic point. *Piri-muridi* is not a research topic. It is a question of the heart. And you will find nothing about *piri-muridi* in books as long as you have not gone through the experience yourself.

The relationship between the *pir* and his *murid* is a secret. Even if someone does make this secret known, you will not understand anything. You will not understand because you are interested in asking why and how. You will understand only if you concentrate on trying to believe in the *pir*. This is a question of power. The power of God has spread all over the world. How can you even begin to understand this power?

To understand *piri-muridi* one has to understand love. One

has to get lost in that love. Only then will one begin to understand what *piri-muridi* is.

Nonetheless, some tried to explain this experience of *piri-muridi*.

How to explain *piri-muridi*? It is a question of experience. You have to experience something within yourself when I speak. Only so will you understand. I will tell you my experiences and leave you to understand them. I do not believe, though, that anyone can understand anything through the experiences of someone else. You will have to bring your own experiences into play to understand what I am talking about. In this way you will be able to discern between right and wrong. If not, anyone can tell you anything and you will believe him. I will tell you what I know because Moinuddin Chisti said three things about *piri-muridi*, the road that takes us close to God. He said, "Feed the hungry, give to those in need, and aid the helpless." Only human beings do these things, not animals. Moinuddin Chisti could have said, fast, pray the *namaz*, perform the pilgrimage, etc., but he did not. Those are the normal duties incumbent on every Muslim. Moinuddin was talking about the additional duties. The additional duty is to be human.

Other *murids* and *pirs*, sought to define *piri-muridi* in different ways. To demonstrate how it is a means of experiencing one's servanthood, and an occasion for renewing one's surrender to God, *piri-muridi* was compared to the woman's lot in marriage.

Piri-muridi is practice. Anyone can read a book. But not everyone can put what it says into practice. For instance, you alone know how long it takes you to reach the Nizamuddin *dargah* from your residence. You know what happens to you on the way. I don't. I don't even know how to ride a bicycle. You know through practical experience. In the same way the *murid* has to get practical experience. He has to learn to love his *pir* in whatever form he may see him. In the course of living with his *pir*, he sees him in every form. He sees his good and bad qualities. But he does not have any connection with the faults of the *pir*. Just as a wife keeps her husband even though he goes to prostitutes every evening, the *murid* has to love and keep his *pir*. The wife cannot correct her husband. If she dares to even ask him why he is going to prostitutes, he will shoot her. Won't he? And if she goes and does what he is doing, if she goes to other men, then too he will kill her. Or he will throw her out. The husband can do whatever he likes to do, but not the wife. If she tries to do what she likes to do, or what she sees her husband doing, she will receive a beating, or she will be killed. She cannot even criticize or correct her husband. This is slavery. The *murid* has to become like the wife. He has to make himself the slave of the *pir*. Only when he commits himself to live the life of a slave has *piri-muridi* begun.

Piri-muridi is like marriage, with the *murid* taking the place of the wife. Once married, she is stuck with her husband for life, be he dark or fair, sickly or healthy, good or bad. She has to do whatever he tells her, good or bad. She cannot complain. If she does not like her husband, what he does, or what he orders her to do, there is nothing she can do about it. She has to stomach everything with a smile. Similar is the *murid's* position and status. He has chosen and committed himself to a *pir*. There is nothing he can do if he does not like his *pir*. He is stuck with him for life, and he has to do whatever the *pir* tells him to do, good or bad, pleasant or unpleasant. It is no use complaining. It is useless to say that he made a wrong choice, or that he had committed himself to the *pir* with his eyes closed. He has to concentrate on obeying and be true to his commitment.

Piri-muridi consists in surrendering oneself to the *pir*. The *murid* learns to behave like a slave. He has to learn to become like the elephant that carries people about. But the *pir* does not beat him. He trains him. He may get angry with him. If the *pir* does not get angry how will the *murid* find the way? It is necessary for the *pir* to get angry with his *murid*. But *pir* must also love his *murid*.

Piri-muridi consists in making the *murid* surrender himself to
the *pir*. The *murid* is made to surrender himself for the sake of
God. When the *murid* surrenders himself, his life changes.
Hence, *piri-muridi* can be understood only in action. If you
surrender yourself to me I will be able to show you what *piri-muridi* is.

Piri-muridi is the way of remaining under the influence of
guidance.

A *murid* once asked Nizamuddin, "What is *piri-muridi*?"
Nizamuddin smiled. Then he pointed north and told him to
walk. The *murid* began to walk in that direction. He did not ask,
"Where should I go? For how long should I keep walking? He
did not ask any questions. He just kept walking in the direction
pointed out by Nizamuddin. In this way he reached Lahore.
There was a *hakim* there who loved Nizamuddin and had spread
word that anyone who came from Nizamuddin, should be sent
to him. So this man was directed to the *hakim*. The *hakim* treated
him with great respect. When it was time for the *murid* to leave,
the *hakim* gave him one thousand gold coins to take to
Nizamuddin.

On the way back, the man stopped at a wayside inn where
a beautiful dancing girl attracted his attention. He could not
resist her. Satan had set his mark upon his heart. The *murid* went
up to her and asked, "What will you charge to sleep with me for
one night?" The woman said, "As many gold coins as there are
flowers in my shawl". He agreed. She took him to a room and
laid the shawl on the floor. The man began to put the gold coins
with him on the flowers. In the process the bag was emptied.
Even then, he did not remember that the money was meant for
Nizamuddin. Satan had captured him. God made Adam with
great love. Yet, Satan misled him. Allah said to Satan, "Your
work is to misguide men and my work is to keep them on the
right path. I will do my work. You do yours." Allah keeps all
men on the right path through the prophets, the saints, and the

pirs.

Since the *murid* had fulfilled his part of the contract, the woman sat down on the bed and waited for him. But, when the *murid,* blinded with lust tried to approach her something pushed him back. He tried again and was again pushed back. At the third attempt he managed to embrace her. But when he embraced her he saw Nizamuddin sitting in her eyes. Then the woman slapped him. With the slap, Satan left him. The slap was not meant for the *murid.* It was meant for Satan. After receiving the slap the *murid* fell in a faint. When he came to he realized what sin he had been about to commit and ran away, leaving everything behind. The woman could not take money for nothing. Hence, she collected the gold coins and followed him till he reached Nizamuddin. When he came into Nizamuddin's presence, Nizamuddin said, "Have you experienced *piri-muridi?* Satan made a great effort to lead you astray. But I saved you. *Muridi* is like this, that you obeyed me when I ordered you to go. You did not ask, why should I go, how far should I go, etc. You just obeyed. This is *muridi.* And *piri* is this, that when you were about to sin with this woman, I saved you. It was I who slapped you and made you unconscious." Then both of them asked for forgiveness. And what did Nizamuddin do? He married them to each other and gave them the bag of gold as a wedding present. He made the forbidden permissible. Sex is forbidden only as long as there is no marriage relationship. This is *piri-muridi* and you will find everything about *piri-muridi* in this story.

It is a difficult and frustrating experience that yields rich fruit when least expected.

A very learned man lived in a village. He had brought up his children well and had become very wealthy. He was also highly respected in the village. One night Allah said to him in a dream, "You have done what society and religion required of you. But you have not been able to recognize Me. You have never searched for Me." After this dream he got the urge to see Allah.

In the morning he called together his whole family and said, "I have fulfilled my duty towards you, society, and religion. But I have not met Allah. I do not know where He is. So, I will leave you and go in search of Him. You go on living the good life that I have prepared for you, but allow me to go in search of Allah. I am old and will soon die." The family prepared for him a farewell feast.

After the feast he left the village and entered the jungle, a jungle so dark that one could not make out the difference between day and night. Slowly, he grew weak for lack of food. This weakness was made worse by the wounds he received from the thorns that tore at his flesh. One day he became so weak that he fell down and could not rise again. In this state he fell asleep for twenty-four hours. When he awoke he had just enough strength to lift his head and look around. He saw a fire in the distance. He began to crawl towards it hoping for human succour. As he neared the fire he saw three *sadhus* squatting beside it. Their wild appearance made him afraid, and he remembered the stories he had heard about strange men who inhabited the jungle and destroyed all who dared to approach them. But he did not have the strength to get up and run away. He remained prostrate where he was and prepared for death. The three *sadhus* [sometimes a *pir* is called a *sadhu*] began to speak among themselves. One said, "I have heard that one man has entered our jungle." The second said, "He is already here. Look, there he lies." The third said, "Since he is already here, call him to us. Let us know why he is here." The first *sadhu* called to the man to join them. The man crawled towards them and lay prostrate: he did not dare to sit with them. They asked him who he was and why he had come there. He told them everything. Then they said to him, "You must be hungry. Go to the next garden. In it there is only one tree with three apples on it. Eat one of these apples. As soon as the man ate the apple, he found all his former strength returning to him. Also, his face became full of light. It was Allah's apple. He was no longer an old man.

When he returned to the three *sadhus* they said to him, "You are a good man and you have a family. Go back home because you will find Allah there. Why have you come here? To commit a sin? Go home. There your wife and children will gladly look after you and you will have the time to recite the names of God. Why have you come to experience hunger in this jungle? Go home. Do not sin by staying in this jungle." He said, "I do not know the way home. I am lost. How will I go home?" They replied, "We will show you the way. But when you reach your village you will do something for us. Go to the king of your country and say to him, 'I saw three fires in the jungle. Three kings sit beside those fires. A fourth fire there is, which is dying out. Unless you return and stoke your fire, not only your fire but the other three fires also will die out. Give the message to no one but the king. If you reveal it to anyone else, you will die." Then they sent him to pick the two remaining apples. They told him to eat one immediately. He was to eat the last apple only after returning home. He was not to give even a piece of it to anyone else.

On eating the second apple, he fell into a deep sleep. One of the *sadhus* blew over him and clapped his hands so that he was immediately transported to his doorstep. In the morning his son found him there. He began calling to all the people of the village telling them that his father had returned from the jungle as a young man. People came running to see this strange phenomenon, an old man turned young again. But the old man was oblivious of all their stares. He was fast asleep, and nothing they did would awake him. Then the three *sadhus* in the jungle clapped their hands and he awoke. On seeing his house and his fellow villagers around him, he remembered that he still had to eat the third apple. He indicated through signs that they should leave him. He went into his house, locked the door and ate the third apple in secret. And he began to look even younger. All who saw him said, "He has truly met God." He spent the whole week entertaining guests and forgot the work the *sadhus* had assigned him. They reminded him of his mission in a dream. The next day he set out for the king's palace with his son.

The son was stopped at the first gate but the father was allowed to pass through all the seven gates. When he reached the king's room, the king stood up and embraced him. He then led the king into the adjoining room and gave him the message in secret. On hearing the message, the king remembered who he was. He also realized that he had finished his work in that country. If he did not return, not only would the other three fires die out, but also the whole world would be destroyed. So, he crowned his son king, lay down, pulled a white sheet over himself and died. His body remained in the palace, but his spirit went back to where the three *sadhus* were sitting. The people were confused. They did not know how or why the king they loved and respected died. The old man was bound to keep his knowledge of the matter secret. But one day, someone forced him to divulge his secret. When he finished telling his story, he became an old man again.

Now I too have left everything in order to search for Allah, for the saint, for the beloved. The Beloved also is at home. He is in my father and mother also. One day the Beloved will catch me and show Himself to me. When that happens I will go mad. This is all there is to *piri-muridi*.

Piri-muridi also consists of getting to know the *pir*.

Do you know Junaid, the great *pir*? He could walk over the waters. Once, one of his *murids* expressed a desire to walk over the waters. Junaid told him that walking over the waters was not for him. But the *murid* kept pestering him. Finally, the *pir* gave in. He said to him, "Hold this end of my cloak and recite, *'ya Junaid'* loudly." Then they began to walk across the river. After some time, the *murid* noticed that the *pir* was reciting, *'ya Allah'*. He thought to himself, "He is reciting, *'ya Allah'*, and I, who am walking behind him am reciting, *'ya Junaid'*. This is *khufr* and a very big sin." Hence, he too began to recite, *'ya Allah'*. But he began to sink into the water and shouted for help. Junaid turned around, pulled him out and said, "I told you to recite, *'ya*

Junaid', and not, *ya Allah*. Now carry on reciting *'ya Junaid'*."
They continued walking over the water. This happened three
times. When they crossed the river and were standing on firm
ground the *pir* in anger said to the *murid*, "You are a very
stubborn man." The *murid* replied, "You yourself recite, *'ya
Allah'*, and you tell me to recite, *'ya Junaid'* behind you. How
can this be? This is *khufr*." The *pir* replied, "Get to know your
pir first, and then you will come to know Allah. As long as you
do not know and understand your *pir* how will you ever know
Allah?" This is *piri-muridi*.

Piri-muridi is training geared towards the attainment of spiritual
knowledge.

"*Piri-muridi* is like this. A child is admitted into a school so that
he can gain some knowledge. You may read all the books in the
world, but without a teacher, you will not understand anything.
A teacher means systematic learning. A teacher makes one
mature. It is a matter of input and output. We have natural
talents. These talents have to be recognized and then developed.
They can be developed only if many things are put into the
student, only if he is given input. *Piri-muridi* gives this input so
that we can approach God. It is a way by which a person
recognizes God, understands the meaning and purpose of this
world, and realizes who made the whole world.

Men of science say, "We can do this and we can do that."
God says, "Wrong. Can you take yourselves apart and put
yourselves together again?" Man cannot do this. Man cannot
take himself apart and reconstruct himself in such a way that he
can function like before. Man may repair a fracture, but that part
will never function as before. Allah says, "Only I can do these
things."

Piri-muridi is a matter of teaching. The *pir* teaches his *murid*.
He makes him mature. He is made mature by being told to stand
up, sit down, do this and that. It is like getting admitted into a
school so that the teacher can make one mature. You have

intelligence, knowledge, etc. But the teacher will give you homework. He will make you work. He does this so that the talents that are hidden within yourself may be revealed and developed. Why do people go to school, college, and university? Just for this reason. If a person has no teacher nothing can happen. A child cannot walk at first. It keeps falling. It needs someone to help to enable it to walk. And it continues to need that help until it can walk without falling down and hurting itself. It is the same with the use of the brain and everything else that we have.

Piri-muridi is not concerned with book knowledge. It deals with spiritual knowledge. If you love a girl and are lost in love of her, you cannot express your entire love in words and actions. What you express in words and actions is nothing in comparison with what you feel. This inexpressible feeling concerns the heart. It concerns knowledge that is in the heart. That is why it is called hidden knowledge. *Piri-muridi* deals with hidden knowledge. It helps us to learn and understand through constant practice. For instance, if you respect Amir Khusrau, only your heart knows how much you respect him. This personal heart knowledge by which you know that you respect him is called spiritual knowledge. *Piri-muridi* gives this spiritual knowledge.

The human body is the house of God. Not everyone knows this through direct experience. Those who do, are said to possess the third eye. One can experience God in oneself only if one cleanses oneself and learns to turn one's mind habitually to God. Only then will one shine within. One's third eye will be cleansed and one will have a hot line to God. You will shine like the light and you will look at a man only once to tell what sort of person he is. But this cleansing of oneself and the habit of constantly remembering God can be attained only if one annihilates oneself in one's *pir*. Next, one will have to annihilate oneself in the Prophet. Only then will one be able to annihilate oneself in God. And this can be done only in *piri-muridi*.

Piri-muridi is the way by which people learn how to lead a life that will result in salvation or paradise.

Piri-muridi is like this. You may know of Adam and Eve. Eve was made from Adam's rib. The rib is crooked. Hence, woman is crooked and a Satan. See what is written in the Bible. God forbade Adam from eating the fruit of the pomegranate tree. But Eve plucked that fruit and ate part of it. Then she spoke in soft and seductive tones and, thus, soothed Adam until he forgot the source of that fruit. And he too ate. She deceived him and he sinned. As soon as they had eaten the forbidden fruit, their clothes fell off their bodies and they found themselves stark naked. Then the angel Gabriel took Eve and put her in Saudi Arabia. Adam, he put in Sri Lanka. Sri Lanka was very dark, full of thick jungle. Adam grew afraid and called aloud to God. God sent Gabriel to find out what was wrong. Adam told him that he was frightened and hungry. Gabriel brought grains of wheat and told him to eat. After that he told him that he had to work. First, Gabriel taught him how to grind the remaining wheat into flour, how to knead it into dough, and how to make *chapatis*. Adam ate some of the *chapatis* and those that were left over were sent to Eve. Then Gabriel taught Adam how to plough using two oxen so that he could grow the wheat himself. Some time later, when Adam was ploughing, the oxen refused to move forward. Adam began to whip them. The oxen cried out to heaven. God again sent Gabriel to find out what was wrong. The oxen said to him, "Adam is beating us without trying to find out why we refuse to move forward. There is a great stone in the earth, and the plough will break if we continue to pull." Gabriel scolded Adam and told him to remove the stone. In this way Adam was given everything by God. The *pir* stands in the place of the angel Gabriel, while the *murid* stands in the place of Adam. He has to be taught how to live a life worthy of paradise.

Piri-muridi is the means by which the *murid* is saved from the wrath of the law, and also the means by which he is able to lead a good life. *Piri-muridi* consists in doing what the *pir* tells one to do. The *murid* obeys his orders because he believes that his

obedience will lead him to paradise. The *murid* becomes mad
out of love for his *pir*. He walks on the path pointed out by his
pir, and does only what his *pir* tells him to do. In *piri-muridi* the
murid is drawn into a special relationship with the saints,
irrespective of whether he himself does good works or not. This
is a very great thing. *Piri-muridi* consists in this: The *murid* accepts
to follow the *pir*. And he tries to internalize the *pir's* teaching.
The *pir* is a guide. The *pir* brings the *murid* into the way of the
Quran, and in such a way that he begins to love it and live
according to its teaching.

Piri-muridi* is a process by which the *murid* is taken to the
station of the *pir*. The *pir* brings the *murid* to his own station by
advising him, by telling him what good works he should do and
what evil he must avoid. He behaves like the *murid's* father. Will
the father not pull his child out of the fire? The *pir* does
everything to make sure that the *murid* will go to paradise. He
becomes the *murid's* father when he buys him. Just as when you
buy something and that thing becomes yours, so also the *pir* buys
the *murid* so that he becomes his own. The *murid* is his, not to
be mistreated, but to be saved and, to be given everything that
belongs to the *pir*. He can do this because he has special power.
One day the *murid* himself will realize that the *pir* has led him up
the correct path. Finally, when he has led the *murid* to his own
station, he will make him a *pir*, and himself die. Just as parents
are free to give all their possessions to any one of their children,
so too the *pir* is free to give his power to any one *murid*. The
Wahabis tell us to go directly to God. It is true that God is the
only one who gives everything. But then something else is also
true. Look at that building. If you want to go up to the roof you
will need something. You will need a ladder, or a staircase. In
the same way, if you want to reach God you will need
something. You will need the path. *Piri-muridi* is the path.
However learned you may be, you will not be able to reach God
if you do not use that path. That is why the *piri-muridi*
relationship is necessary for everyone.

Finally,

> *Piri-muridi* is a relationship which one takes up because one desires something intensely. For instance, an addict to tea or tobacco does not feel happy until he gets the tea or tobacco; when he gets the tea or tobacco he is satisfied. A person enters *piri-muridi* to ensure that he will not suffer any punishment in the after life. This life does not matter. The next life is what matters.

To recapitulate: The general assumption that *piri-muridi* cannot be described, while being a genuine difficulty experienced by some *murids*, may be a way of saying that practice is more important than theory or understanding. This mode of operating seems to rest on the Sufi principle that doing leads to understanding, or practice leads to inner transformation and knowledge. Practice cannot, however, lead to understanding unless the one who practises reflects on his experience and tries to come to some understanding of it. The *murids* in the Nizamuddin Dargah give much evidence of reflecting on their experiences by drawing on the rich store of stories and beliefs contained in the oral tradition, on experiences they have had in the past and on experiences they continue to have in the present as they live out their lives in the larger society.

The *murids* may compare their difficulty in explaining the experience of *piri-muridi* with the difficulty of explaining the experience of cycling long distances. One who cycles such distances regularly knows how to balance, has practical knowledge about the difficulties and dangers involved and how to avoid them. But as long as he does not reflect on this experience with a view to explaining it to himself and to others, he may find it difficult to explain this experience to someone who does not know cycling. Fortunately for us, the *murids* reflect on their experience of *piri-muridi* by contrasting and comparing it with other experiences. For instance they may compare the master–slave relationship that *piri-muridi* is with their own experience of marriage by making the *pir* take the place of the husband and the *murid* that of the wife. The husband can do what he likes. He may visit prostitutes, drink and do all kinds of wrongs without anyone being able to do anything about it. Not even the wife can correct him because she does not have that right over him. Further, she cannot pity herself, emulate her husband's evil ways, or criticize him. If she does any of these things, she will be beaten, killed, or discarded by the husband. She has to bear everything with a smile, and behave as if she has not noticed her husband's wrong doing. The *murid* may also compare *piri-muridi* to a man who enters a thick jungle: A man goes into a thick jungle and loses his way. Lack of food and the wounds that he receives from the undergrowth and thorns further weaken him until he is brought to the point of believing that he will die without having gained anything. It is in that moment of utter desperation that he begins to receive the reward for all his efforts.

Hence, *piri-muridi* is not the master–slave relationship in which the *pir* is merely a task master and a tyrant. It is true that a *pir* can be a taskmaster and a tyrant, but he is more than that. He is a father, who like the *murid's* father loves him and wants to bequeath all his spiritual wealth to him. But he can do so only after training the *murid* so that he can be mature enough to handle the responsibility that comes along with that inheritance. Hence, the *murid* has actually sold himself to a father, a new parent. The frustrating experience of training for maturity is also likened to the experience of being educated in a traditional Muslim school where the student is completely at the disposal of the teacher. Or the experience of being trained may be compared with that of the prophet Adam, who after the fall from paradise was transported to a strange and dark place, the jungles of Sri Lanka. He did not know how to grow and cook his food and had to be taught these elementary tasks while experiencing much fear and hunger, by the angel Gabriel in order that he might take up his responsibility as vicegerent. Hence, *piri-muridi* is also compared to a ladder or a staircase that takes the *murid* to the top of a building (the desired end, union with God via union with the *pir*).

STAGES IN *PIRI-MURIDI*

I have divided the socialization process that *piri-muridi* is into different stages.

The First Stage: Choosing a *Pir*

Since the *pir* is the official locus of the self-manifestation of God the social actor, the *murid* has the liberty of choosing someone whom he can consider as the locus of God's self-manifestation. He is expected to choose his *pir* from those who are normally recognized as *pirs*, whether *khandani pirs* or *pirs* who have received the *khilafat* from their own *pirs*. But the process of choosing a *pir* is difficult. The seeker is repeatedly warned that many self-avowed *pirs* are false *pirs*, representatives of the divine name misguider.

Why are you asking about *piri-muridi*? *Piri-muridi* does not exist today. Everyone just wants to make money. *Maulvis, mullahs, pirs, pandits* and priests are all busy doing evil. Everyone has gone astray. There was a time when everyone had his own nature and was faithful to it. But today, no one knows anyone's nature because people do not live up to their responsibilities.

The spirit of self-abnegation has disappeared. People no longer seek to tame the lower self. The *pirs* care more about wearing expensive and glittering clothes, eating good food and going about in cars.

Do not think that the *pirs* you meet in this *dargah* are true *pirs*. They are largely uneducated. They are sinners and dirty within. They have no powers, they only pretend to have it.

The *pirs* that you see here are not *pirs*. They have no mercy. They are only greedy for money. They do not even have knowledge. They will prevent you from earning your living and tell you to start begging. They have turned *piri-muridi* into business. It is no longer a respectful relationship.

Do not go to these *pirs*. They are more interested in making money than in fulfilling their duties as *pirs*. Very few *pirs* practise what they preach. A long beard, fingers studded with rings, and going about in taxis and cars does not make a *pir*. These are fakes. They may be turning the *tasbih* with their fingers. Their tongues may be moving in their mouths. But their minds are elsewhere. They are thinking of ways of earning more money. This is not worship. True worship consists in keeping God before one. Only God should matter to one.

Why do people become *pirs*? To earn money. What else is there to it! After all, everyone has to eat. To become a *pir* means to become rich. These *pirs* misguide people. They look at their clients, judge their background and then talk accordingly. Hence, if they say ten things, at least four of them are bound to be true.

These bogus *pirs* attract people in this way: One man has an idea. And he is able to convince one man in a hundred that what he is saying is true. That one man will follow him even if the remaining ninety-nine are against that particular *pir*. As time passes, the *pir* may be able to convince two or three more people that what he says is right. He has progressed from one to three. After that he will force these three followers to do certain things for him, things that will make him famous. In return for these services, he gives them certain benefits, like money, a place to stay on his land, etc. This is how he operates. Both the *pir* and his *murids* are crooks and self-centred. They both give each other economic, political and social support. The *murids* advertise the name of their *pir* wherever they go.

Or the seeker may meet people who tell him of their bad experiences with *pirs*.

One thousand years ago, the lords used to boss over people and force them to live like animals. There are men in the Muslim community also who are like these lords. They insult others. God is not on our tongue. By what authority, by what power do they insult others? A man who has been insulted more than he can bear finds it difficult to surrender to anyone. If the person who insults asks, "Who are you?" he will reply, "I am like you. Allah has created you and the same Allah has created me. You did not create yourself. Allah did. You cannot say you are a *pir*.

Allah created you and has made you a *pir*. How dare you torture other men? Who has given you the authority to punish me? Why do you do this? You do this because you have forgotten the power of Allah." Where there is no humanity, I tell you, there is no spirituality.

Listen I have suffered much. I came here by the grace of Allah. On the first night, I was robbed of all my money and clothes. The next day, one *pir* asked me from where I had come. I asked him to give me a job so that I could earn some money and eat. He offered me ten rupees. I told him I would like to earn my bread. I am not a beggar. He said he would try to get me a job. I took the ten rupees and ate the first and only meal of that day. The next day he said that he could not get a job for me. Then he offered me Rs.300 so that I could go back to Bangladesh. I told him I would earn that money. Taking money from him would be begging. My Prophet also worked when he wanted money. He never begged. Why should I beg? I should be like him. So he gave me a job. I had to write letters for him from morning to night for twelve rupees a day. But he did not pay me. He did not even give me food to eat. I had to go to sleep hungry. Next morning I asked him for three rupees. He said, "I have no money." This has been going on for the last two weeks. Now I am ill. The only way out is to beg for the three hundred rupees and go back home.

I came to find a *pir*. But I only found inhumanity. How can these people be the saints of God? It is a sin to become their *murid*. Mohammed is the last Prophet. And the Quran is the perfect book. It tells us everything about our lives. It tells us how to run our business, our conjugal life, etc. But we Muslims do not put it into practice. We do not even open the Quran. We do not read it. We do not discuss what is written in it. We talk about ways of earning more money, ways of torturing men, ways of robbing others so that they have to die of starvation on the roadside. I am going back and will never return.

That *pir* took two thousand five hundred rupees from me four months ago and I am still unwell. He made me drink the

water from the *baoli* in which lepers and all kinds of sick people
bathe. From that day onwards I got even more ill. That *pir*
cheated me. What am I to do? I go to another *pir* and he refuses
to treat me until I throw out all the *tawizes* the first *pir* gave me.
But I have paid so much money for them.

Such unhappy experiences may lead some people to give up the idea
of becoming a *murid*.

I gave up the idea of becoming a *murid* because all the *pirs* I met
are second class *pirs*. They call themselves *pirs* to earn money.
They know nothing about the Sufi path, or about religion.

I wanted to become a *murid*. But I did not find a single good
man. I will not find a good man. It is difficult to find a good man.
Every *pir* I have come across has some defect or the other. A
perfect *pir* is a saint. He has no faults. He is the man who has
the mercy of God within him. He loves people. Such men do
not exist today.

Some others initiate the *piri-muridi* relationship with a dead *pir*,
the saint.

I keep going to where *pirs* live and work. But I have not become
the *murid* of any *pir*. I have made the saint my *pir*. I have made
him my *pir* by giving myself to him in my heart. Officially I am
not a *murid* because I have not surrendered to a living *pir*. But
one can also do this: One can stand before Allah, and while
standing before Him say in one's heart, "I give myself to you
before Allah. Now you are my *pir*." This is possible because true
pirs do not die. They only draw a veil between themselves and
us. With the living *pir* not much happens. There is no *piri-muridi*
with them. They only know how to get angry. What is the use
of their anger? I have no need of their anger.

Quite a few people fear the demands made of a *murid*.

It is very difficult to be a good *murid*. One has to do so many things. One has to pray and worship much. One has to stay with one's *pir*. I do not have the time for all this.

It is very difficult to become a *murid*. Before one becomes a *murid* one must wash one's mind with soap. One must become pure. This is too much for me just yet. So I have not yet become a *murid*. When one becomes a *murid* one must be different from others.

Many of this category find a way out by becoming the *murid* of a dead *pir*, the saint.

Unquestioning obedience to a *pir* is not possible. Obedience to him should concern only spiritual matters—not concern worldly matters. If a *pir* asks his *murid* to marry someone, the *murid* should not be bound to obey. Obedience in all matters is a thing of the past. Today, the *murid* should be allowed to make his own decisions. That unquestioning obedience is a characteristic of classical *piri-muridi*. I am a *murid* because I have certain feelings. These feelings no longer incline me to search for a living *pir*. *Piri-muridi* has two aspects, the official and the unofficial. Unofficial *piri-muridi* means that the individual retains his individuality. You do not do what the *pir* orders unless it agrees with your conscience. Official *piri-muridi* is complete obedience in all matters. In the unofficial form of *piri-muridi*, the *pir* is a saint, or dead. This contract is safer. It is safer because *piri-muridi* also involves fraud. The *pir* can rob the *murid*, specially today. Today *piri-muridi* is more false than true. The *pir* can say, "I had a dream in which the Prophet said..." He can say anything and the *murid* has to believe and obey him. Because of all these problems I have chosen Nizamuddin as my *pir*. Nizamuddin is alive, not dead. All the dead are still living but the saints are more alive than others. They have entered another mode of existence. And they still continue to help us.

Many, however, do not lose heart. They continue to search for an authentic *pir*.

Sultans are one kind of people and *faqirs* another. But the *faqirs* look just like the sultans. So it is difficult to recognize them. The saints are great, not because they prayed the *namaz* and kept the fast. They are great because they spent their lives in serving the people. To observe the five pillars is important. But more important is to love. Nizamuddin was one great person. I believe that such great men exists today. There are *pirs* who can clean the heart. I am searching for such men.

These *pirs* cannot be recognized by their external appearance.

One does not recognize a *pir* from his clothes, or his appearance. Once, a man dressed in rags was standing near a gutter. He was picking up the muck from the gutter and eating it. A police inspector came along. Striking him with his stick he said roughly, "Go away. Why are you eating muck?" At that moment a well-dressed man came along, saluted the man in rags and said, "*Pir* sahib, pray for me." The inspector exclaimed in astonishment, "You are a *pir*!" The *pir* merely picked up some more muck from the gutter and offered it to the inspector. The inspector saw that it was not muck, but *halwa*. He touched it and found that it was hot. He tasted it and found that it tasted like *halwa*. So he fell at the *pir's* feet and said, "I want to become your *murid*." The *pir* said, "I will make you my *murid* if you pass a test. Go and bring me a kilo of scorpions." The inspector thought it a simple task because he had many men under him. But try as they would, they could not collect the required kilo of scorpions. Finally, the inspector had to go humbly to the *pir* and tell him that he had failed the test. The *pir* began to make fun of him, "You are a police inspector and still you cannot collect a kilo of scorpions. You think that you are a very big man and that you have the right to order everyone about. You think that you have the right to beat people for no reason at all. But you are nothing. You cannot bring me even a kilo of scorpions. This

is such an easy task and yet you have failed. You are useless.
None the less, I will help you. Go to the grave of your
predecessor and open it. There you will find more than a kilo
of scorpions. Bring me one kilo." The inspector went to the
grave and on opening it found it full of scorpions. He collected
one kilo and brought it to the *pir*. Then the *pir* said, "Did you
see all those scorpions in his grave? They sting him night and day
for all the sins he committed as inspector. The same fate awaited
you. But I decided to save you."

Before choosing a *pir*, The prospective *murid* would like to test
him. But how does one test a *pir*?

One cannot say to a *pir*, "Show me your power. I want to see
if you have any faults." To that, the *pir* would reply, "How can
you judge me when you are not fit to judge yourself? First go
and correct yourself and then come and judge me. Follow what
I tell you. Only then will you know whether I have power."

They solve the problem by observing the *pirs* and their *murids*.

We can find out if a *pir* has power when we observe his *murids*.
If the *murids* are not liars, the *pir* has power. The behaviour of
the *pir* and his *murids* reveals his power.

There are many *pirs*. It is difficult to know which of them
is false and which is true. All trees look alike. How does one find
out the difference between them? One looks at their fruit, their
flowers and leaves. The trees may look alike but their fruit,
flowers and leaves are different. There are good *pirs* in all *silsilahs*.
A good *pir* should be able to show his power. I have not been
able to find any *pir* who has power. How does one find out
whether a *pir* has power? One stays with him for a few days.
Then one can see for oneself whether he has knowledge,
goodness, etc. His goodness can be seen in his works, and in his
attitude. One must watch and find out whether he is bent on
making money or whether he desires to do the will of God.

The *pir* must know how to deal with people. His way of talking and dealing must be good. If not, he is not a true *pir*. This does not mean that he cannot be hot-tempered or that he cannot punish people for wrongdoing. But his dealings with people must be good.

One has to watch the *pir*. I chose this *pir* because when people talk rudely to him, he replies with kindness. He is always calm, and he follows the Quran, the *sharia* and the *hadith*. He does not pray the *namaz* to be seen by men. I lived with him and found him praying the *namaz* at 2.00 a.m., when no one is watching. He is a holy man.

I stayed with my *pir* for one year. During that time I did not catch him telling a single lie. Then I watched to see whether he observes the five pillars, especially the *namaz*. When one finds that he does pray the *namaz*, one must try to find out if he tells the truth. If he tells the truth, one must watch and see how he earns a living. Is he stealing or is he earning money in an unlawful way? This may be enough for some *murids*. But others may want to know whether he has power. How does one go about finding out whether he has power? I will answer this question with a story. Once, two men walked into Nizamuddin's *khanqah* at lunch time and refused to eat. Since they refused the servants, the great men who were eating came and offered food to them. They still refused to eat, and in a very insulting manner. Word reached Nizamuddin, and he himself came to serve them. He sat with them for a long time trying to convince them that they should eat something. But they refused to eat. Finally, Nizamuddin said to them, "This food is far better than what you ate in the jungle." On hearing this the two men looked at him in astonishment and accepted the offered food. Then they became his *murids*. They realized that he had the power to know what they had done secretly in the jungle. If Nizamuddin did not pray the *namaz*, tell the truth, and earn his daily bread honestly, how did he get this power to see the secrets of men's hearts? He did all the other things also. That is why he was the ideal *pir*.

A *murid* may unduly test the *pir* and, antagonize him.

The other night I had gone to Paschimpuri. A man tested me
there. He put in my pocket a bottle of liquor and a video cassette
of blue film. People were searching for that cassette. Why did
he do this to me? He made me walk a long way. Then we caught
a bus. We caught a bus because he said that he had no money
to pay the rickshaw fare. It was 11.45 p.m. I told him that I had
the money. But he said, "No, no, you have come to my house.
Thank you for taking all the trouble to come to my house. I must
take you back to the *dargah*." The bus stopped at Punjabi Bagh.
Then I sat in a rickshaw. There were policemen in our bus, and
I did not know what was in my pocket. I thought that it was
medicine. I kept it in the inner pocket of my coat. At Punjabi
Bagh I took a rickshaw and told the man that he could
accompany me to the Nizamuddin Dargah if he so wished. He
said, "No Baba, I have the money. I will pay the rickshaw fare."
When I entered my office he said, "Baba, you are an evil man."
I asked him why he said that. After all, I am a *pir faqir*. He said,
"I tested you, and you failed the test. The cassette in your pocket
has a blue film on it, and the bottle contains liquor. You trusted
me so much that you carried it all over Delhi." I replied, "I do
not trust you. I trust my *pir*. But you have attacked and insulted
me." "No," he replied, "I was looking at the others in the bus.
They were all staring at you and they wanted to attack you. But
none of them had the courage to do so. Suppose someone
attacked you, what would you have done?" I replied, "My *pir*
protects me. He will not allow any evil to harm me." Then I
told him to go away and never to return. I told him that our
relationship was over. On hearing this, he got frightened,
caught my feet and asked for forgiveness. I let him go scot free.
What harm can I do him? I am a *pir*. I put the bottle in my pocket
because he told me that it contained medicine. He committed
a sin by putting those things in my hands and then in my pocket.
If anyone else knew what was in my pocket, he would have

complained to the police and they would have come to arrest
me. He thought the police would arrest me just like that. But
nothing of the sort happened. And he was surprised that nothing
happened. When I go about I keep on reciting something or the
other. I have the blessing of my *pir* and he looks after me. I
thought this man wanted to become my *murid*. That was why
I agreed to visit him.

Finally, after a long period of testing, watching, and listening to
what the *pirs* and their *murids* have to say about *piri-muridi*, those
searching for a *pir* may conclude that all *pirs* can lead one to God.

One has a problem with choosing a *pir* because they are like the
fingers of the hand. All are *pirs*, but each *pir* occupies a different
station. The light of God is found in all stations. Each of them,
whatever his station has the light of God within him. Further,
it is impossible to know the station of a *pir*.

Choosing a *pir* is like falling in love with a girl. In the eyes
of the lover a particular girl may be beautiful, while another may
see nothing special in her. She may even appear ugly to him.
Each man has his own personal taste and way of looking at her.
A *pir* is like this girl. He may be everything to one man, but
nothing to the man sitting next to him.

When a man is attracted to anyone, he goes to him. He goes
to him because he begins to believe in him, or he is at least willing
to believe in him. And once that happens he gets involved with
that person for the rest of his life.

One comes to know the real *pir* only if one learns how to
have faith and how to trust. It is a question of the heart.

People today do not know how to believe. They have no
faith. They are fools. They want to test the *pir*. The medicine
is the same, but what do people say? They say that this doctor
is better than that one. And they have to pay the better doctor
fifty rupees, while the ordinary doctor asks only for three rupees.
The medicine in both cases is the same. Why do they call one
doctor better? They do this because they believe in the

expensive doctor. They believe in him even though he and the
ordinary doctor give the same medicine. What is a specialist? It
is a matter of believing. The doctor feels the patient's pulse,
examines his chest, and does many other things. And while he
is doing all this the patient tells him everything about himself. He
tells the doctor what is wrong with himself. And what does the
doctor do? He listens to what the patient is saying. Then he tells
the patient the very same things. The important thing is to
believe.

Hence, it is no longer a question of finding a *pir* who has no faults.
It is a question of finding a person whom one can come to consider
as the locus of the self-manifestation of God.

A person has to find out as much as possible about the *pir* before
becoming his *murid*. He should search for his good and bad
qualities. Only then can he decide whether he can surrender
himself to that *pir*. After he becomes a *murid* he is not allowed
to look at his *pir's* failings.

And if the *pir* fails to meet his expectations after he becomes his
murid, he should trust in God.

You may have taken all the trouble to find a good *pir*. But it is
quite possible that you have made a mistake. Your *pir* may be
a fake *pir*. May be he knows nothing. You may know more than
he. But then you will not be held responsible for choosing the
wrong *pir*. This is because your faith is correct. It is the *pir* who
has cheated you. That is why all your sins and faults will be piled
on the head of the *pir*.

Those who have not yet found a *pir* use another method. They
pray for a *pir*.

There was a time when I roamed about like a mad man in search
of a *pir*. Finally, when I was about to give up, I prayed to Allah

during the Friday *namaz* to send me a *pir*. I told Him that I would become the *murid* of anyone He sent to me. When I left the mosque, one man attracted my attention. I thought to myself, "I should at least meet him." I went up to him and said, "If you wish to drink tea, please come to my humble dwelling." He followed me to my room and while I prepared the tea he asked me where I came from. I told him that I am from Bihar, and that I had been roaming about for the last ten years. He asked me whether I was anyone's *murid*. I told him, "I have not become a *murid*, but I still want to become one." He said, "Become my *murid*." I replied, "I am not worthy of such a great honour." But he would not listen. He just made me his *murid*. I am his *murid* for the last three years and I am very happy with him.

I was desperately searching for a *pir*, but I did not know where to search. One day I went into the shrine of Nizamuddin and asked him to give me a *pir*. That night I had a dream in which I saw my father giving me to a certain *pir*. That *pir* does not live in Delhi. He lives in Pakistan. But it so happened that when I went to the *dargah* the next day, I saw him. He had come to Delhi to visit his *murids* and to pay his respects to Nizamuddin. I went up to him and asked to become his *murid*, and he immediately took me as his *murid*.

My father used to spend the whole day sitting at the shrine of Nizamuddin. He had prayed to Nizamuddin to give him a *pir*. And he believed that if he kept on sitting there, he would receive a sign by which he would know which of the men coming to the shrine was to be his *pir*. One night he heard the words, "Go to Ahmedabad." And a face appeared before him. The next day, he asked people about Sufis in Ahmedabad, and was given the name of the most famous *pir*. Armed with this name he set out for that city. He did not know that *pir's* address. Nor did he know whether he was the one whose face appeared before him in the dream. When he arrived in Ahmedabad, and was leaving the station, a *tongawala* called out to him. When my father ignored him, he went after him saying that he would take him to the right place. Finally, my father gave in and sat in his *tonga.* And the *tongawala* took him straight away to the right *pir's* house. My father had not told him the purpose of his visit. Nor had he given him the name of the *pir* he wanted to meet. The *tongawala* stopped in front of a particular house and told my father to get down. As he was getting down he saw a man emerging from the house. His was the face that had appeared to him in the dream. Before my father could say anything, the *pir* said, "So you have come! You have come in order to be polished." My father was even more astonished when he heard the *pir* say this because it was exactly the thought in his own head. Then the *pir* said, "Come, I will polish you." And he made my father his *murid.*

I was about to set out for Saudi Arabia. My brother had prepared my passport and he had also bought my ticket. I had given up the idea of becoming a *murid.* But the week before I set out, I had a dream in which I saw a *pir* with three *murids* sitting around him. One of those *murids* was myself. In the morning I told my father that I could not go to Saudi Arabia. I had to become a *murid.* I had to go to the shrine of Moinuddin Chisti and find my *pir.* There I found this *pir.* He invited me to come to Delhi and to stay with him for a few days. When I came here, I told him everything about myself and he made me his *murid.* I have been with him ever since.

Sometimes, *pirs* may give people formulae to recite to find a *pir.* One *pir* thinking that I wanted to find a *pir,* told me to recite every night, "*Kulwallah Allah ul samadlamia Ali aulamia kul lahun dhona Ahad*". Others have been told to pray for forty consecutive days and then wait for Allah to send someone. During that time they have to pray all the five *namazes* and give alms to the poor.

Not everyone has to pass through a frustrating experience to find a *pir.* Many find their *pir* without difficulty.

My father was a *murid.* He took me along whenever he visited his *pir.* He wanted me to become a *murid* of that *pir.* I was a child then and enjoyed the outing. But in the process I developed the habit of going to that *pir.* This was the lesson my father taught me. Later, when I grew up I felt attracted to him and became his *murid*.

I have a *pir*-sister who had a very evil husband. He was the town ruffian and a smuggler. But one day he got a heart attack. My *pir*-sister approached our *pir* and asked him to cure her husband. He took a cardamom, recited something over it and told her to make sure her husband ate it. He ate it and was cured. What the doctors could not do, my *pir* did with one cardamom. After that my *pir*-sister's husband also became a *murid* of my *pir* and gave up his evil ways.

I am a *murid* for the last twelve years. Earlier, I knew nothing about *piri-muridi*. But my friends were *murids*. And they told me that it was a very good thing. One day one of them took me to his *pir* so that I could see *piri-muridi* for myself. This *pir* treated me like a son. He said that he would look after me and remain my father even after I die. I liked him very much. Hence, I became his *murid*.

My *pir* called to me one day as I was passing by his office and asked me to become his *murid*. He told me that my heart is clean and that I would profit much by becoming his *murid*. I accepted.

A *pir* once came to my house and told my mother that he wanted to train one of her children to be a *pir*. My mother gave me to him. I was nine years old then. When he looked at me, I said, "I am your child now." Then he took me. Later on my mother took me back and forbade me from meeting him. But I had come to love the life of holy men. I loved to remain awake the whole night praying, and to see the thousands of pilgrims flocking to the *dargah*. Hence, I continued to visit him. My brothers used to beat me every time I went to him. But that did not discourage me. Slowly, I began to learn many things and whatever I learnt remained in my head. He gifted everything to me. Today I do not need to ask for advice when I am writing a difficult *tawiz*.

I was not really interested in *piri-muridi*. Also, I never visited this *dargah* even though I passed by it often. But one night I had a dream. I did not understand it, but it troubled me and made

me search for something, I did not know what. One day I
happened to enter this *dargah* and pass by this office. When I saw
him and his office, I realized that this was the man and the place
that I had seen in my dream. I entered the office and sat down
in one corner. The *pir* asked me, "Who are you?" I gave him
my name. Then he kept me waiting for a very long time until
he had finished with all his clients and guests. After all of them
left, he turned to me and I told him my dream—That I had seen
an old man who looked just like him sitting in this office and
praying for me. I believe that one should become the *murid* of
him who prays for me, who spends his time reciting the names
of Allah. And here was a man who was already praying for me.
I had to find him and become his *murid*. But the *pir* said, "I
cannot accept your dream as true. I too need to have a dream
that will verify your dream. I will be told if I am to become your
pir." I continued to visit him, however, and one day he made
me his *murid*. He was a very holy man and a great *pir*.

Finally, the *murid* learns to interpret his desire to become a *murid*
as the result of a call of a *pir*. Hence, he can say,

The real *pir* is everywhere. There are very many such *pirs*. The
pir called, I heard and then I began to search. And one day, after
a long and painful search I found the *pir* who called me.
   I heard the call, but I did not understand what it was. I began
to visit the different *pirs*. I saw with my eyes and listened with
my ears, but I did not speak with my tongue. One day I found
my *pir*. I could not say anything in front of him. I just felt that
this was my *pir*. Then I began to visit only him and sit with him
for hours on end. And one day he made me his *murid*. Finding
one's *pir* is a matter of one's fate.

To recapitulate: One who sets out in search of a *pir*, is constantly
warned and indeed finds that the *pirs* he comes across are ordinary
men with the failings and the mentality of the normal run of men.
He may even be told and also feel that they are crooks. He may meet

people who recount their own sufferings at the hands of *pirs*. But if he does not lose heart and continues to visit the *pirs* and *murids* and listens carefully to what they have to say, he realizes that the true *pir* and even the perfect man is hidden by the forms of these ordinary and weak *pirs*. He strives to overcome his frustration, and searches for the perfect *pir* with renewed vigour. He finds that all *pirs* can lead him to God. Hence, it becomes more important for him to try and find out whether he can submit completely to a particular *pir* with love and devotion. If he cannot find such a *pir* he resorts to prayer, to God or to a saint, and subsequently finds a *pir*. Once the *pir* is found and submitted to in *bai'a*, the *murid* reinterprets his whole search as an unconscious response to the call of that *pir*. Those who lose heart at the beginning or in the middle of their search, either choose a dead *pir*, the saint, as their *pir*, or give up the idea of *piri-muridi*. Of course, not all have to go through this frustrating and troublesome experience of finding a *pir*. They may submit themselves to the *pirs* of their fathers. A person may also submit himself to the *pir* of his wife who cured him of a serious illness, or to the *pir* of a friend, etc.

Those in the process of searching for a *pir* may present their various conceptions of the *pir* in terms of stories and images that they pick up from *pirs* and *murids*. That the *pir* appears as an ordinary and even sinful man even though he may not be a sinner leads them to compare him with a mad beggar who stands in a gutter eating muck. But this empirical observation is actually an illusion: He is not a beggar and not eating muck. He is a *pir* and eating *halwa*. He is manifesting the repulsive image only to provoke someone, who would normally avoid a *pir*, into interacting with him. Hence, finding a true *pir* becomes a question of encountering him and somehow forcing him to show his true colours. The seekers find the way of testing the *pirs* by comparing them to trees: All are trees. But trees can be distinguished by their leaves and fruits (the *murids*). Thus, the constant visiting, watching and listening to *pirs* and *murids*, in the belief that external action is the manifestation of inner nature. The seeker realizes that *pirs* are like the fingers of the hand: All are fingers and function as such even though they look different. Or that *pirs* are like medical doctors who have the ability to cure diseases, irrespective of the belief of the patient because a particular disease has a particular medicine. But people make the distinction between specialists and general physicians, and put greater faith in the specialist. All they gain by doing this is the heavier bill for the same diagnosis and the same medicine.

All *pirs* can lead to God. Choosing a *pir* then becomes a question of falling in love: Different men may look at the same woman with different eyes. Some find her ugly, a few may find her repulsive, but there is one who finds her beautiful and a pleasure to be with because he loves her. The *pir* is like that woman and the seeker is like the men who behold her. His dislike for or his coming to like a *pir* is more a function of his own way of looking at the *pir* than a function of the characteristics of the *pir*. If he still cannot find a *pir* that he likes and can come to love, he resorts to prayer, deciding to accept whoever is indicated with faith and trust, since he firmly believes that the prayer will be answered.

The Second Stage: *Bai'a*

When someone decides to become the *murid* of a particular *pir*, and that *pir* accepts him, he undergoes *bai'a*, or the initiation rite.

Bai'a is a contract between the *pir* and his *murid*. Through it, the *murid* commits himself to obey all the commands and wishes of his *pir*, and to respect him in every possible way; while the *pir* commits himself to guide his *murid* to God by taking his abilities and his capacity into account. The *pir* makes a commitment to lead his *murid* in the way of Islam, to protect him always even after death, and finally, to advise him on how to fulfil his daily responsibilities. The *pir* undertakes to pay attention to every aspect of the *murid's* life.

> *Bai'a* means that the *murid* has sold himself to the *pir*. It is the way of truth because in the resulting relationship the *murid* learns good things. The *pir* teaches the *murid*. He makes him understand many things and helps him to attain knowledge. In *bai'a* the *murid* becomes the disciple of the *pir*. He surrenders himself totally to the *pir*. Thus, he becomes a man of the Quran.

The *pir* is the knowledgeable one who takes the *murid* forward by giving him everything he has.

Bai'a is meant to inspire faith in both the *pir* and the *murid*. This ceremony helps them to believe in each other. Consequently, the *murid* can follow the *pir*, and the *pir* can tell him secrets. Without *bai'a*, the *pir* will not tell the *murid* the secrets, and the *murid* will not surrender himself to the *pir*.

The *bai'a* rite consists in giving one's hand to the *pir* as a sign of self-surrender to him while he recites the *kalima*.

The *bai'a* goes like this: The *pir* takes the *murid's* hand. All *pirs* do this. Then he gives him a lesson. He tells the *murid* to always tell the truth, not to cheat, not to dishonour anyone, not to act like a fool, not to wish evil on anyone, to remember Allah always, and to make an effort to follow his teaching.

In case of a female *murid*, she and the *pir* hold opposite ends of a handkerchief or a shawl while he recites the *kalima*. The *pir* does not normally hold the woman's hand because as one *pir* said,

Satan is ever ready to tempt everyone. Hence, the Quran says that a man should not touch a girl who is over ten years old.

There are also other variants of the *bai'a* rite.

The *pir* holds your hand and recites the *kalima*. Also, he covers your head with his shawl or towel. The *murid* may also recite the *kalima* with him. This finished, the *pir* will give the person some advice. This is called the lesson. The *pir* will tell his *murid* to do good works. He may also say, "When you continue to visit me I will progressively teach you the secrets of God and of spirituality. I will explain the contradictions that you will come across as you progress. For example, I will explain how man can be God. I will teach you that man is not God, but that God is in man and with man. Then I will tell you what Allah has done for you and what He expects of you. Once, you have mastered everything, I will make you a *pir*."

In *bai'a* the *pir* holds the *murid's* hand for the following reason. When the first companions were making the *bai'a* with the Prophet, they put their hands in his hands and promised to serve him. At that moment Allah said, "This is not the hand of the Prophet. It is My hand. You see the hand of the Prophet: that is *zahir*. But in actual fact it is My hand: this is *batin*." Allah was saying that they were making the *bai'a* with Him and not with Mohammed.

Or the *pir* may not take the *murid's* hand. He just tells the person at he has accepted him or her as his *murid*.

Where do you live? [the *pir* asked a woman who had come to that particular house along with her husband because the *pir* had agreed to pay a visit]. "In Haryana," [replied the woman]. Do you have my visiting card? [asked the *pir*]. "No," [replied the woman]. [The *pir* ordered one of his *murids* to give her his card and then said,] I take you as my *murid*. Do you accept? "Yes," [replied the woman with great happiness]. [The *pir* continued,] You must do this. Look at me. Look at my feet. Now look at my torso. This is my beard. This is my forehead and this is my crown [his cap]. Always keep these five things in your mind. Also remember that when you recall me in this way, I am with you. If you remember me in this way and ask me to come to you, I will hear your call and come. What I have told you should be kept secret. Also, you must belong only to one *pir*. Just as you have only one husband and cannot consider another man as your husband also, so too you can have only one *pir*. If you remember your guru, wherever you are, he is there with you. You have to believe in me and see me. Why do we keep our hearts clean? You keep your heart clean so that your *pir* can come and sit in it. Wherever you look you will see me if you keep me in your heart. Whatever task you undertake, however difficult or troublesome, will be successful. The *pir* shows God to you. God is everywhere. But the *pir* gives the key to the lock and tells you that you should go through a particular door. He who loses nothing gains nothing. Remember your guru. And when you have difficulties do not go and tell others, I have this and that difficulty. You must remember that your way is through your *pir*. When you get married, you must show that you are married. In the same way when you take a *pir* you must show that you are a *murid*. You must keep your guru before you. The face of God is in the form of your *pir*. This face of mine is the face of God. The light of God is in it. Hence, no one will be able to bring down any evil upon you, wherever you may be. You must always say to yourself, my *pir* is with me. Then go and stay where you like and do what you like. Only remember this, do everything together with your guru. I have made you my *murid* because I like you. Since I like you, I have not only made you my *murid* but also told you all these things. [Then the *pir* said to all those present,] Why did I come to like her? Why did I make her my *murid*? This is the first time I met her. I came to like her because when I entered this house she had her hands folded in respect. No one else displayed such respect.

The instruction during the *bai'a* ceremony varies according to the needs and station of the *murid* as judged by the *pir*.

My *pir* recited the *kalima* over me. Then he told me to recite the *kalima* always and to pray the *namaz* regularly. He told me that this is my main duty. Then he told me never to tell lies. He did not teach me to do anything else. Hence, I carry on reciting the *kalima* and praying the *namaz*. And whatever he sends me I eat.

When I took the *bai'a* with my *pir* he said to me, "You have one big fault that you must correct." This was the same fault that my parents and relatives were constantly pointing out. I had stubbornly refused to listen to them. But when the *pir* told me to correct myself I obeyed. I was a drunkard. Then the *pir* gave me good advice. He told me that I must stop begging. He ordered me to ask only Nizamuddin for what I needed. In this way, he said, I would have everything I wanted and more than I needed. Finally, he told me to correct myself before seeking to correct others. He said that I would know how to correct others only after I had learnt how to correct myself.

During the *bai'a* the *pir* gave me the following lesson: Just as a teacher in the school teaches the students, I will teach you how to walk on a particular path. I will teach you this because it is good for you. If you obey me you will enjoy good fortune in future. You will not suffer misfortune, and you will not have any difficulties in future. If you walk on the path I indicate, you will remain in good condition. One thing you must always do— never tell lies. Second, you must never rob, and third, you must not look at any woman with an evil intention. These three things are fundamental to your new way of life. If you do what I tell you today, you will have no problems. Your path will be cleared of all obstacles. And even if you do not get anything in this world, you will get everything in the afterlife.

A *pir* told a *murid* at a *bai'a* ceremony,

Once a year go to the *urs* of Moinuddin Chisti. Give gifts to the poor. It will be good for you. You will always be healthy. Feed the poor, not yourself. I do this. That is why I am respected. I watch the whole world. Remember, if you do any evil, my name will get spoilt. People will hold me responsible for all your sins. If you are good and serve people, I will be respected. I pray for everyone, but there are some who are not on my list. That brother of mine is not on my list. The one who is on my list will come and sit with me and demonstrate his love for me. If you do not really accept me, all the great things that you may do will not profit you. May be, I will give you nothing. But remember that I pray for you. I do not pray that evil befalls you. I pray that you may prosper and be successful in everything you set your hand to. If you are not greedy, you will get everything. If you are greedy, nothing will come your way. You will have only greed and nothing else. You will be useless if you are greedy.

I became a *murid* when I gave my hand to my *pir*. Then he
told me that I am his *murid*. I have to do all that he tells me to
do and many other things which I cannot tell you. When he
took my hand in his hands, he recited the *kalima*, and the *darud*
over me. Then he gave me the following lesson:

A believer is annihilated in Allah's love. Baba Farid, who is
buried in Pakistan, worshipped for forty years but he did not get
what a *murid* gets from his *pir*. Hence, he went to Moinuddin
Chisti who is also called Gharib Niwaz. Moinuddin asked him,
"Son, why have you come to me?" Baba Farid replied, "I have
come to meet you. What else can I do? You know everything.
What more is there to say?" Moinuddin Chisti replied, "Yes, I
know everything. But the sea is not with me. There is a *pir* by
the name of Qutbuddin Bhaktiyar. Go to him. He will guide
you." Baba Farid went to him and could not believe his eyes
when all he saw was a boy of twelve playing with a ball. He
thought to himself, "This is but a child. How can I become his
murid?" Nevertheless, he said to him, "I have come to work
under you." Qutbuddin shouted, "Go away. Go back to where
you have come from." So he returned to Moinuddin who
insisted that he go back to Qutbuddin. Baba Farid began to weep
and said, "But sir, he is only a child. He is still playing with a
ball." Moinuddin replied, "So what if he is playing with a ball!
Were you not naked when you were a child? What did you not
do when you were a child? You learnt to respect your parents,
yourself and your body only much later. Go back to him." Baba
Farid returned to Qutbuddin. This time Qutbuddin ordered
him to fetch his ball. And every time he kicked it, this grown-
up man had to run and fetch it. After Qutbuddin had finished
playing, he asked, "Why have you come to me?" Baba Farid
replied, "Great sir, you already know why I have come to you."
Qutbuddin replied, "I am but a child. How can I know
anything?" Baba Farid shed tears and replied, "Even though you
are a child, I accept you. I will become your slave." Qutbuddin
said, "Leave me alone." Baba Farid said, "If you send me away,
where shall I go? Moinuddin Chisti has sent me to you. I will

not leave you, come what may."

After this, my *pir* gave me a sentence from the Quran and told me to recite it every night. I cannot tell you what it is. Finally, he gave me good advice like, do not rob, do not tell lies, do not beg, and do not spend money that does not belong to you.

A *pir* said to a *murid* who had just taken *bai'a*,

Now you are on the path of a Sufi. As a Sufi you should not care for the things of this world. You must be like the saints who were lost in worship. They got all they wanted because they were lost in the remembrance of God. Today, the world has gone astray. People are not interested in worship. As a Sufi, you must seek to bless all God's creatures. Do not covet anything that belongs to someone else. If you are covetons like others you too will build big houses. But this is not the work of a Sufi.

A Sufi's work is to kill the stomach. Do not leave your worship. Continue to remember God. Others are lost in the affairs of this world. They think only about money. A holy man is not interested in politics. His work is to pray for everyone. You must remember that when good things happen to others, they have happened to you also. If good things do not happen to them, how will good things happen to you? If you think in this fashion, everyone will respect you. We think in this fashion. That is why the government respects us. The government says, "Only the people of this place are good people." Hence, they themselves come to us. And before they come the police phones and informs us that they are coming. All these ministers know us personally. Our policy is to pray for everyone. That is why we are successful. If you do not pray for everyone, you will not be successful. You will remain underdeveloped and people will complain to God that you are not doing your duty by them.

Another *pir* said to another *murid* on a similar occasion,

It is written in the Quran: when the Prophet was throwing

stones at his enemies, Allah said, "It is not he, but I who threw the stones." There are many points to be learnt from this statement. If Allah wills you will find what you seek. You will get what you desire slowly. I know what you want. I know everything. You have to make the line your own. Once you are on this path, everything should be forgotten, your country, your family, everything. You must try to reach this station. Try to annihilate yourself. If you keep on reciting the names of Allah and if you annihilate yourself, you will reach Allah. After that there will be nothing else for you. Everything will have gone back to its origin. Everything will be as nothing before you.

When I keep my mouth wide open and breathe out, hot air comes out. But if I purse my lips and blow through them, cold air comes out. What kind of thing is this mouth? If you look at yourself you will find so many wonders in yourself. In the whites of your eyes, there is light. The eyes are so small. Yet, they can see things lakhs of miles away. They can see the moon, the sun, and the stars. What is there in the eyes that can see all these things? They have so much power. Who made them? What kind of person is their Maker? Then look at the Maker. Try to see what He is, and what His occupation is. You will come to know all these things by looking at yourself. Then read the Quran, and you will find out that you are not an independent existent. You are a form. Everything is just a form.

No one has talked to you in this way till today. Have you been listening? According to the Quran, your body is a beautiful form that has been made. You are put into this form. Your body with its face, hands, eyes, etc. is the beautiful form into which you have been put. It is not man. It is a form. And the One who has put you into it has written within it, "I have made this one the first of my creatures. He is the ruler of all creatures." And Allah has made the creatures prostrate themselves before you. But there are also human beings who are worse than animals. They also are in the form of men. And Allah alone knows who is the first, who is an animal, and who is Adam.

I will make your whole system run on love. I will clean your heart. Just as a blackened vessel has to be taken to the tinsmith for tinning, so too I will clean you. The name Allah is hot; and if you are impure it can make you mad. I will put the name into you only after cleaning you. Then Allah will make you understand why you have come into this world, what is your work, where you have come from and where you will have to return. This is so with everyone, but it is not for everyone. Allah Himself says in the Quran, "I am closer to you than your jugular vein." In the same way, the Prophet is closer to you than your jugular vein. The *maulvi* will not tell you this. This jugular vein is the life of *nafs*.

Finally,

One is permitted to become the *murid* of a person who is in his proper senses—not of someone who is mad, however holy he may be. If a man is so close to God that he loses all consciousness of himself, how will he guide others? Take Hallaj. He said, "I am God." Many people told him not to say this. But he did not listen. He was completely immersed in God and did not know what he was saying. That is why he was killed by stoning. How can such a person be a *pir*?

To recapitulate: *Bai'a* is the rite at which the *murid* sells himself to the *pir*. The selling of the self is symbolized by placing the right hand in the right hand of the *pir*, holding one end of a handkerchief while the *pir* holds the other end and recites the *kalima* and the *fathiha*, or by simply saying yes to a *pir's* expressed desire that one become his *murid*. In this rite the *pir* also undertakes to train the *murid* so that he attains union with God. And the rite ends with the *pir* giving advice which may consist of a series of dos and don'ts drawn from the *sharia*, a warning not to commit a certain sin (e.g. robbing, drinking, telling lies, etc.), or instruction on mystical theory, depending on the station of the *murid* as judged by the *pir*.
During the rite, the *pir* may try to reassure the *murid* of his guidance by comparing himself to a doorkeeper who will give him

a key and tell him what door he has to open and enter. And he may remind the *murid* of the public nature of his commitment by comparing the *bai'a* rite to a marriage ceremony which is publicly witnessed to by the wife who colours the parting in her hair and wears a chain of black beads around her neck. The *murid* likewise has to witness to his relationship with his *pir* by taking all his complaints and problems only to him. If visiting the *pir* is physically impossible, he should remember the *pir* imaginally, believing that when he remembers the *pir* in this way the *pir* is really present and listening. Finally, the *murid* cannot be disappointed in his *pir*, even though like Qutbuddin he may appear to be a child who still plays with a ball, because he is a *pir* and as *pir* is fully qualified and capable of leading him to God.

The Third Stage

Once the person becomes a *murid*, the *pir* usually orders him to stop doing something. And he makes the *murid* promise to obey.

> The first station is repentance. One has to promise that one will not do a particular thing from that day onwards. It is a very big sin to break one's promise. One becomes impure, and one's heart receives a stain.

Disobedience, however, is very common at the early stages of *piri-muridi*. It is believed to result in loss of faith. Hence, it has to be dealt with immediately.

If the *pir* sees his *murid* losing faith in himself he has to do something about it. For instance, the *pir* may tell his *murid* not to rob. And he promises not to rob, but disobeys. If the *pir* ignores this act of disobedience, the *murid* will say, "My *pir* is useless. I can do anything I like and he will do nothing to me. He does not even know that I have disobeyed." So, the *pir* begins to mean nothing to him. The *murid* has lost faith in his *pir*. And when the *murid* has lost faith in his *pir*, he has lost faith in God. He has lost his path to God. So, the *pir* must never allow his *murid* to disobey him.

The *pir* gives the *murid* to understand that he knows of the act of disobedience, that he does not tolerate disobedience, and that he has the power to destroy him.

When I became a *murid*, I promised my *pir* that I would give up the work of a *goonda*, [ruffian]. But I did not obey completely. Once, I was carrying a gun on my person. I had returned to Delhi by air with that gun. At the airport the police checked me with a metal detector, but did not catch me. If one is clever enough, one can fool the detector. But this knowledge is secret. Besides that special covering over the gun, I was wearing many layers of clothes as it was the cold season. Hence, the gun was well hidden. On hearing that the *pir* was there, I went to meet him. But as I was approaching, he shouted, "Are you not ashamed to carry such a dangerous thing about?" When I was close to him, he told me where the gun was hidden, its name and make. I was completely surprised. What the metal detector and the police with all their body searches could not find, my *pir* saw from afar. The metal detector did not find the gun because of the power of my *pir*. But then he did not let me go. He corrected me. I have not carried a gun ever since. With what eye did he see the gun? He is a very powerful *pir*. From that day onwards, I was afraid to do anything wrong. He is able to see everything.

This *murid* mentioned much later that the *pir* lived in his house whenever he visited Delhi as he knows his father very well. What is important here is that he had succeeded where the *murid's* family members had failed.

As the relationship progresses, the *pir* may order the *murid* to do him a favour. Even then he may have to frighten the *murid* into obeying.

[When a *murid*, a businessman, walked into the office of a *pir*, the *pir* asked,] Have you brought what I ordered you to bring? "What?" [asked the *murid*]. Ghee, [shouted the *pir*]. "Oh that! I have already distributed the ghee. I told you that earlier,"[replied the *murid*. The *pir* kept him standing and began to speak,] Some things are really astonishing. They are no ordinary matters. But they can be understood only after deep reflection. [The *murid* intervened,] "Tell me about it." [The *pir* shouted,] A business-men who is robbed realizes how weak and useless he really is. But tell him that you need something for the work of God, and he becomes tight-fisted. "But I already told you everything about the ghee," [protested the *murid*. The *pir* replied,] Listen, I am not stupid. [The *murid* intervened again,] "I agree, but I have talked to you about this ghee before. I have already settled this matter with you. And now you are bringing it up again." [The *pir* continued to speak,] He who is not ready to give today will be more than ready to give on the morrow. If you do not bring that tin of ghee tomorrow, I will punish you in public. It may be that others do not see through you. I do. You do not know me. But I know Delhi. You think of feeding only the *kafirs* [non-believers]. Remember that I have to feed the whole world.

"What?" [asked the *murid*]. What did I say? [asked the *pir* sweetly, and then continued,] Listen, I am not dead. There is a lot of life in my body. [The *murid* protested,] "I have not said anything. I am not justifying and protecting myself. And yet, you say all these things to me." [The *pir* continued,] You have to give up your precious tin of ghee. "All right, I will do that," [agreed the *murid*. The *pir* threatened,] If not, I will shave your head. I will make you penniless. Remember, "All right, I will obey you," [said the *murid*]. [The *pir* added,] Further, you will have to come here at 11.00 am. And you will have to help with the cooking. You will also help with the serving of the food.

"But..." [protested the *murid*. The *pir* cut him short,] I also can roam about like you. But out of fear of Him who rules the world, I have to sit here and serve. If I want to hide from Him, where can I hide? He is everywhere. He has ordered me to feed

everyone. I have experienced everything. And I have experienced everything by sitting here day and night. Remember,
you said yes once before and did not bring the ghee. Now you
say yes again. This time if you do not bring the ghee, it can only
mean that your wealth has been gained through impure and
unlawful ways. Nothing bought with impure wealth will come
here. If your money is unclean, do not bring the ghee. Do not
bring impure money into this *dargah*. It is of no use to this *dargah*.
It is only fit for the work of Satan. If your wealth is lawful and
holy, it will love to come here. It is fit for the work of this place.
Have I said anything wrong? "What you say is true, very true,"
[responded the frightened *murid*. The *pir* added,] I am not talking
simply. I have seen this happen. Once a man visited me, and
on seeing how many people I feed, promised to give me a sack
of sugar. But that sugar did not come. Later, I got the sugar from
someone else. That man's wealth was unclean. That is why the
sugar that he gifted me did not come. Only Satan will eat that
sugar. Then he came here to beg for forgiveness. But what could
I do for him. He went bankrupt. A Hindu gave me money to
go to Mecca. When I reached Mecca and was performing the
pilgrimage, that man appeared before my eyes for a fleeting
second and then disappeared. He sent me for the *hajj*, and in the
bargain, he himself made the *hajj*. I have experienced all these
things. Do you think that I am dead? I have enough energy to
go to Mecca again. But I will go there only if I receive the order
from the All-high. What did I say?

"You have said everything that is true," [replied the *murid*.
The *pir* then said,] All right, sit down. You have received
enough punishment for now. [As soon as the *murid* sat down,
he asked,] How many hands do you have? "Two," [replied the
murid. The *pir* said,] What are your two hands in front of His two
thousand? What a great thing it is to know that He has two
thousand hands while we have only two hands! A man came to
me this morning and told me that he was in need of a thousand
rupees. I told him to take everything I have. When one gives,
one must give generously. What did I say? "You have spoken

rightly," [responded the *murid*. The *pir* added,] You are a miser.
When miserliness exceeds bounds, it is useless for you to come
here. "Certainly, of course, of course," [responded the *murid*.
The *pir* continued,] Remember Nizamuddin's arm is very long
and his grip is very strong. You do not even have the strength
to go directly to him, but he has the strength to go directly to
God. What did I say? "Absolutely right," [said the *murid*.].

Because of possible chastisement, the *murid* begins to fear his *pir*.
He may try to keep away from him as much as possible.

I seldom visit my *pir*. When he comes to Delhi, I go and visit
him because that is expected of me. But as soon as I greet him
I look for an opportunity to leave.

   I see my *pir* in dreams. He does not say anything. He only
wants me to know that he continues to look after me. I see him
in dreams because I love him—just as I would see a girl in my
dreams if I loved her very much. My *pir* prevents me from doing
wrong. But I have not gone to meet him for many years. It is
possible that I will commit a sin before I see him. That will not
be good. Also, my *pir* may order me to do something. When
a *pir* commands the *murid* has to obey. It is possible that I will
not be able to obey him. And it would be a sin not to obey. My
pir has not yet ordered me to do anything special. It is better to
keep it like this.

But the *pir* urges his *murid* to continue visiting him:

You have come after a very long time. Will someone beat you
when you come to me? Will you die when you take the trouble
to visit me? How old are you? You are still very young. I will
give you happiness and peace of mind. I do not want to take
anything from you, you fool. I know everything. I know what
is happening to you at this moment. Someone is playing with
your life. Now tell me what has happened. Tell me why you
are so sorrowful. What can anyone do to you without my

permission? As long as I am alive no one will be able to harm you. They will try, but will not succeed. You must believe me. Only then will you be happy. Remember, your burden is my burden because you are my child. Be happy and live in peace. I am not your *pir* for nothing.

And when a *pir* finds a *murid* obedient and faithful to his promises, he expresses his joy.

You have done a great thing for me. Till today I did not believe that anyone follows the dictates of his religion. Now I know that there are some people in this world who follow their religion. Till today, my love for you was not complete. It was only partial. But today, my love for you is complete. My house is your house also. Come and eat here whenever you like. You have kept your promise. This is a strange thing in today's world.

The *pir* gave that *murid* his blessing and special instruction. He also gave him a *vazifa* to recite and told him how it could be used to help the people he met in his daily life. Normal instruction, as explained earlier, consists in listening to what the *pir* and his more advanced *murids* say to the clients and the *murids*, and to what they have to say about the *pir*, the *murid*, *piri-muridi*, and their own experiences; and in watching the behaviour of the *pir* and his more advanced *murids*.

The *pir* also sets a good example for the *murids*. Once a woman, who had been divorced by her husband, came to a *pir*. A fervent *murid* was sitting with him. She said to the *pir* :

I have three children, and my husband has divorced me. He divorced me because I am looking after my sister who is very ill and has no one else to care for her. I asked him to have a little patience: she will get well again. But he refused to understand. He divorced me, left the children with me and disappeared. He told me he wanted to perform the *hajj*. He has gone to enjoy himself. I told him that his *hajj* would be invalid if he divorced me and left me with the children just because I have to look after

my sister. Where will I get the money to feed my children and
my sister? And who will pay the rent? He is a *maulana* and keeps
such a long beard. But his heart is made of stone. What does he
think of himself? He may know the Quran in Arabic. But he
cannot fool me. I have read the Quran in Urdu, and I know that
he has done wrong. [Then she began to cry. The *pir* asked her
where she was staying. And after receiving the answer he said,]
"You must not start living a sinful life. I will help you to get
married again". But I cannot leave my sister until she gets well
again, [protested the woman]. "Oh, I am sorry, I forgot, [said
the *pir* and then continued,] I will pay the rent. You must
remember me whenever you are in trouble, and I will help you.
Carry on looking after your sister and when you are in trouble
come to me. I will help you. But you must live a holy life. If
you fall in love with a man come and tell me, and I will arrange
your marriage. Do not do anything with him outside marriage.
I am a *qazi* and I can perform marriages. [Then the woman began
to criticize her former husband. The *pir* stopped her by saying,]
I do not listen to such talk and I do not put my goodness into
anyone's hands. If he has done wrong he will suffer the
consequences. It is written that he who does wrong eats the flesh
of his dead mother. Why should we concentrate on the evil that
he did? Go now and come tomorrow. [Then the *pir* turned to
his *murid* and said,] See what kind of people live in this world".
[The *murid* replied,] "I have seen good things." [Then the *pir*
told him that he fed the hungry once a week and asked him to
donate money or raw food so that he could feed more of them.]

When the woman subsequently came to collect the money, the *pir*
almost drove her away. But she refused to give up hope, continued
to visit him and sat in his office for hours until he finally gave her
something. Nevertheless, the *pir* had impressed that *murid* at the right
moment by setting a good example. It is not uncommon for a *pir* to
stop demanding money for *tawizes* when an important and fervent
murid is with him. He will just tell the person to give what he or she
wishes to give, and that too only after the client has asked how much

he or she should pay.

The *murid* may occasionally slight the *pir*. But the *pir* can say nothing even if he is deeply hurt. He can only wait for the *murid* to return apologize, and thus renew the relationship.

The other night, one of my *murids* asked me to look after some goods while he went to get labourers. When he returned he began to check the goods. I asked him why he was checking. Did he think that I would rob some of his goods? He replied, "Where will one find an honest person like you? This checking has nothing to do with you. I am checking for another reason." But what that reason was he did not say. He is like the others who come here. They do not believe fully. How can I give such people anything?

"All right, I am going," [said one female *murid*]. Did you have anything important to discuss? [asked the *pir*]. "I wanted to talk to you," [she replied]. Then do this [said the *pir*]. Come on Friday evening. "Whether I come or not does not matter to you. Why have I fallen so much in your eyes that I sit here and you do not care for me?" [asked the *murid*. The *pir* answered,] You have come to sit here on your own accord. I did not ca'l you. [The *murid* said,] "I sat here for so long and you did not bother about me." [The *pir* replied,] You came here because you had the time to come. "That is not true," [protested the woman and walked out in a huff. When she had gone, the *pir* said,] She got angry over nothing. She got angry because I did not stop talking to you and start talking to her. She may be angry with me. But then there is something else to think about. She has not come to visit me for one and a half month. Whatever she may think of me, she should remember that one does not forget the person one loves. When she came today, she found me talking to you. She should have the sense to realize that I cannot drive you out to attend to her. If she wanted, she could have started talking to me as soon as she came. She could have drawn me to herself. But she just came and sat here. If she just wants to sit, she can sit here for as long as she likes. She came to fulfil her own need. And when she could not fulfil her need she just got up and walked away.

If she behaves in this way, she will get nothing. To get anything here, she has to learn to love. If I do not love my *pir* … if I just go there, then suddenly get up and walk away, why will he even remember that I came to visit him? Love is essential. One must come with love and leave with love. Then only can the *pir* do something. She did me no favour by getting angry. She is angry now, but after three or four days, she will forget that anger. Then she will phone me and ask me how I am, and say of her own accord, "You know that day I came to you and you did not look at me … " And I will tell her, "Put your hand on your heart and ask yourself whether you were angry with me or with yourself. You came and sat down silently. And then you got up and walked out. You were angry with yourself. If you want to leave me you are free to do so. If for some reason you were angry with me you should have told me why."

How long did she sit here? Not even fifteen minutes. She will definitely come back. If not tomorrow, then when she has difficulties. She will come back to me because my stamp is on her. Some stamps are indelible. The stamp that I have put on her can never be destroyed. She may have something against me. But then she will remember this: She will remember my respect for her, the way I have behaved with her, and that I have always desired only her welfare. And she will remember that she came regularly to me for one year. She will also remember that I never looked at her with evil intentions. When she remembers all these things, she will praise me lakhs of times. She may say that I am not able to do her work … that I am a useless *pir*. But that is the will of Allah, not mine. A holy work cannot be stopped whatever anyone may do. One day it will reach its fulfilment. I have begun the holy work with her. And it has to reach its end. It may take one day or a few years. But it will be be successful finally. I could have made a lot of money from her. But I did not. I did not seek to rob her. I did so much for her and she does not care for me. She spoke with anger and for no reason. Now

her heart will be troubled. She will not be able to sleep tonight.
She will be in tension for the next few days. And she will have
peace only after she phones me. I know what medicine will cure
her.

Subsequently, the *murid* does come back and apologize, and the
pir forgives. Hence, the *murid* can say,

The *pir* is always forgiving. He does not condemn. His work
is to bring us on the right path.

After going through all the ups and downs of the relationship,
the *murid* begins to say,

Before becoming a *murid* I was a smuggler, a drunkard and a
robber. But after becoming a *murid*, I left all those things
automatically. My *pir* changed my life. He took me away from
the path on which I was walking and put me on this path.
    If I saw a man smoking a cigarette I would follow him until
he threw it away. Then I would pick up the glowing stub and
smoke it with utter contentment. My father or my brothers were
not short of money. But if I saw you smoking a cigarette, I
would follow you even for three miles until you threw it away.
Even if I could take only one puff out of the stub you threw, I
was happy. This was how I was twenty years ago. I remember
now what I used to do then. My account book is with me and
I go on filling this account book. Now I talk to people and sit
here. I spend my whole life trying to make those I meet happy.
I am no longer interested in taking anything from anyone. I have
learnt that it is important to understand oneself. If I do not
understand myself, how will I understand others? What is the
use of talking about what I have not seen? I speak about myself.
My *pir* taught me this. He has done great things for me.
    One must keep one's heart clean. Then only one will
progress. One will be led step by step to Mohammed. If one's
heart is not clean what can the *pir* do? The *pir* is necessary to

make the mind and heart of the *murid* clean. He does this through his power.

Once the *murid* reaches this stage,

The *pir* will leave him on his own. It is up to the *murid* to do something to draw the attention of the *pir* to himself. He can either increase or reduce the respect people have for his *pir*. If a cycle repairer does not repair a cycle properly, the customer will ask him who taught him so badly. The teacher loses respect. But if he repairs properly the teacher gains in respect. If the *murid* increases the respect of his *pir*, he can call the *pir* and show him how he has increased the respect for him.

Most *murids* remain at this stage all their lives because of their family and business responsibilities. Only a few *murids* make it to the next stage.

To recapitulate: At the beginning the *pir* tries to bring the *murid* to the stage or station of repentance by ordering him not to commit a particular sin, or not to repeat a personal weakness. Aware of the *murid's* initial tendency to disobey, he watches the *murid* and when he finds him disobeying frightens him into obeying. Later, he may ask the *murid* for a favour; and if he disobeys he forces him to obey by threatening to humiliate him in public and even to destroy him. When the *murid* avoids him out of fright, he is extremely kind and affectionate towards him and encourages him to visit him by reminding him of his role as protector and guide. If the *murid* slights the *pir*, the *pir* waits for him to return and apologize so that he can forgive him. Consequently, the *murids* find that their constant association with the *pir* has transformed them into better human beings. They begin to continually praise their *pirs* and believe them to be extremely powerful and good men. Most *murids*, however, remain at this stage because of family and worldly responsibilities. Only a few make it to the next stage.

The Fourth Stage

At this stage the *murid* decides to give up everything and live with his *pir*. If family responsibilities do not permit this, he spends as much time as possible with the *pir* because he realizes that,

> One cannot understand the *pir's* words just by listening to him. One begins to understand only when one begins to live with him. One must see with one's eyes, hear with one's ears but not speak with one's tongue. Then one gets everything and one begins to realize how profitable it is to become a *murid*.

Or, he begins to see that,

> One gets the line, not merely by making an intention and becoming a *murid*, but by continuous striving. The line does not come just like that. One must give up everything. One has to give up one's heart, one's mind and everything else. One has to lose oneself in one's *pir*. One has to give everything to one's *pir*. Only then can one get the line, and receive the connection with God.

But in the course of living with, or spending as much time as possible with the *pir*, the *murid* comes to see his sinful side and consequently, struggles to reconcile this aspect of the *pir* with his former image of him. The *murid* may, for example, find his *pir* committing adultery.

> My *pir* committed adultery. What could I do? What could I say? If I saw someone else doing it, I would have taken a stone and broken his head. But this was my *pir*. What could I do? But there has to be a hidden meaning. If there is no hidden meaning, why did it happen before me? I must remember that if I point a finger at someone else there are three other fingers pointing back at me and saying that I am three times as great a sinner. Let the *pir* do what he likes. I will not take the punishment for his sins. My duty is to treat all who come to me with love.

Look at Nizamuddin Aulia. Once, when he was roaming about in the jungle robbing travellers, he met Baba Farid. He said to him, "What precious things are you carrying with you? Give me everything you have." Nizamuddin was a great sinner. He did many wicked things, and he committed many sins. Baba Farid replied, "Nizamuddin, go and ask your parents whether they are willing to suffer for all the sins you commit. After all, they live on what you earn by robbing and killing." Nizamuddin thought to himself, "This man talks sense." But he said to Baba Farid, "Yes, and when I go to ask this question, you will run away. You are a very clever man." Baba Farid said, "No Nizamuddin, I will not run away. If you do not believe me, tie me to a tree."

Nizamuddin tied him to a tree and went home. Baba Farid had upset and confused him. One question kept coming to him, "How does this man know my name? I have never met him before." When he reached home, he said to his mother, "You eat from what I rob. Will you take a part of my punishment?" She said, "Why should I? I fed you and brought you up so that you would be responsible for yourself. I did not bring you up in order to suffer for your sins. Now I have grown old and depend on you for food. Hence, you feed me. How you earn the money is your business, not mine." His father also answered similarly. When Nizamuddin returned to the jungle he found Baba Farid free of the fetters and sitting comfortably in the shade of a tree. Nizamuddin fell at his feet and said, "I have committed so many sins. I have somehow to reduce my punishment. I want to change my life." Baba Farid said, "The *pir* who could have forgiven you is dead. But you can do one thing. Recite the following name day and night while sitting at the foot of this dead tree. When you see this tree come to life again you may understand that your sins are forgiven. You may then know that God has forgiven you."

Nizamuddin sat under the tree and began to recite the name. Close to that tree was a graveyard. It belonged to a village about two miles away. A girl had died there. Her lover, who wanted

to marry her, could not bear the news of her death and went mad.
He entered the graveyard, dug out her body and had intercourse
with it. Nizamuddin sat watching as he recited the name. He had
already spent a few days under that tree. He did not feel hungry
because God had become his master and himself used to feed
him. On seeing what the man did with the corpse, Nizamuddin
fell into a rage and went and killed the man. He was so angry
that he said to himself, "Even if I commit one more sin it does
not matter. I have already committed so many murders. I can
always ask for forgiveness." After he had killed the man he
buried both bodies in the same grave. Then he returned to the
dead tree to continue the recitation of the name. But when he
reached the tree he found that it had come to life.

On seeing this he got confused. He said to himself, "I have
committed so many murders. Those murders made me a sinner.
But with this murder I have become pure again." And he
became a saint. He got the direct connection with God. If he
had not murdered he would have failed the test. He passed the
test by murdering. This is a matter of religion. He himself had
committed so many sins. But when he saw this man commit that
sin with the corpse he thought to himself, "This man will
commit many more sins in the future. He must be killed. Only
his death will prevent the occurrence of those sins in the future."
Hence, he killed him. If you see someone having intercourse
with a woman who is not his wife will you not do something to
him? And if you can do nothing, will you not call someone else
who can do something about it? You will do this because you
cannot bear to see what that man is doing to the woman. And
suppose you kill that man in the heat of your anger, God will say,
"See, that man was committing sin and this one prevented him
from committing more sin. He does not fear men. How can this
man be a sinner?" My *pir* is not a sinner. I am not fit to judge
him.

A *murid* may find his *pir* running after money.

If you do not give this *pir* something he will not even look at you.
Look at all these poor people. No one cares for them. But when
a rich man comes, he gives him tea, talks nicely to him and gives
him a *vazifa* to recite. He does all this because that rich man gives
him lots of money. What can the poor people give him? He
wants only good food, expensive clothes, and money.

But the *murid* learns to justify the *pir's* greed, sometimes with the
pir's help, and says,

A time will come when *baba* [*pir*] will not behave like this. He
will behave differently. He will sleep anywhere and eat
anything. and the whole world will come to him. *Baba* has
power. But if he does not try to earn a living today, his family
will starve. He is concerned only with good things and the truth.
But this is the world. The *pir* is also a man. He has children and
a wife. He has to work hard to feed them and look after them
properly. But he is still the Truth. When my *pir* goes out to make
murids, thousands come to him. This world has no religion. It
has only money. People come to the *pir* because they respect
him. My *pir* cannot live the life of the great saints just now
because he has to look after his family. But one day, he will be
free from this responsibility. Then he will forget that he is
married. He will forget that he is in this world. That time has
not yet come. [The *pir* began to speak,] "I have asked for ten
years to earn my living. One year is over, nine more remain.
My children are still young. But by that time they will be able
to look after themselves and their mother. It is necessary that I
look after my children now. To care for my children now is part
of my act of worship." [The *murid* continued,] When that time
comes, *baba* will not care for anything. He will talk very little.
People will come and prostrate themselves before him and
remain like that until he tells them to rise. He will tell them why
they have come. And he will see to it that their desires are
fulfilled. He will not care for food or drink. Then he will be dead
while still alive. [The *pir* said,] "Then I will be a *khwaja*." [The

murid continued to say,] His wife and children will keep a respectful distance from him. He is actually all this even now. But the time has not come to make the *batin* [or hidden] manifest.

A *murid* may also feel that his *pir* gives him nothing. At first, a poor *murid* may think that his poor background has something to do with this attitude of the *pir*.

I sit at my *pir's* office and recite the *kalima* and also, *subhan Allah*. If my *pir* speaks to Allah about me, my condition will improve. I will get everything. But he has not yet told Allah to give me anything. See, you are a big man and I am small. I am a small man because I am poor. If the *pir* looks at me, Allah will make me a *pir*. If you give money to the poor, it is actually Allah who is giving. And Allah gives through you. Allah tells you to give to the poor. That is why you give. The *pir* is like this. But my *pir* has not given me anything till today. I am still his slave. I still have to serve him. The *pir* makes one his slave. And if he does not give anything to one in this life, he will give something in the next.

If I have something to give him, it is possible that he will teach me. If I give him a hundred rupees, he will make a hundred rupee prayer for me. He will pray for each member of my family. But if I give him five rupees, he will make a five rupee prayer for me. I have nothing. Hence, I serve him in every possible way. I do everything for him out of love. One day he will realize how much I love him. Then he will give me a *vazifa* to recite. In this way he will put me on the line. But he has not done anything so far. He does not give me the line because he knows that I have no money to give. Where should I go? No one will give me anything.

He may impute this to his lack of education.

The *pir* has power. But he uses his power only for those who are educated and rich. Who will waste his power on an illiterate man? Why should the *pir* waste his time on me when I do not know how to read and write? If he takes the trouble to purify me, he will be known as a friend of sinners. He treats me like a servant before his guests. I do so much for him. I serve him and all the members of his family and yet he does not care for me.

He may even attribute this apparent discrimination to his own straight forwardness.

The honest get into trouble in this world. What is God? He has decreed that men should tell lies. If you tell lies you will prosper, eat well, wear good clothes, etc.

But soon enough he learns to give meaning to the frustrating experience of receiving nothing because he meets the *khalifas* of his *pir* and sees that some of them are as poor and uneducated as himself.

Today, I got up and took my princes, my *pir's* children, to school. After school I took them to the shopping centre at Bhogal. Then I took them home. That done, I came here and began to attend to the guests. When my *pir* is not here I have to sit and talk to them, answer their questions, and serve them water and tea. I also help the sick to go to the toilet. Have you understood? I have to do what the *pir* and his guests ask me to do. The other *murids* also order me about. I have to serve everyone. This is my duty. I am responsible in this office as long as my *pir* is not here. When he comes and sits here my responsibility ends. Today, I have not had time to have breakfast or lunch. When my *pir* is not here who will feed me? I have to obey those who are here. I cannot say anything to them. At night also I may not be able to eat. But before going to sleep I will talk to Allah. I am happy like this. I have much strength within me. And if I eat I will become lazy. I will have to visit the toilet and the urinal. To do all this I will have to leave the house of Allah.

A *pir* may have lakhs of *murids*. But out of those lakhs only three or four will be real *murids*. These three *murids* will serve their *pirs* and take all the insults. They will be the ones who are giving. They will also serve and take the insults from their *pir*-brothers. And they always think, "These are my brothers. I must continue to serve them." These real *murids* support their *pir*-brothers in this way. Hence, they make Allah happy. And because of this they will find the line. I believe this. I have given up this world, and Allah has given me much power. I have not read the Quran, yet I have been able to see and do great work. Those who understand and know this, recognize me. They do not talk to me with their mouths. They talk to me with their eyes. They come here, look at me, communicate with me through their eyes, and then go to the *dargah*. I have seen so much. I have seen people laugh at me. But I have also met people who are happy to see me. Some treat me badly. They mock at me and my poverty. Those men have fallen. He who scoffs at me or slights me has fallen into sin. He will be caught and troubled by the police. I have seen this happen. I myself will not beat or insult anyone. I will never curse anyone. My blessing is the *khwaja baba*. I will never destroy or wish evil on anyone. I will feed others. This is my duty.

Further, by listening to the praise these poor and uneducated *khalifas* heap on his *pir*, by observing their respectful attitude towards him, and by listening to what they have to say about the path, the *murid* begins to realize that they received the *khalifa*, and the secret instruction, not by criticizing his *pir* but by learning to see him as Allah (the locus of divine self-revelation) in the positive and negative aspects of his personality. Consequently, the *murid* begins the long process of learning to see his *pir* as Allah. He begins to accept the humiliating treatment as part of the special training. And, even if the *pir* does not give, Nizamuddin, the perfect man, whom also the *pir* represents, will give him everything.

My *pir* is Allah. If one has Him, one does not have to worry about the world. A sleeping man does not know what is happening. If Allah comes into him and teaches him His word, he will learn to put it into practice. Then whatever he says will come true. He will have faith within himself. He who becomes a true *murid* will find that Allah comes into him and gives him strength. The *pir* humiliates the *murid*. But he also gives him everything.

He who receives this word of God will not run after wealth. He will find all that the world values meaningless. He will go to the jungle. He will be called mad; and people will drive him away. He will have no place to lay his head. He becomes like this because he practises his religion. The world will hate him. But whatever he says will come true. In the wilderness one will find very good *pirs*. This *pir* is nothing before them. Even so, he is good. He is the type of *pir* that one finds in modern places. *Pirs* of the jungle do not exist any longer. They belong to a lost age. *Pirs* used to live like that a hundred years ago.

The important thing is to practise one's faith. God alone can make one practise one's faith. And he who has learnt to practise his faith has become truly religious. I am watching everything. I know everything about my *pir*. I know what he does in which place. But I do not give away *tawizes*. I only want to become a man who practises his faith. When I die, this world will be dead as far as I am concerned. My *pir* cannot give me anything. God alone can give. What will this *pir* give me? He will give me a wife and wealth. Then I will have children and become a man of this world. That I do not want. He who seeks, finds. I can get hundreds of women if I want. But I do not want women. I want a pure heart.

When I serve my *pir* I know that I am serving Nizamuddin. I am serving Moinuddin Chisti. Whatever I do for my *pir* I do for them. They will reward me. I serve Allah by serving my *pir*. What do I have? I have nothing. Allah is everything. Yet I have everything I could wish for. I do not suffer from want. I have been captivated by religion. Religion is within me. Faith is within me. I accept Moinuddin Chisti and believe in him

though I do not see him. I have faith in my heart. Have you
understood? What will remain when I die? I know that in the
end I will have to leave the world just as I came into it. I do not
want anything for myself. I pray for the whole world. What will
I keep with me? Others hold on to their things. What does my
pir have? What can he give me? I stay with him and obey him.
What will he give me? He has the connection. Hence, he can
give me everything. It is like this. This is the saints' service
house. I have come to Nizamuddin, the beloved of God. And
how do I serve him? I serve him by serving my *pir*. If I do good
day and night, and if I spend my life in service then, when Allah
wills, the good that I do will enter my heart. It will enter my
heart when I sleep. My *pir* cannot give me anything. If I have
a pure heart, the beloved will enter my heart. He will guide me,
he will show me what I am to do. But who is my beloved? My
pir is my beloved. He will enter my heart in a dream. I have no
power yet. My *pir* has power.

I want nothing. I only want to meet people. Even if I die,
my spirit will continue to meet people. I have accepted my *pir*.
I do not recognize Allah. I recognize and accept only the
representative of the Prophet [the *pir*]. You may ask, "What,
you do not recognize Allah?" I will answer, "What is Allah?"
Allah is a name. This name also has a form and an appearance.
You may say that you cannot see Allah. But I see Allah. I serve
and feed him. I can understand Allah only in this way. If I do
not accept my *pir* I have not seen Allah. I do not rob. I do not
talk behind anyone's back. The one who backbites will find that
he has lost Allah. I am a servant.

Finally, he is able to say in front of his *pir*,

He who recognizes his *pir* has recognized God and Mohammed.
The *pir* who likes you is your Allah, your Mohammed. He who
has become Allah is a *pir*. We are all men. But when someone
recognizes Allah, Allah comes to him in a dream. That man who
comes to him in a dream has become Allah for him. This *pir* is

my Allah, my Mohammed. [The *pir* of this *murid* said,] "What
he has just said is a great thing. It is the fruit of much training.
The training is like this. Have you heard the name of Hallaj? He
had a sister who was very beautiful. She fell in love with
someone and she used to visit him every night. She had become
the *murid* of a *pir*. She surrendered herself to him, and she visited
him every night. When they were together, two cups would
come down from heaven. She drank from one and her *pir* from
the other. Then she would leave. But the people made a big
noise. They began to say, 'Hallaj's sister is a prostitute. She visits
a man every night.' But all they used to do was to drink from
the cups that came down from heaven. And while they drank
they used to talk. The talk used to take place from heart to
heart."

Once the *murid* has begun to see his *pir* as Allah, or as the locus
of the self-manifestation of God the social actor, the *pir* begins to
instruct him.

The *pir* watches over the *murid*. When he is sure that he can trust
him, he shows him how to write *tawiz*. The *murid* begins to
write and distribute *tawiz*. The *pir* continues to watch him. If
he still finds him trustworthy, he shows him how to write even
more powerful *tawizes*. And when he is completely satisfied
with this *murid*, he gives him all his power. This power is given
from heart to heart. This may take ten to twenty years.
    When I visit my *pir*, he gives me pen and paper. Then he
shows me how to write a new *tawiz*. He makes me write the
tawiz very many times. In this way the power of my *pir* comes
into me.

Consequently, people begin to approach the *murid* for works of
power whenever the *pir* is not available.

I was standing at the gate of the *dargah* this morning. Suddenly
I saw two Afghani women walk towards my *pir's* office. I ran

to the office and told them to wait as my *pir* would be coming soon. But they could not wait because they had to make preparations for the marriage of one of their daughters. They had brought a big mirror along. They put it in my hand and told me to put power in it. I asked them whether they had forgotten to invite my *pir* for the marriage. They said that it was the duty of the boy to make all the arrangements. I saw that they were speaking the truth. I held the mirror to my chest, and began to recite a verse of the Quran silently. I closed my eyes and began to breathe in and out very forcefully, and as I breathed thus, the power that is within me was transferred to the mirror. They gave me twelve rupees and went away. I put the money into the *pir's* drawer and left for some work. Two visitors of the *pir* saw all this and told him of this. When I returned, I found my *pir* very happy. He took me for a walk and gave me betel leaf to chew. Then as we were walking back to the office, he gave me some money to distribute to the poor. I am very happy today.

As the *murid* progresses he slowly learns of the personifications of the divine names, the meaning of the *pir's* power, and of the way in which his *pir* lives in his heart.

They say that in the course of living with the *pir* one gets the ability to talk to the *jinn*, the *hamzas*, the *devas*, etc. But where are all these things? Each *pir* gives a different description of them. They also say that they are not present anymore. In this age, only men exist. Where are those other things? Where have they gone? If they existed in any age, they should exist in this age also. They are not seen today because they are within man. Allah has control over each man. He has given each man all the account books. One day man will have to answer for the way he has used each of these account books. If I become a *pir* I will learn to fill all these account books. I will have to do what Allah demands of me. And I will have charge over all these things. Only Allah will be in charge of me.

In my heart I have a mirror. Everyone has. My mirror is

you. You are sitting before me. By looking at you I see myself.
You are my *atma* and I am your *atma*. Listen to what I have said
and reflect upon it. Then close your eyes, and you will see that
what I am saying is true. You will see that you have an eye within
you. And you will see that you are within that eye. It is up to
you to develop that eye. You cannot do this without a *pir*. Allah
has made the world and put a lot in it. What he has not put in
the world he has put in man. You also have it but you do not
know this. The medicine to cure your illness is within you, but
you do not know this. You go to a doctor, a *faqir*, a *maulana*. He
recognizes the medicine that is within you, and he will say
something to activate it and then the disease will go away. The
disease goes away because you have faith in that man. If you do
not believe in him, your illness will not be cured, however great
a doctor he may be. You need to have faith in him. You must
not doubt him.

I am such a thing that I can enter into everyone. I live in
everyone. Do you know how? I enter you by talking to you.
If I do not talk to you I will not enter you. If I talk to you, my
voice will remain in your heart. It is in this way that I am in
people. They search for me but do not find me. But if they hear
me speak they will recognize me and come to me. They will
come towards my voice. Why will they come to me? They will
come to me because my voice is already in their hearts. One has
to go where one's heart leads one. And then one will sit down
in one place for the whole day just to hear that voice. This is
what is meant when one says spiritual. You come and listen to
my words. These words have found their mark. They remain
in you. You remember them. You remember that you had gone
to such and such a man, and that he said this and that. Then you
will be able to visualize how he talks, and hear what he says. You
will find him living in you. You are searching for the genuine
thing. In the course of your wanderings, you may suddenly
come to know the genuine thing. You will realize that the
genuine thing is within yourself. If you search elsewhere, you
find nothing. You will have to believe. You will have to believe

someone. My *pir* may be anything. He may be a robber, a crook, a *goonda*, a violent man, etc. But he is my *pir*. In him I believe. He speaks to me. I cannot say anything against him. If I do, he will no longer speak within me.

The *murid* also begins to experience himself as the possessor of power.

A few days ago a man visited the *markaz* (Tablighi Jamaat). A lot of people went to see him. Everyone accepted what he said unquestioningly. They all said to themselves, "He is the knowledgeable one." I also went. After listening to him for some time, I suddenly got up to say something. Everyone's eyes were turned to me. I began to talk about his history of *piri-muridi*. I told that man what was in his heart. I told him everything about himself, what he did when, and what he got by doing what. Everyone there was astonished. The man himself told me that everything I said was correct. He also surrendered himself to me saying, "You know what is in my heart." What I said came out of me spontaneously. I have the voice and the power within me. When I say good things, the voice, the power and courage comes within me. The man told me that everything I said was correct. He said, "It is not only correct, but also good." The others, however, did not understand what I was saying. They began to question among themselves, "Who is he? What is he? Where does he live? What has he got with him?" The Quran is in my heart. I have never read the Quran. But Allah has put the Quran in my heart. By sitting with the *pir* I learnt that one must never tell a lie, that one must tell the truth, and do good. He taught me to read and how to write *tawiz*.

But this newfound knowledge and the awareness of power may go to the *murid's* head. He begins to criticize his *pir*. He is in danger of losing his awareness of his *pir* as the locus of the self-manifestation of God, and also the awareness of himself as servant.

I am not worried about anything. Allah is everything. When anyone talks to me he is careful because he is afraid of me. No one can talk to me in any way he likes. They cannot talk to me the way they talk to my *pir*. But then, they do not believe in me in the same way as they believe in the *pir*. Why? Because I do not show off like him. I do not talk much. I keep quiet. And the power that is within me goes out and helps the person who comes to me. It makes him happy and gives him peace. People get frightened to talk to me because of the tremendous power that I possess. They know that if they do not behave properly with me they will bring curses upon themselves. It is a question of saying certain things. The things that I say have immediate effect because I have tremendous power. People do not come to me because they think that I have the power to work magic. They avoid me. When the *pir* comes and sits here everyone comes here, but when he is not here no one comes. I have to sit here alone. Magic is like life. For instance, there are the normal Islamic formulae like the *Bismilah*. But if I recite it backwards the person who has played the fool with me will suffer misfortune. When one recites it backwards one must believe fully that the intended effect will take place. Only those who have power within themselves can do it. I have that power. That is why no one plays the fool with me.

This *murid* says that this *pir* is my *pir*. When I came here I listened to the conversation of my *pir*-brothers. I watched their behaviour. Then I made the *pir* understand. I gave him my knowledge. And my *pir's* mind changed. His whole personality changed. His whole mentality changed. I taught him to behave like a *pir*. I showed him what a *pir* has to do. I made him feel ashamed of himself. I showed my *pir* the way.

I do not care for this world because I have received very many things. I have received them not from my *pir* but directly from God. I receive directly from God through dreams.

Hence, the *pir* had to correct this *murid*. He corrected him by giving him difficulties.

There comes a time when the *pir* makes his *murid* experience one difficulty after another in order to kill his *nafs*. As long as the *murid* continues to get angry, the *pir* will continue to give him difficulties so that he loses all consciousness of himself as king.

The *pir* shouted at his *murid* and falsely accused him. On one occasion the *pir* shouted at him for not being in the office when he arrived even though he knew that the *murid* had gone to do the work that he himself had given him.

If you behave like this, if you go roaming about instead of sitting here, I will throw you out. If you think too much of yourself I will have nothing to do with you.

The next day, the *pir's* brother accused the *murid* of roaming about, and wasting his time.

"You were not here when I came a few minutes ago. Where were you? You should have come here early in the morning. But you have come only now." [said the *pir's* brother. The *murid* replied,] I was here the whole morning. It just happened that I had gone out on an errand for the *pir* at the moment when you came to the office. [The *pir's* brother said,] "I do not believe you." Then who kept your slippers and the shoes of the *pir* in the right place, and who cleaned the office? [asked the *murid*. He continued,] I know everything. I know what is happening and what you are up to. I also know how often you came here this morning and what you did here. [The *pir's* brother was silenced and walked out. Then the *murid* said to a visiting *murid*,] I have the power of my *pir* within myself. If I did not have this power how did I get the courage to stand up to his brother? Now I order you to go and have your lunch. I cannot accompany you because my *pir* has ordered me to sit here. And I have to obey him. [Ten minutes later the *pir* walked in and asked the *murid*,] When do you take my children to school? [But before the *murid*

could answer, he told a daughter who had accompanied him to
the office to answer. After she had spoken, he said to his *murid*,]
Make sure you come back straight here after you have taken
them to school and brought them back home. I do not want to
hear anyone saying that you are roaming about.

The problems between this *murid* and his *pir*, and the *pir's* brother
only got worse in course of time. The *murid* began to say,

My *pir* has been misled by his brother. He tells him lies about
me. I was told to bring some passports from a travel agency. I
wanted an authorization letter. He said he would give it later. I
left to take the *pir's* children to school. When I returned to the
office, there was no one here. The *pir's* brother was also not in
his usual place. Hence, I took the *pir's* father to the mosque for
namaz. When I led him back to the house, the *pir* and his brother
were waiting for me there. The *pir* asked me, "Have you
brought the passports?" I answered that I could not get them
without an authorization letter. He knew that there were no
passports to collect. He also knew that I did not have the money
to travel twenty kilometres in order to go and bring them. He
just wanted a pretext to blame me. Then they would throw me
out. But all he was able to do was to make me angry. He made
a fool of me. When cooking rice, one puts salt only once. There
is no need to offer salt to everyone at the table. They have made
me look like a fool. I have been with this *pir* for so long, and what
does he do to me?

My *pir* does not say, "Go have a bath. Take this money and
buy soap." He makes me sit here day and night. That is why
he does not have to worry about his guests. He does not give
me another set of clean clothes. And he does not give me soap.
How am I to have a bath? He criticizes me for not bathing. If
I leave the office even for a few minutes, he scolds me. I have
to tell him what phone calls come and who came when he was
out. I too get tired of sitting here day and night. And whose
orders should I take, his or his brother's? He can make it easy

for me to wash my clothes. But he does not. He only says, "He has enough clothes." There is time. But I am not free to go and wash them because I have been ordered to sit here.

Then the *pir's* brother began to use an employee to trouble him.

Now the *pir's* family has employed another man to serve my *pir*. We both are men of the line. But still there is a great difference between us. His mentality, his understanding is different from mine. Not everyone can serve this *pir*. I could not serve him well enough. How could this man? All right, he wants to serve, but why does he carry tales about me? One must not talk against people behind their backs. What will I feel when someone comes and questions me? I feel that the name of my *pir* is getting spoilt. [The *pir's* reputation is in the hands of the *murid*.] Also, he tries to please my *pir* when the time is right and as a reward he gets something to recite. And I get nothing. Two people cannot stay in the same place.

This man should try to help me instead of competing with me. We should be helping each other, not tearing at each other. I can help him. But he is trying to boss over me, and I over him. How can we work together? He is doing what they told him to do. He is giving me as much trouble as possible to make me go away. He is trying to incite me to fight with him. Then he will blame me. But he is nothing. He cannot give me anything. He cannot take anything from me. He cannot beat me. He cannot make me good.

Subsequently, the *murid* began to react. He began to shout at the man and even threaten him.

You are here to spy on me. Go and do your own work. And do not interfere with me. If you play the fool with me, you will die.

This only made his position worse. In the view of the *pir*, this *murid's* social power and pride lay in his long hair and beard, which gave him the status of a holy man. Hence, one day he found a pretext to cut it.

> The *pir*, myself and some others had gone to a hotel. Some policemen came there and asked who I was. My *pir* told them that I belonged to his group. They went away. Then the *pir* told me to return to the *dargah*. When I returned here, I was in a terrible state. My *pir* was angry with me. He came later. When he saw me sitting on this side of the office, he entered by the other door and sat far from me. Before leaving, he told me that he would return and cut off my hair. When he returned there were some *murids* sitting here. He told them to get a pair of scissors from the neighbour's house. They brought the scissors. I got up to leave, but my *pir* also got up, caught me by the hand, and led me back to my place. Then he cut off my hair. Then he told them to take me to the barber and have my hair cut properly and to see that my beard was shaved off. I did not say anything. Then the *pir* began to insult me. A *pir* should not talk like this. But this *pir* has also loved me very much.

People who respected this *murid* failed to recognize him without the beard and the long hair. He said,

> By cutting off my hair, he has destroyed me in this town. He has proclaimed publicly that I am a sinner. Now no one will come and ask me to pray for him. I will have to go and begin all over again.
>
> Now that my hair and beard are gone, anyone can do anything to me. They can push me anywhere and kill me also. They can say, "What are you doing in India? You are a Bengali. Tell us what you have brought to India, and what you will take back with you. Show us your passport." They can break my legs, cut off my hands and force me to give them money. The world goes on. Money is everything in this world. It can kill you. But it can also make you something. I have power.

Humaneness is over. There is no humaneness. I am the guest of the *baba*. He who comes here because he believes in the *baba* is his guest. You also are someone's guest. The word will come out of the mouth of the *baba* and I will go mad.

Have you understood? This is my life. It is good that it is like this. What I have not seen is prepared for me. I do not recognize it. And I have not yet gone there. That is my everything. It is my punishment and also my reward. A lot has taken place here. I have become a member of this place. Everyone living here is like my parents, my brothers and sisters. Allah's world is very big. When I was to be born, the *khwaja* sent me to my home so that I could bring joy to my parents. Then he told me to do my duty by them. If one does not obey him he will not leave one in peace all one's life. While doing my duty towards my parents I must have done something wrong. So what happened? He made the conditions such that I had to leave my country. How? I was no longer interested in staying with them. Hence, I had to leave the place. Now, if while staying here, my heart yearns for another place, I will have to leave and go there.

Even so, I am not angry. I am happy and still continue to bless. They may curse me, but I will continue to bless. I also am in need of other people's prayers. But now I do not ask for blessing. My prayer has been answered. I will not greet anyone. I will greet only him who does not cast a shadow with his body [Mohammed or the perfect man]. Allah will say the word and bring about my meeting with him. Then I will not go about with this *pir*. Dreams tell the truth. I have not come to earn silver or gold. But one needs money to live in this world. You need it, so do I. I have to eat and I also have to feed others. You have a profession same as mine. If ten men live on what you earn, definitely one lakh will live on what I earn.

The next day the *murid* said,

The longing that I had kept alive all my life has been destroyed.

When life begins, one is a king: when life is spent, one is a *faqir*. I have got only good things and sweet talk. What was my sin?

Then he began to soliloquize with his *pir* who was absent.

Do you think that I am just a sinner? I got this promotion. You say good things to me but you see my faults at the same time that you see my good points. You cut off my beard and hair. I have become an evil man. You have exposed my sin to the world. I accept what you have done to me. You go on talking. You see and you understand what is happening. But I will not speak. I am at Allah's mercy and will. I am happy with whatever you give me. But then, you go and show the world that I am a bad man. I will not talk to anyone.

An hour later he recommended his soliloquy.

What happened to our relationship? What has happened? I am staying with you. You have taken me as your *murid*. Whatever be the state of my hair, it is you who are responsible for that state. You said something and I returned. And you cut my beard. Then you insulted me with a lot of bad words. Where can I go to complain against you? Even if I complain about you, who will take action against you?

Then he said to himself,

What did he gain by cutting my hair? If he did not like me he should have sent me away. What right has he to cut my hair? If I want I can put him in trouble, in no time. But I fear to do that. I should bless him. What will I gain by destroying his life? He has not been able to destroy me. He can kill me. But what will he gain by killing me? I will gain more than he.

Yet again, he began to talk with his absent *pir*.

Why do you beat me? What is my fault? I am hurt because you
beat me. The fault is yours, not mine. That is why I am not
afraid. Have you ever treated me with affection? Have you ever
asked, "Have you eaten?" No, never. I have been able to eat
because of the money I have earned by cleaning your toilet, by
looking after your shoes, your children, etc. I do not beg from
anyone. I do not intend to open a bank account. All that I have
I give away. You have many big expenses. You have to travel
by air. Whom are you trying to impress? Who will vindicate
me against you? No one will dare to tell you that you are in the
wrong. What is the use of all your money? What I have said
about you cannot do me any ill. It is all true. But I cannot tell
anyone. I can tell only those I trust.

The next day he said,

The time has come for me to die. To get tired of this life is not
shameful for me because I have left the world. But I am still his
responsibility. He is my *murshid*. He is still with me. One cannot
kill him. Because if one kills him there will be no one else. He
who destroys his *pir* destroys himself in the very act. He is a
khwaja. Who can say anything to him? Why should he kill me?
Now the one whom he and I accept is dead. He will also die.
So will all his *murids*. The one he orders about is also his *murid*.
He has lakhs of cooking pots [*murids*]. One cooking pot is
broken. There was a *murid*. He was, but is no more. What has
happened? Another has come and taken his place. Everyday, so
many men come and go. If I am not here, the world will not
stop. Will it not go on? Tell me. After all, does not the world
go on in those places where I am not present? When I am not
there, my spirit is also not there. Where will my spirit then be?
In the grave. So I will still be alive. That is why I am still sitting
here. This is another of my confusions.

The *pir's* brother and employee continued to trouble him. The
people, too, continued to fail to recognize him. So he said,

They may try to beat me. If they do, I do not know what I will do. I am in trouble. But that is just as well. They do not recognize me, but I recognize them. I understand everything about this world. Who can make me understand anything? I am such a man even now. What if my hair and beard are gone? What is within me is still with me. The power that is within me is with me. This air still talks. My *qalb* is within me. I am not mad for their *namaz* and things. I do not pray the *namaz*. I do not want the *tasbih*. I recite on the *tasbih* of my heart. And if anyone sees me doing this the whole world will go mad. The whole world will fall. All who see me, prostrate themselves before me. They ask for my blessing. I do not care for anyone's money. Even if lakhs of rupees come to me, I will spend those lakhs. What has happened, and what will happen, I know. I know everything. Think of the *khwaja baba*. I am his. To make a *faqir* a king and a king to turn into a *faqir* is the game. My reign is over. But that is all right. What am I now? Nothing. It is time for me to go. When I go I will go just like that. I will be as I am now. But then I am trapped by love. This has become my house.

Three days later he decided to leave.

I am thinking of leaving this *pir*. I want you to come day after tomorrow with a camera and take my photo at the shrine of Nizamuddin. I shall dress up for the occasion.

But he had second thoughts.

If I leave this *pir*, where will I go? I shall not find another *pir*. I shall have no one in this world. I do not wish to leave. I will not listen even if anyone calls me to him. It is said that one must hide all that concerns one's *pir*. See with your eyes, hear with your ears but do not speak with your tongue. If you speak with your tongue you will be given a beating in this age. I have received such a high post that if I go away without telling him my life will be ruined. Have you understood what I have said? It is like this. If I go away, he will make a case against me through his magic. It will be so powerful that wherever I am in India I will be caught and thrown out of the country. They will put me in jail. He will do this to me. Who will listen to me then? I have come to take the blessing of the *khwaja*. Is there any *Allahwala* over the police? Do they have any *pir-murshid*? In this age which policeman respects a *pir*? They have pistols, rifles, and sten guns. Thus, they frighten the *Allahwala*. But those same people love me. Even though I had no passport they allowed me to cross the border at night. See what Allah has done for me.

Still it would be a good idea to go away. This *pir* is not my friend. He is my enemy. If I remain here I will remain a slave all my life. If I go I will be free. But who knows, he may allow me to go and then make sure that I always remain a poor *faqir*. He may destroy my family. He has *murids* in Bangladesh. He will give them my name. They will contract a gang in Bangladesh to destroy my family. Such men love to do these things. They love to play. They love to make kings poor *faqirs* and poor *faqirs* kings. What has he done for me? He has cut my hair and beard—and so destroyed me. No one recognizes me anymore. Now I am nothing. I mean nothing to people. The *pir* has given everything to his son. But he makes me wait here. It is better to die. I have no value any longer. I have become a lie.

My *murshid* cut my hair and threw it out. I did the right thing by submitting to him. If I resisted what would have been the use of having a *pir*? I do not have my hair. So what! I am still what I am. I am not less than I was. Now I have to sit here until the *pir* returns. If he does not return I will have to sleep here. Nowadays I do not work for the *pir's* brother. Let other people beg. I will not beg like them. If my brother visits this *dargah* and sees me begging how will he feel? I will not beg. I have my self-respect. I cannot beg like them. I am in the *dargah* of a king. I am the *khalifa* of Nizamuddin. I serve in his name. I do nothing of my own accord. I have to receive the *khalifa* from this *pir*.

Then I can go and do something. Whether my *pir* has power or not I do not know. He who has this power does not talk about it. He is busy doing his work. Everything is the same for him. It makes no difference to him whether people come to him or not. If he has to go hungry, it does not matter. And if he eats his fill it still does not matter. When such a man says anything it happens. It happens because Allah works through him. My *pir* is this kind of man for me because he is my *pir*. Whether he actually has such power I do not know.

If the *pir* sends me away after calling and blessing me, I will go with every blessing. But if my *pir* drives me away without his blessing, all that I have gained till now will also be lost. I will have nothing. If he blesses me and sends me to my parents, if he sends me away with love, and if he tells me what I should do when I go home, I will gain everything there is to receive. But if he drives me away, I will have nothing. This is the thing. My *pir* has made me a king. So why will he not crown me king? I have faith. I believe that he will make me a king one day. My *pir* is a man. Yes, my *pir* can make me a king with a single word. He can put me on the path with one word. I have accepted him and I believe in him. I would not have stayed here for so long if I had not accepted him and believed in him. I will wait longer because I believe in him in my heart.

I am trapped by love. One cannot attach the leaf of one tree to another tree. It will not live on the new tree. Your blood is red; so is mine. They are the same. Yet, they are different. The doctor's instruments will show the difference. I cannot leave this *pir* and take another. He has made me angry. What else has he achieved? Nothing else. I cannot go. My heart does not allow me to leave.

Once he decided to stay, he began to look on his difficulties as a test set by his *pir*.

One *pir* made many *murids*. One day he said to himself, "Let me see which of them is really my slave. I want to see which of them is fit to take my place. Hence, I will test them." To test them, he went into a temple and after prostrating himself before the idol sat down. The *murids* saw him doing this. Half of them left him saying, "This man is not a *pir*. He is possessed by Satan. He is mad." The *pir* set out on a long journey with those who remained. When they reached a town, the *pir* entered the house of a prostitute. On seeing this all but three of his *murids* left him. With these three he set out on another long journey till he reached a high mountain. He began to climb the mountain. Half way up, two *murids* fell down and died. They had begun to doubt their *pir* in their hearts. Only one *murid* made it to the peak with his *pir*. The *pir* looked around, and on seeing only one *murid* said to himself, "The other two did not trust me. That is why they fell down and died. Only this one trusted me fully." These are the tricks of a *pir*. How can he make all his *murids pirs*? He will make only one of them a *pir*. This is the way of the *pirs*. I must not fall by the wayside. Oh Allah, help me.

I respect this *pir-murshid* and I obey him. I came here, I found my *murshid* and I stopped here. My king is playing with my emotions. I cannot talk about it, and I cannot show you what is being done to me. I know what is happening. But I will not speak. I am a man of the *dargah*. I will not talk. I will not display anything. People come here and say, "You know everything. You can do anything." I have to learn to kick the world. I was tempted to leave this world and to make a new one. Now I have said no to that temptation. The old will remain. The new cannot come. There is no need to break and destroy. It is not allowed. There is something that wants to take me by the hand, feed me and give me everything. I must open myself to it.

I must not say anything. One has hair and another does not. What is mine? Nothing. Everything belongs to my *murshid*. This is the frolic of the guru, of the *pir-murshid*. What can I say? No one has any rights before him. No one can say anything before him. Look with your eyes, hear with your ears, but do not speak with your tongue. This is the order. Ornaments are forbidden. This is the path. I have to see him play with me. Not

everyone has a *murshid*. This is also one kind of cleaning. Allah
is true. He sent the Prophet into the world to clean it. Have you
understood what I am saying? I am an ordinary man. What kind
of man am I? I am the slave of a king. I came to take blessing.
One day I will go, I do not know when. I do not know anything
about myself. If I knew everything about myself I would not be
a slave. If my *pir* is happy, I am happy. If he is angry, I am angry.
Everything is the game of the *pir-murshid*. When one tastes one
banana, one must remember that there are many more bananas
to taste.

When my *pir* comes to the office, he will come to do some
good work. He will talk from his heart. I will prostrate myself
before him. I will say, "What happened will not be repeated. I
do not want money. I will not go anywhere. I will not fight with
anyone. I will remain here with you." Have you understood?
Then he will take me here and there. And I will have to stay here
with him. But if we get angry with each other, we will have to
say good-bye to each other, and I will go the same way as I came
here, with nothing. If the *khwaja baba* sends me away, my
enemies will mean nothing to me. No sin will remain, and no
fear. Who will feed me and who will dare to beat me? Who is
my friend and who is my enemy? Nothing of this will remain.
All will be forgotten. It will be as if I never experienced evil.
Why do I say this? I say this because my fate is in the hands of
my *pir*.

I will try to remain here. My *pir* is angry with me. I will try
to behave in such a way that I will not have to leave him. I had
a wish to leave. But now, even if my *pir* continues to be angry
with me I will not leave him. I will not leave when my *pir* is
angry. When my *pir* is happy, my heart also is happy. If he is
not happy with me, it is as if I am dying. If he is not happy with
me after I have stayed with him for so long, leaving him is like
dying. I will no more criticize my *pir*. He also should not talk
about me. He has to say only one thing. When he says that I
will be changed. I will speak with a different spirit. Then I will
be able to make people better. I am already at that post. But my

pir has kept me with him and will not let me go. I have not committed such a grave sin that he will take away everything that I already have. There is no one like my *murshid*. [The phone rang. The *murid* picked it up and found himself speaking to his *pir's* wife. After the phone call was over he said,] My *pir* has begun to love me again. His wife phoned me and told me to come and pick up my washed clothes. So I will go and collect them. In the morning, I will bathe and then wear them. If I do not do that there will be another fight with my *pir*. It is good that I clean myself. My *pir* has every right to test me.

I have everything within myself. Allah is with me. But I do not know how He is within me. I cannot recognize Him. If I could, I would be a *pir*. Since I do not recognize Him in myself, I must live with this *pir*. In this *pir* I see the Allah that is within me.

The *pir* once asked me to make a sacrifice. I kept on wondering, "What sacrifice does he desire?" He meant my hair and beard. When I had the long hair and the beard many people used to come to me and ask me to pray for them. Now no one comes to me. Hence, no one gives me money. This morning someone came and asked me, "Where is that person with the long beard?" I did not tell him that I am that person. I just said, "That person is gone. I am his brother." And the man went away. So what, if I have no beard and long hair! I am still what I was. My essence is in me, not in my beard. I may have changed outwardly. But what is within me is the same, and still there. What has changed? Nothing. I am still living here. I am still the *murid* of this *pir*. I still serve my *pir*. And he still feeds me. My sacrifice was my beard and my hair.

My *pir* is everything to me. I understand everything because of my *pir*. You must become a *murid* if you want to understand what I am saying.

What is *khwaja*? The rose is at first a bud. Then it becomes big. And as it grows big, it begins to open out until it looks like a flower. When the bud becomes a flower, it has become a *khwaja*. In the same way some men become *khwajas*. When I become a full human being, I too will become a *khwaja*.

To recapitulate: At this stage the *murid* gives up everything in order to live with his *pir*, or he spends as much time as possible with him. Consequently, he begins to see the *pir's* faults and sins, and finds it difficult to reconcile this aspect of the *pir* with his former image of him as a good and powerful *pir*. Nonetheless, he learns to cross this hurdle and see the *pir* as the locus for the self-manifestation of God (or as Allah and Mohammed). The *pir* begins to train him in esoteric knowledge and in the art of writing *tawiz*. This makes the *murid* conscious of possessing power. He becomes proud, and begins to consider the *pir* as inferior to himself. The *pir* corrects him by giving him every manner of trouble so that he becomes humble and once again learns to treat him as the locus of the self-manifestation of God.

The *murids* describe the series of transformations that take place in themselves at this stage by using a number of stories and images. When the *murid* sees his *pir* committing adultery and finds it impossible to continue respecting him, he compares him to Nizamuddin. The great *pir* (in the story consulted or manufactured) was a robber and murderer before he met Baba Farid. The latter gave him a divine name to recite in order to earn forgiveness of his sins. But in the course of the recitation Nizamuddin commits another murder. Contrary to his expectation, however, that this murder would entail additional penance, he finds that he has been forgiven all his sins. Hence, a confusing situation arises: the other murders made him a sinner, but this one made him pure. Applying this analogy to his own situation, the *murid* finds that he cannot judge his *pir*. For all he knows, the adultery he witnessed may have made his *pir* as white as snow.

Feeling frustrated because the *pir*, rather than train him, treats him like a free servant, and feeling jealous of the richer *murids* who are given *vazifas* to recite and spiritual instruction, he compares the *pir* to a merchant who displays differently priced wares on the shelves of his shop. The *pir* sells prayers which are priced according to their value, inclusiveness, and power. There are hundred rupee prayers and five rupee prayers. The richer *murids* get spiritual instruction and *vazifas* because they give the *pir* much money and expensive gifts. He, however, can pay the *pir* only with physical labour which carries a low market price. Hence, he gets nothing or nearly nothing, only the value of a five rupee prayer. Nevertheless, the *murid* sees that many of the *khilafas* of the *pir* are as poor as himself. This fact together with their praise and reverence for his *pir* forces him to change his opinion of the *pir* and seriously apply himself to the task of seeing him as Allah (the locus of the self-manifestation of God).

But when he does achieve this and is rewarded with instruction and power, he becomes proud. Consequently, he is troubled and chastised publicly. He compares his new situation with that of a king who suddenly finds himself a poor *faqir* at the whim of an uncaring and conceited *pir* who is answerable to no one. Since he refuses to abandon his pride, he is shorn of the external symbols of his power and holiness (his hair and beard) so that people who respected him and approached him for spiritual favours no longer recognize him. The disgraced *murid* compares himself to a cooking pot that is broken and thrown aside, and decides to leave his *pir*. But unable to take that step, he compares himself to a leaf of one tree (his *pir*), that cannot be attached to another tree and live. He compares the *pir* to the blood that courses through his own veins and is of a rare type. He believes that he cannot have new blood of another blood group (another *pir*) transfused into himself and still live.

Realizing that he cannot leave his *pir* without doing great harm to himself, he searches for some acceptable explanation for the *pir's* behaviour. He finds appropriate the story of a *pir* who deliberately appears as a bad man and an uncaring *pir* by visiting prostitutes, prostrating himself in temples before idols, and then climbing up a steep mountain, unconcerned about the fate of the *murids* who still follow him. Most of his *murids*, either leave him or fall off the mountain and die. Ultimately, he is left with only one *murid* to whom he bequeaths the *khilafa* and all his power. The troubled *murid* determines that he will be like that *murid*. Consequently, he interprets the actions of his *pir* as a trial, and as a correction of some failing of his. Hence, he is able and willing to accept his own faults: he admits his pride, resolves to humble himself in front of his *pir* and see him as Allah. Discovering the liberation that results from the acceptance of the *pir* and his own weakness, he compares himself to a rose bud that takes a lot of time to open out and display itself as a flower. He hopes to open out like that flower one day, and he is certain that when that happens he will become a *pir*.

The Final Stage

At this stage, the *murid* begins to realize that everything and anything can be a *pir*, or the locus of divine self-revelation. I was able to find only one *murid* who seemed to have reached this stage, and I could meet him only once.

My *pir* is dead. It is good that he is dead. It is good for my faith that he is dead. But he died after telling me the last truth. He told me that anything can be a *pir*. How shall I explain this great truth? My *pir* once told a man who came to meet him that he already had a *pir*. When the man looked at him in astonishment, my *pir* explained that his wife was his *pir*, and that he was his wife's *pir*. He was the *murid* of his wife and his wife was his *murid*. It took me a long time to understand what the *pir* was saying.

On another occasion, he told me this story. Once a mad man, who wanted to make the *hajj,* went to the port to board the ship. But everyone told him that he would not be able to board the ship unless he took a *pir*. There was not much time left for the ship to leave. While the man was wondering who would accept him as his *murid,* he saw a stack of hay in the middle of a field. He ran to it, got down on his knees, caught it with both hands and said, "I surrender myself to you." Then he got up and told the stack of hay, "You are now my *pir*, and I am going on the *hajj*." Just before the ship set sail, he managed to stow himself away in one of the holds. When the ship was far out at sea, he revealed himself to the captain and the other passengers, who treated him with much love. One day the ship hit a rock and began to sink. The captain asked all the *murids* to pray to their *pirs* for help. But nothing happened. Then he remembered this mad man, and told him to also remember his *pir*. The

man sat down in one corner, and recalled that stack of hay. And
the stack of hay came and blocked the hole made by the rock.
The ship was thus saved. When the ship reached a port it was
lifted out of the water for repairs. And they found that stack of
hay blocking a gaping hole. On seeing this the captain lined up
all the passengers and asked each of them to describe their *pir*.
When the mad man described his *pir*, the captain knew that this
particular *pir* had saved the ship. When the ship was repaired, he
left all the passengers behind and allowed only the mad man to
accompany him as he set sail for Mecca.

Allah is everywhere. He is in everything. I understood this
only after my *pir* died. That is why I say it is good that he died.
My faith has increased. May Allah help you to understand this
great truth.

To recapitulate: At this stage the *murid* begins to see everything
as *pirs* or as the loci of the self-manifestation of God. This is explained
by using examples (as given by a *pir*) because it is believed that
reflection on them helps *murids* to reach this stage. A *pir* once told
a man that there was no need for him to become his *murid* because
he was already a *murid*—the *murid* of his wife, who was his *pir*. And
he also was a *pir*—the *pir* of his wife who was also his *murid*. At
another time this *pir* told the story of a mad man who took a stack
of hay as his *pir*. And it was this stack of hay that blocked the hole
in a sinking ship at the request of that *murid* in order to save his life
and the lives of all those on the ship. In other words, it does not
matter who or what the *pir* is. What really matters is the ability of
the *murid* to treat something as a *pir* (the locus of the self-manifestation of God) irrespective of whether it is a human being or some
other existent thing.

CONCLUSION

Piri-muridi aims at union with God. The desired union with God is usually depicted in Sufi circles as attainable by passing through an ascending hierarchy of stations and states with the application of spiritual exercises and discipline. Available knowledge of the ascending hierarchy of stations and states as given in Sufi literature is, however, incomplete and inadequate: There are many lists, each of which gives a different number of stations and states; the various stations and states occupy different positions in the lists of different Sufi orders and mystical writings; and there is no complete description of all the experiences together with the method for arriving at their meanings or names. Hence, it is difficult if not impossible for an average person to recognize his present station, and plan progress to the next one without external help. Sufism has designated the *piri-muridi* relationship (or the relationship with an experienced person called the *pir*) as the external help available to those who wish to achieve union with God. And it is popularly believed that those who display progress on the spiritual path while being outside an empirically observable *piri-muridi* relationship have an esoteric or hidden *piri-muridi* relationship with a dead saint, or Mohammed.

The origins of *piri-muridi* are lost in history. It is sometimes depicted as instituted directly by God, sometimes by a prophet, and at other times by holy Muslims who wished to save the Muslim community and the world from destruction by leading men and women on the right path and giving them an experiential knowledge of their faith. It would appear that the relationship is basically a teacher–student relationship.

Works on Sufism containing passing references to *piri-muridi*, support this understanding of the *piri-muridi* relationship. On the other hand, however, they demonstrate that the relationship is much more than just a teacher–student one. They describe the *murid* as utterly dependent on one particular *pir* for all spiritual attainment (or

for all progress towards the desired union with God), and explain that
this desired end is attained only through the annihilation of the *murid*
in the *pir*. Sometimes annihilation in the *pir* leads to union with God
via two additional stages, annihilation in the founder of the order and
annihilation in the Prophet. Both these annihilations are dependent
on the mediation of the living *pir*.

This other aspect of *piri-muridi* is supported by small studies.
They show that God is central to the *piri-muridi* relationship. Further,
the *murids* consider union with the *pir* as a goal together with the goal
of union with God. They seem to combine the two goals in such
a way that union with the *pir* is equated with union with God.
Obviously, the *murid* believes the *pir* to be God in some way. The
pir, however, is only a man and, thus, according to common Islamic
understanding completely different from God. The *murids* display
full awareness of the humanity of the *pir*. He suffers like them, and
like them is working towards his own union with God. As man he
is a model. He is God in the sense that he represents and transmits
Him to the *murid* in the form of the states of Glòry and Peace. These
states are induced through *bai'a*, *adab*, the purificatory exercises,
dhikr, the meditations and the imaginal form of the *pir*. The states
make the *murid* aware of his dependence on the *pir* and, consequently, on God. Thus, not only do we have a contradictory
definition of the *pir*—he is God and yet, not God—but we also find
that the *pir's* mediation of God is central to the *piri-muridi* relationship. Hence, it would seem that the *piri-muridi* relationship is
basically a relationship between God and the *murid* through the
mediation of the *pir*. It rests on the *murid's* desire for union with God,
the *murid's* belief in the *pir's* ability to mediate God to him, his
willingness to surrender himself to God in the person of the *pir*, and
the *pir's* acceptance of him.

God, however, is non-empirical. Hence the problem of dealing
with the *piri-muridi* relationship sociologically. A survey of the
literature on the sociology of religion demonstrates that religion may
be understood as a system of meaning the working of which is similar
to the human social system. Religion is similar to the human social
system in that both are appropriated, maintained and handed down

by specific groups, and both are the basis for interaction among social actors. Further, religion uses the vocabularies and concepts of ordinary human language to describe the roles of the supernatural and human social actors, and for actually interacting with the supernatural human actors. Religion also uses the dominant pattern of human social interaction to describe the interaction with supernatural actors. And finally, the mode of interaction between human and supernatural actors is similar to the mode of interaction used in indirect human social interaction, i.e. typifications and categories. These typifications and categories are found in the theologies of specific social groups. The theologies or collections of typifications give the type of God that is encountered in religious experience, the sort of relationship that the human actor can expect with such a God, and the interactional styles that are appropriate for interaction with Him. Thus, we have a theoretical and methodological basis in sociology for explaining the *piri-muridi* relationship in terms of the relevant typifications that describe God and human beings as social actors, give the kind of relationship that the believer can expect and hope for, and the interactional styles that are considered appropriate.

An examination of the mystical social system as described by Ibn Arabi, who was referred to now and then by my respondents, led me to see the divine names, the roots, supports and realities given in the words, phrases, verses and *surahs* of the Quran and in the *hadiths*, and the names of all existent things as the values in terms of which all existent things interact with each other and with God. These values also explain the nature of the existent things because all things are the institutionalized forms of these names and display their effects and properties. The values are arranged in hierarchies, in paradigms and in syntagms of binary opposites, which give norms like wrath leads to mercy. Further, these interrelationships among the names are believed to explain all forms of inequality (physical, biological, intellectual, social, etc.), and are believed to be the source of all transformation and change in the universe. Consequently, knowledge of these divine names, their interrelationships, and their effects and properties in existent things is a major part of what is considered the real and the secret knowledge.

In the case of the human social system as explained by Durkheim and structural-functionalists, one is faced with the problem of human freedom and creativity. In the mystical social system too we have a similar problem: If everything is determined by the divine names, their interrelatedness, and their effects and properties, where then is the freedom of the human person? And why should a person be held responsible and punished for any wrong that he does? Ibn al-Arabi tries to solve the problem by saying that the real problem is ignorance, i.e. the normal person does not know that he is influenced by the divine names, nor does he know how is is influenced by them. Consequently, he thinks that he is the cause of the effects and properties displayed in himself and the other things in the universe. This ignorance is not the effect and property of any divine name. It is the result of non-existence. Hence, it is this ignorance—and not the effects and properties of the divine names, whether judged as good or evil—that is punishable. And it is in knowing the divine names, their interrelationships, and their effects and properties, and in acting in accordance with this knowledge that human freedom is exercised and demonstrated, i.e. the effects and properties of the divine names are both epistemological and ontological.

The mystical social system also tells us how God can be considered as a social actor. God may be approached in two ways: as God in Himself (called the Real) and as God the social actor (called Allah or the All-merciful, and also by the other ninety-nine divine names). As God in Himself, He is unapproachable and unknowable. But as God the social actor, He is not only knowable but also observable in all existent things and even in ourselves as constantly responding to our actions. He is observable in all things and ourselves in the effects and properties of the divine names and roots which are considered as the roles of God the social actor. Since human beings also act in terms of the divine names and display their effects and properties in themselves and others, the human and divine social actors are similar. This similarity, however, does not imply equality because God in Himself is completely different from human beings. Consequently, great emphasis is placed on constantly reminding oneself that He is the Independent, the Incomparable, and Unknowable. However similar He may appear, He is always the Master, never the servant.

The perfect human social actor in this mystical social system is called the reality of Mohammed. It is also called the microcosm, the Perfect Man, the Universal Man, and Allah. It is believed to be the divine consciousness that God manifests to Himself in His state of absolute Unity, the essence of the universe or macrocosm, the unifying principle of the cosmos, the active principle on which depends the existence of all other universal essences, the hearing, seeing, hands and feet of God, and finally, the universal essence of each and every existing human being. Consequently, the perfect social actor is the mirror image of God the social actor. But since God, the object that is mirrored in the Perfect Man is non-empirical, one can be easily misled into thinking that the empirically available image is the object, or that man is Master. Hence, the stress on always remembering that the perfect human social actor stands before God as servant who always receives everything from God, even when he stands before the universe as Master, or as God's orientation to the universe.

This concept of the perfect social actor can be turned into a reality in the lives of individuals. Those who have succeeded have been called perfect men, prophets and saints. The chief characteristic of the perfect individual social actor is that he has no ego, personal will or desire of his own. Consequently, he is constantly aware of receiving everything from God at every moment (i.e. he is constantly aware of his servanthood), and also aware of constantly manifesting God the social actor to others (i.e. his awareness of being Master does not interfere with or eclipse the awareness of his servanthood before God). He also knows of the ways in which all existent things receive the effects and properties of the divine names and manifest God to each other and to himself. Since he has no will of his own, but wills only what God wills, it is said that he is the hearing, seeing, hands and feet of God, and that God is his hearing, seeing, hands and feet. Further, he is perfectly content with his concrete situation, whatever that might involve: riches or poverty, honour or insults, being well fed or hungry, etc., and even paradise or hell. Finally, he follows the external law, the *sharia*, in order to constantly remind himself of his servanthood before God. Hence, he cannot be easily recognized and is described as hidden while existing in this world. This stage is the highest in Muslim mysticism and the much sought after union with God.

The perfect man is also described as free because freedom is not the ability to take away all the obstacles that prevent one from exercising one's own will, or that prevent the awareness of being Master. Freedom is the ability to remove all those obstacles, especially one's ego, that prevent one from doing the will of God, or that prevent one from being aware of how one receives everything from God and manifests only Him. Hence, punishment is due, not to the displaying of the effects and properties of the divine names, be they the names of mercy or the names of wrath. Punishment is due to the lack of constant awareness that one is nothing but servant since one is only an institutionalization of the divine names, and thus, only the locus of the manifestation of God the social actor at every moment of one's existence.

Piri-muridi inasmuch as it tries to attain union with God, or inasmuch as it tries to turn the *murid* into a perfect man, is an institutionalized form of socialization that aims at forcing the *murid* to give up his awareness of manifesting himself (his ego) so that he can take on the new awareness of manifesting God at each and every moment of his life. It tries to make him aware of his servanthood. And it achieves this by giving the *murid* an official locus of the divine self-disclosure, the *pir*, and by prescribing the rite of self-surrender (*bai'a*) and a set of practices and beliefs (*adab*) with respect to the *pir*. The living out of *bai'a* and *adab* inculcates in the *murid* a consciousness of complete dependency on the *pir* even for his personal qualities, with the result that he finds himself manifesting, not himself but his *pir*. From here it is a short step to realizing that by manifesting the *pir*, he is actually manifesting God the social actor.

Examination of the field data shows that the *pir* is the official locus of the self-manifestation of God as far as the *murids* are concerned. As the official locus of the self-manifestation of God, the *pir* is expected to manifest the effects and properties of the divine names of Mercy and Guidance in his own life, in the lives of his *murids*, and in the lives of all those who come to meet him. If he manifests the effects and properties of the divine names of wrath, then he must be able to help himself, his *murids*, and his clients to understand how that particular manifestation of wrath leads to mercy. The *pir* is keenly aware of his responsibility to manifest the effects and properties of the divine names of mercy, and he strives to make this a reality in his own life, and in the lives of his *murids* and clients by giving them *tawizes*, encouragement, advice, etc., and by doing good deeds. But the *pir* is also keenly aware of his own sinfulness. Hence, he is like his *murids*, and also needs an official locus of the self-manifestation of God. He finds this locus in his own *pir* and/or a saint. Finally, all those involved in the *piri-muridi* relationship recognize that the locus of the self-manifestation of God is the only way by which they can come to know God.

Consequently, the *murids* strive to learn how to treat the *pir* as the locus of the self-manifestation of God the social actor. This striving also involves manifesting the effects and properties of the names of mercy to all those they come in contact with, even to those who are outside the *piri-muridi* relationship. For instance, the *murids* strive to serve their neighbours. They also help those who visit the *dargah*, not only by showing them around the *dargah*, attending to their needs, explaining what they do not understand, and introducing them to their own *pirs*, but also by being courteous and gentle with them. If they cannot help them, they just sit with them while praying silently so that they may experience peace and find some solution to their problems. Those *murids* who have been trained to write *tawizes* give them freely to their neighbours and to those who are in trouble. But if they find that their *tawizes* do not help a particular person, they take the person to their own *pir*, believing that he will be able to help him or her. And while they serve these visitors, their neighbours and other people in these various ways, they constantly remind themselves that they are rendering service to their *pir* and, thus, pleasing him.

It was this spirit of service and the desire to manifest the effects and properties of the names of mercy, on the part of both, the *pirs* and *murids*, that enabled me to conduct this research fruitfully while remaining outside the *piri-muridi* relationship. I was often advised to become a *murid* in order to participate in and observe the relationship more closely. However, such a move (besides being unethical, since I do not subscribe to their beliefs) would have restricted me to one *pir* and his circle of *murids*, thus narrowing my field of research in the Nizamuddin Dargah. It would have also increased the length of the field work to twelve years (by the reckoning of the *pirs* and *murids* themselves) by involving me in a lengthy socialization process which would not help me to observe and analyse the *piri-muridi* relationship as understood and practised by those who already participate in the relationship. It would have given me a subjective and limited personal experience of the relationship with one *pir* that would have had to be widened only after the socialization process would be considered over by that *pir*. Further, the constant suggestion by *pirs* to give up the research would have become binding had I become a *murid*. Finally, I find that reminding the *pirs* and *murids* that I am outside the *piri-muridi* relationship acts like a soothing balm on their injured feelings resulting from the fact that I cannot meet them for long periods of time, now that the field work is over. While conducting the field work, however, I behaved like a *murid*, following the *adab* whenever applicable (e.g. sitting near the door, never extending my feet or turning my back towards the *pir's gaddi*, listening respectfully to what the *pirs* and the more advanced *murids* had to say even when I found it utter nonsense by the standards of modern science and medicine, willingly extending a helping hand whenever needed even when it involved a great amount of effort and time, etc.). Consequently, the *murids* and *pirs* invited me to their rites, took me on some of their visiting rounds, invited me to their houses, and shared with me what they consider the secret knowledge.

Coming back to the *murid's* relationship with his or her *pir*: the *murid's* continuous effort to see him as the locus of the self-manifestation of God goes through, what I have called five stages. The first stage is the process of choosing a *pir*, where the *murid* may come to realize that any *pir* can be the locus of the divine self-revelation. The second stage is *bai'a* where the *murid* voluntarily submits himself to a particular official locus of divine self-revelation. In the third stage the *murid* comes to know the *pir* as the hearing, seeing, hands and feet of God, learns to obey him and to see all that he has and receives as coming to him through this locus of divine self-revelation. In the fourth stage the *murid* goes through the painful process of seeing his *pir* as the self-manifestation of God, not only in his good qualities, but also in his bad ones and consequently, reaffirms and deepens what he has learnt in the third stage. He may also find himself manifesting his *pir*, and may attain union with him. Finally, in the fifth stage, the *murid* learns to see all things as *pirs*, as the loci of the self-manifestation of God the social actor.

Each stage involves a progressive giving up of the ego and a fuller living out of human servanthood. Until the fourth stage, the *murid* learns to live out his servanthood with respect to the *pir*. In the fifth stage he learns to live out his servanthood with respect to all things which he now sees as *pirs* or as loci of divine self-disclosure. And to the extent he is able to maintain this way of looking at things he maintains or loses his union with God.

The *murids* and *pirs* also explain their experience of *piri-muridi* in terms of the social relationships and experiences they share with the larger society in order to understand the *piri-muridi* relationship in greater depth, and attain greater familiarity with its concepts and its mode of operation.

At the beginning, when a person is in the process of searching for a *pir*, he is told and even finds that the *pirs* are sinners. He is also told that the *pirs* are not sinners. That the *pirs* appear as ordinary and even sinful men even though they may not be sinners leads the person to compare them with a mad beggar who stands in a gutter eating muck. But this empirical observation is actually an illusion: The *pir* is not a beggar and not eating muck. He is a *pir* and eating *halwa*. And he is only manifesting the repulsive image in order to provoke someone, who would normally avoid a *pir*, into interacting with him. Hence, finding a true *pir* becomes a question of encountering him and somehow forcing him to show his true colours. The seeker finds a way of testing the *pirs* by comparing them to trees: All are trees. But trees can be distinguished by their leaves and fruits (the *murids*). Thus, the constant visiting, watching and listening to *pirs* and *murids* with the belief that external action is the criterion for judging inner nature. Consequently, they find that *pirs* are like the fingers of the hand: All are fingers and function as such even though they look different. Or *pirs* are like medical doctors who have the ability to cure diseases, irrespective of the belief of the patient because a particular disease has a particular medicine. People, however, make a distinction between specialists and general physicians, and put greater faith in the specialist. All they gain by doing this is the heavier bill for the same diagnosis and the same medicine.

All *pirs*, therefore, can lead to God. Choosing a *pir* is a matter of falling in love: Different men may look at the same woman with different perspectives. Some may see her as plain, some others as ugly; a few may find her repulsive, but the one who loves her finds her beautiful and a pleasure to be with. The *pir* is like that woman and the seeker is like the men who behold her. His dislike or liking for a *pir* is more a function of his own way of looking at the *pir* than a function of the characteristics of the *pir*. Consequently, if he still cannot find a *pir* that he likes and can come to love, he resorts to prayer, deciding to accept whoever is indicated with faith and trust, since he firmly believes that the prayer will be answered.

Once the *murid* has chosen a *pir* he sells himself to him (but without accepting money in return) in a rite called *bai'a*. During the rite, the *pir* may try to reassure the *murid* of his guidance by comparing himself to a door keeper who will give him a key and tell him what door he has to open and enter. And he may remind the *murid* of the public nature of his commitment by comparing the *bai'a* rite to a marriage ceremony which is publicly witnessed to by the wife, who colours the parting in her hair and wears a chain of black beads around her neck. The *murid* likewise has to witness to his relationship with his *pir* by taking all his complaints and problems only to him. If visiting the *pir* is impossible, he should remember the *pir* imaginally, believing that when he remembers the *pir* in this fashion the *pir* is really present and listening. Finally, the *murid* cannot be disappointed in his *pir* even though like Qutbuddin he may appear to be a child

328 Piri-Muridi Relationship

who still plays with a ball: notwithstanding appearances, he is a *pir* and as a *pir* is fully qualified and capable of leading him to God.

After the *bai'a*, however, the *murid* is encouraged to discover and define for himself the hidden aspect of the *pir*. His external manifestations are the rings with stones of different colours that adorn all the fingers of his right hand, the place where he sits (usually the precincts of a *dargah*), the instruments of his trade (*tawiz* paper, inks and pens, books on astrology and *tawiz*, etc.) and the reverence displayed by the persons who visit him. The *murid* is invited to consider this hidden aspect of the *pir* as a short examination question that requires a lengthy answer. That the *murid* usually does not have access to any written tradition that explains what the *pir* is, is no impediment. In fact, as the *pir* and more advanced *murids* discourage the *murid* from using the written word as a means of understanding the *pir* (or answering the question). They advise him to come to an understanding of the *pir* by attending to his own personal experience of him. And they explain hów he should use this experience to gain the required understanding of the *pir*. He has to use this experience in the same way as he uses his experience when solving riddles. Consequently, the *murid* contrasts and compares his experience of the *pir* with his other everyday social experiences in order to arrive at definitions of the *pir*, which he constantly revises as his familiarity with his *pir* and his acquaintance with the beliefs and practices (*adab*) surrounding the *pir* increases. These definitions are expressed in stories and statements of belief.

The *pir* is compared and contrasted with the *murid's* experience of his own father. The *pir* is father in the sense that he commands respect and obedience, is ever watchful in order to save the *murid* from troubles and difficulties, constantly cares for, helps and educates him. But he is more than a father because his responsibility over the *murid* extends even after death, until the last judgment. The *pir* is also compared to a *maulvi* who teaches the faith. But unlike the *maulvi*, he practises his faith. Hence, he knows the difficulties involved in putting that faith into practice and the ways of overcoming them. Thus, he has power not possessed by the *maulvi*. Since the experience of the *maulvi* as guide and teacher is not adequate to understand the *pir,* the *pir* is further compared to Mohammed, the Prophet, who gave the revelation, the Quran, and showed the revealed way of putting it into practice, the *sunna.* The *pir,* however, is subservient to him because far from bringing any new revelation and practice, he is restricted by the Quran and by the *sunna* (practice) of the Prophet. He is compared to the flying horse, Buraq, who took Mohammed into the presence of God (the *miraj*): Just as that flying horse took the Prophet into the presence of God, the *pir* takes the *murid* to the Prophet, and also into the presence of God. And the *pir* as intercessor is compared to the secretary who takes a visitor's request to the prime minister.

The *murid* observes that a *pir* has two main characteristics. These are the characteristic of worship and that of service. He tries to understand the characteristic of worship (the process of becoming a possession of God) by comparing it to a mill that grinds grains of wheat into flour. And he tries to make others understand his own experience of the *pir's* attitude of service by recalling the selfless devotion of a mother who serves her child in every possible way even when that service involves going hungry, sleeping on a wet bed, etc. Also she serves without desiring any future remunerative reward from the child.

The *pir's* duty of leading the *murid* to God is likened to the training of a sweeper in the etiquette and ways of higher society: It is not enough to give him a three-piece suit and have him sit at table in a five-star hotel. The greater necessity is to train him in the appropriate ways of behaving in that society. Acknowledging the *pir's* responsibility in this matter the *murid* calls him father, recalling his experience of his own father seeking to ensure his spiritual and material welfare while he was under his care. Finally, when the task of leading the *murid* to God is seen to near completion, the *pir* is likened to the women who dress, adorn and beautify a bride on her wedding day.

As his relationship with his *pir* grows, the *murid* may find him and his fellow *murids* explaining the *pir's* power through different images drawn from the *murids'* and clients' life experience, for instance, the example of cooking: The wife can produce a very good meal with ordinary ingredients, but the husband will produce a meal that no one can eat, even with superior ingredients. This expertise of the wife is like the power of the *pir*. A *pir* and/or a *murid* may also explain this power by using the example of our normal way of looking at things: we may see the same female human in different roles—as woman, mother, daughter, wife—at different times or she may be all these things to different people looking at her at the same moment. But her correct meaning at any particular moment can only be one of these. The *pir* knows her correct meaning at each particular moment. Hence, he can deal correctly with her at each and every moment. In this lies his power. Sometimes the power of a *pir* is referred to as a *tamasha* (a big show) that creates faith so that the watchers open themselves to his good influence and go away feeling that they are better off than before.

The *pir* may also tell the *murid* of his consciousness of being a *murid*, in spite of being a *pir*, and of his continual need for the care and guidance of his own *pir* because he knows himself to be a sinner, an ordinary man who can be discouraged, led astray, etc. The *pir* may present this relationship with his own *pir* by comparing himself to an electric bulb that cannot take the high voltage coming on the overhead high tension wires. Receiving that voltage and current directly would burn him out because he is still impure and a weak human being. But he still receives voltage and current because of his relationship with his *pir*. His *pir* is the step-down transformer that reduces the current and adapts it to his individual capacity so that he can still give light, or manifest the mercy of God to those around him, irrespective of his personal and private weaknesses. In his function of manifesting the effects and properties of the names of mercy the *pir* may also compare himself to a gardener, who rather than let the plants planted by someone else die, waters and cares for them so that they may grow and one day bear fruit. He reminds himself of his responsibility to manifest mercy by comparing himself to the saint Nizamuddin, who continues to care for and shower blessings on the thousands who continue to flock to his shrine.

Thus helped by his *pir* to solve the riddle of the *pir*, and faced with his *pir's* greater demands for better and more dedicated service, the *murid* may abandon his quest to understand the *pir*, and turn his attention to more important and pertinent questions. He may try to understand more deeply his own role as a *murid*, and the *piri-muridi* relationship.

The *murid* is very much aware that he has sold himself into slavery. But since he has no prior experience of slavery, he tries to present this relationship to himself in terms of the experience of buying and possessing animals and things: He compares his situation to that of a cow or goat that is being led away by its purchaser. One end of the rope is around its neck and the other end is in the hands of the new owner. As a *murid* he himself has tied one end of the rope around his own neck and given the other end to the *pir*. He also compares his situation to that of a pot that is bought after much examination so that it can fulfil the purposes of the buyer, the *pir*. He has sold himself to the *pir* and hopes that the *pir* will put some precious thing (esoteric knowledge) into him (It may be worthwhile to recall here the pots of gold and precious stones in the story about Ali Baba and the forty thieves). And he compares his efforts to please the *pir* with the efforts made by an ideal *murid*, Amir Khusrau to please an ideal *pir*, Nizamuddin Aulia. Amir Khusrau, a courtier, stooped to disguise himself as a dancing girl, and danced and beat a drum in front of his *pir*, in order to appease his anger, make him laugh, forgive him, and feel pleased with him again.

The *murid* may try to understand his increasingly felt need to remain in association with his *pir* in terms of the relationship between God and Mohammed: God too was in need of a companion, and hence, He made Mohammed from his own light. But the *murid* is not God and he needs the *pir* also for guidance and support. His need for a *pir* may be expressed by comparing the *pir* with the collar on the neck of a dog: dogs sporting collars are left alone because the collar tells people that its wearer belongs to someone. Dogs without collars, on the other hand, are kicked about. Similarly, being associated with a *pir* keeps away Satan, misguidance and the misfortune that he can bring. The *pir* is a sign that one belongs to a special group that has to be treated with respect. Finally, the *murid* may explain his need for association with his *pir* by comparing him to a

walking stick that prevents an old and frail man (the *murid*) from
falling and hurting himself—the *pir* prevents the weak *murid* from
falling into misguidance and into the clutches of Satan.

When trying to understand the *piri-muridi* relationship, the *murid*
may encounter difficulty. He compares this difficulty with the
difficulty of explaining other normal experiences in his life, for
instance, the experience of cycling long distances. One who cycles
such distances regularly knows how to balance, and has practical
knowledge about the difficulties and dangers involved and of the
ways of avoiding them. But as long as he does not reflect on this
experience with a view to explaining it to himself and to others, he
may find it difficult to explain it to someone who does not know
cycling. Consequently, the *murid* reflects on his experience of *piri-
muridi* by contrasting and comparing it with other experiences. For
instance he may compare the master–slave relationship that *piri-
muridi* is with his own experience of marriage. The husband (the *pir*)
can do what he likes. He can visit prostitutes, drink and do all kinds
of wrongs without anyone being able to do anything about it. Not
even the wife (the *murid*) can correct him because she does not have
that right over him. Further, she cannot pity herself, emulate her
husband's evil ways, or criticize him. If she does any of these things,
she will be beaten, killed, or thrown away by the husband. She has
to bear everything with a smile, and behave as if she has not noticed
her husband's wrongdoing.

The *murid* may also compare *piri-muridi* to a man who enters a
thick jungle: He loses his way in the jungle. Lack of food and the
wounds that he receives from the undergrowth and thorns further
weaken him until he loses hope of living. It is in that moment of utter
desperation that he begins to receive the reward of all his efforts.
Hence, *piri-muridi* is not a master–slave relationship in which the *pir*
is merely a task master and a tyrant. Even if he is a task master and
a tyrant, he is more than that. He is a father, who like the *murid's* own
father loves him and wants to bequeath all his spiritual wealth to him.
This he can do only after training the *murid* so that he is mature
enough to handle the responsibility that comes along with that
inheritance. Hence, the *murid* has actually sold himself to a father,

a new parent. The frustrating experience that training for greater maturity involves is likened to the experience of being educated in a traditional Muslim school where the student is completely at the disposal of the teacher. Or it is like the experience of prophet Adam, who after the fall from paradise was transported to a strange and dark place, the jungles of Sri Lanka. He did not know how to grow and cook his food and had to be taught these elementary tasks by the angel Gabriel, while experiencing much fear and hunger, in order that he might take up his responsibility as vicegerent. Hence, *piri-muridi* is also compared to a ladder or a staircase that takes the *murid* to the top of a building (the desired end, union with God via union with the *pir*).

Having attained much understanding of the *pir*, of his own role as *murid*, and *piri-muridi*, the *murid* may advance to the next stage where he is forced to undergo a number of traumatic experiences (for instance, awareness of the sinfulness of his *pir*) that change him. The *murid* describes the series of transformations that take place in himself at this stage by using a number of stories and images: When the *murid* sees his *pir* committing adultery and finds it impossible to continue respecting him, he compares the episode with that in Nizamuddin's life. Nizamuddin (in the story consulted or manufactured) was a robber and murderer before he met Baba Farid. The latter gave him a divine name to recite in order to earn forgiveness of his sins. In the course of the recitation Nizamuddin commits another murder. But contrary to his expectation that this murder would entail additional penance, he finds that he has been forgiven all his sins. Hence, a confusing situation arises: the other murders made him a sinner, but this one made him pure. Consequently, the *murid* finds that he cannot judge his *pir*. For all he knows the adultery he witnessed may have made his *pir* as white as snow.

Feeling frustrated because the *pir*, rather than training him treats him like a free servant, and feeling jealous of the richer *murids* who are given *vazifas* to recite and spiritual instruction, he compares the *pir* to a merchant who displays differently priced wares on the shelves of his shop. The *pir* sells prayers which are priced according to their value, inclusiveness, and power. There are hundred rupee prayers and five rupee prayers. The richer *murids* get spiritual instruction and *vazifas* because they give the *pir* much money and expensive gifts. But he can pay the *pir* only with physical labour, which has low market value. Hence, he gets nothing or nearly nothing, only the value of a five rupee prayer. The *murid*, however, sees that many of the *khilafas* of the *pir* are as poor as himself. This fact together with their praise and reverence for his *pir* forces him to change his opinion of the *pir* and seriously apply himself to the task of seeing him as Allah (the locus of the self-manifestation of God).

But when he does achieve this understanding of his *pir* and is rewarded with instruction and power, he becomes proud. Consequently, he is troubled and chastised publicly. He compares his new situation with that of a king who suddenly finds himself a poor *faqir* at the whim of an uncaring and conceited *pir* who is answerable to no one. Since he refuses to abandon his pride, he is shorn of the external symbols of his power and holiness (his hair and beard) so that people who respected him and approached him for spiritual favours no longer recognize him. He compares himself to a cooking pot that is broken and thrown aside, and decides to leave his *pir*. But unable to take that step, he compares himself to a leaf of one tree (his *pir*), that cannot be attached to another tree and live. Further, he compares the *pir* to the blood that courses through his own veins. It is of a rare group. He believes that he cannot have new blood of another blood group (another *pir*) transfused into himself and still live. Thus, realizing that he cannot leave his *pir* without doing great harm to himself, he searches for some acceptable explanation for the *pir's* behaviour. He finds as appropriate the story of a *pir* who deliberately appears as a bad man and an uncaring *pir* by visiting prostitutes, prostrating himself in temples before idols, and then climbing up a steep mountain unconcerned about the fate of the *murids* who still follow him. Most of his *murids* either leave this *pir*, or fall off the mountain and die. Ultimately, he is left with only one *murid* to whom he bequeaths the *khilafa* and all his power. The troubled *murid* determines that he will be like that one *murid* who perseveres till the very end and attains everything. Consequently, he interprets the actions of his *pir* as a trial, and as a correction of some failing of his. Hence, he is able and willing to accept his own faults: he admits his pride, resolves to humble himself in front of his *pir* and see him as Allah. Discovering the liberation that results from this acceptance of the *pir* and his own weakness, he compares himself to a rose bud that takes a lot of time to open out and display itself as a flower. He hopes to open out like that flower one day, and he is certain that when that happens he will become a *pir*.

It is just a matter of time before the *murid* can attain union with the *pir*, and receive the mandate to make *murids*, i.e. become a *pir*. Once he attains union with the *pir* he may pass on to the final stage of *piri-muridi*, where he begins to see all things as *pirs*, or as the loci of the self-manifestation of God. Seeing everything as *pirs* is explained by using examples (as given by a *pir*) because it is believed that reflection on them helps *murids* to reach this stage. A *pir* once told a man that there was no need for him to become his *murid* because he was already a *murid*—the *murid* of his wife who was his *pir*. And he was also a *pir*—the *pir* of his wife who was also his *murid*. At another time a *pir* told the story of a mad man who took a stack of hay as his *pir*. And it was this stack of hay that blocked the hole in a sinking ship at the request of that *murid* in order to save his life and the lives of all those on the ship. In other words, it does not matter who or what the *pir* is. What really matters is the ability of the *murid* to treat something as a *pir* (the locus of the self-manifestation of God) irrespective of whether it is a human being or some other existent thing.

Each stage involves a progressive giving up of the ego and a fuller living out of human servanthood. Until the fourth stage, the *murid* learns to live out his servanthood with respect the *pir*. In the fifth stage he learns to live out his servanthood with respect to all things which he now sees as *pirs* or as loci of divine self-disclosure. And to the extent he is able to maintain this way of looking at things he maintains or loses his union with God.

These in short are the components—the cosmology, the lived encounters, the entire repertoire of metaphors, images, stories, memories and recollections wherein the *piri-muridi* relationship is produced and reproduced. The present attempt is limited to exploring only some aspects of the relationship. As a matter of fact there exists a wide area of *rumoor* (secrets) which the respondents refuse to part with. Hence, a more creative methodology verging on even forcing the researcher to relinquish his/her identity may be worth venturing into.

BIBLIOGRAPHY

Abbasi, Razia. 1964. Makhdum Abdul Wahid Sewistani and His Ancestors, in *Al-Hikam*, Hyderabad, Pakistan: Shah Wali-ullah Academy, December, 1964, pp. 65 ff.

Ahmad, M. G. Zubaud. 1946. *The Contribution of Indo-Pakistan to Arabic and Persian Literature from Ancient Times to 1857*, Lahore : Sh. Muhammed Ashraf.

Ajmal, Mohammed. 1984. "A Note on Adab in the Murshid-Murid Relationship", in Barbara Daly Metcalf (ed.), *Moral Conduct and Authority: The place of Adab in South Asian Islam*, London: University of California Press, pp. 241-54.

Ali, Hazrat. n.d. *Dua-e-Kumal, Dua-e-al-Amaan*, Yousuf N. Lalljee (compiler). Bombay: Esquire Press.

Ali, Zahid. 1989. A Critical Study of Malfuzat Literature in Persian (Sultanate Period). University of Delhi, Dept. of Persian, (unpublished).

Althusser, Louis. 1971. *Lenin and Philosophy and Other Essays*. London: NLB.

Ibn Arabi, Muhyiddin. 1985. *Ismail Hakki Bursevi's Translation and Commentary on Fusus al-Hikam*, 3 vols. Bulent Rauf, R. Brass, K. Rollemache (tr.), Oxford: Muhyiddin Ibn Arabi Society.

Arasteh, A. Reza. 1980. *Growth to Selfhood: The Sufi Contribution*, London: Routledge and Kegan Paul.

Archer, John Clark. 1980. *Mystical Elements in Mohammed*, New Haven: Yale University Press.

Bellah, R. N. 1964. "Religious Evolution", *American Sociological Review*, 29: pp. 358-78.

Berger, P. L. 1973. *The Social Reality of Religion*. Harmondsworth: Penguin.

Berger, P. and Luckmann. 1976. "Sociology and Social Research", in T. Roland Robertson (ed.), *Sociology of Religion*. Harmondsworth: Penguin Education.

Bowering, Gerhard: *The Prophet of Islam*,

Brooke, Tal. 1982. *The Hidden Side of Sai Baba, Avatar of Night*. Delhi: Vikas.

Chittick, C. William. 1983. *The Sufi Path of Love: The Spiritual Teaching of Rumi*, Albany: State University of New York Press.

———. 1988. "Death and the World of Imagination", in *The Muslim World*, 78, 1, January, pp. 51-82.

———. 1989. *The Sufi Path of Knowledge: Ibn Arabi's Metaphysics of Imagination*, Alabny: State University of New York Press.

Cole, Stephen. 1976. *The Sociological Method*, Chicago: Rand McNally College.

Cressesy, D. R. 1953. *Other People's Money: A Study in the Social Psychology of Embezzlement*. New York : The Free Press.

Crow, Frederick E. SJ. 1985. (ed.): *A Third Collection of Papers by Bernard J. F. Lonergan, SJ.*, New York: Paulist Press, and London: Geoffrey Chapman.

Al-Dashti. 1985. *23 Years: A Study of the Prophet Career of Mohammed*, F. R. C. Bagley (tr.), London: George Allen and Unwin.

Davis, Howard and Walton, Paul (ed.). 1983. *Language, Image, Media*. Oxford: Basil Blackwell.

Dehlawi, Hassan. n.d. "Fawa'id-ul-Fu'ad" in *Islam in the Modern World*.

Delhi the Capital of India (rev. ed. of All About Delhi, (G. A. Nikestan and Co., Madras, 1918)

Von Denffer, Dietrich. 1976. "Baraka as Basic Concept of Muslim Popular Belief", in *Islamic Studies*, 15, (3), pp. 167-86.

Digby, Simon. 1986. "Tabarrukat and Succession among the Great Chisti Shaykhs of the Delhi Sultanate", in R. E. Frykenberg (ed.), *Delhi through the Ages: Essays in Urban Historical Culture and Society*, Delhi: Oxford University Press.

Douglas, M. 1966. *Purity and Danger*, London: Routledge and Kegan Paul.

Dresh, Paul. 1989. *Tribes, Government, and History in Yemen*, Oxford: Clarendon Press.

Dumont, Louis. 1980. *Homo Hierarchicus: The Caste System and Its Implications*, Mark Sainsbury, L. Dumont, and Gulati (tr.). University of Chicago Press.

Durkheim, Emil. 1965. *The Elementary Forms of Religious Life*, Joseph Ward Swain (tr.). New York: The Free Press.

——————. 1984. *The Division of Labour in Society*. Macmillan Education.

——————. 1964. *Rules of Sociological Method*, Sarah A. Splovey and John H. Mueller (tr.). New York: The Free Press.

Eickelman, Dale. 1976. *Moroccan Islam: Tradition and Society in a Pilgrimage Center*. Texas: Austin, University of Texas Press.

Eisenstadt, S. N. 1974.*Max Weber on Charisma and Institution Building*. London: University of Chicago Press.

Eliade, M. 1959. *The Sacred and the Profane: The Nature of Religion*. New York: Harcourth, Brace.

Ernst, Carl E. 1984. "Esoteric and Mystical Aspects of Religious Knowledge in Sufism", *Islam and the Modern Age*, 15 (4), 201.

Etzioni, Amitai and Lehman Edward W. (ed.). 1960. *A Sociological Reader on Complex Organization*, New York: Holt, Rinehart and Winston.

Fiske, John. 1982. *Introduction to Communication Studies*, London: Methuen.

Geertz, Clifford. 1971.*Islam Observed: Religious Development in Morocco and Indonesia*, London: University of Chicago Press.

——————. 1960. *The Religion of Java*, London: University of Chicago Press.

——————. 1975. *The Interpretation of Cultures*, London: Hutchinson.

Gilsenan, Michael. n.d. *Recognizing Islam: An Anthropologist's Introduction*, London: Croom Helm.

Goode, William and Hatt, Paul K. 1986. *Methods in Social Research*, New York: McGraw-Hill and Kogakusha.

Grunebaum, G. E. 1972. "The Place of Para-Psychological Phenomena in Islam". in S. A. J. Zaid (ed.), *Malik Ram Felicitation Volume*, Delhi: Rajadhani Book Binding House.

Gurevitch, Michael, Tony Bennett and others (ed.). 1982. *Culture, Society, and the*

Media, London: Methuen.

Hall, Stuart. n.d. "The Rediscovery of Ideology: Return of the Oppressed in Media Studies", in Michael Gurevitch, Tony Bennett, and others (ed.), *Culture, Society and Media.*

al-Halveti, Sheikh Muzaffer Ozak al-Jerrahi. 1981. *The Unveiling of Love: Sufism and the Remembrance of God,* Muhtar Holland (tr.). London: East West.

Haq, Muhammed Enamul. 1975. *A Study of Sufi-ism in Bengal,* Dacca: Asiatic Society of Bangladesh.

Harcourt, Captain A. 1886. *New Guide to Delhi,* United Service Advertiser Press.

Haralambos, M. and Robin Harold. 1980. *Sociology Themes and Perspectives,* Delhi: Oxford University Press.

Hearn, Gordon:. 1920. *The Seven Cities of Delhi: A Description and History,* Calcutta: Thacker, Spink.

Hosain, Hidayet. 1932. "A Treatise on the Interpretation of Dreams", *Islamic Culture,* 6, p. 568.

al-Hujwiri, Ali B. Uthman al Jullabi. 1967. *The Kashf al-Mahjub: The Oldest Persian Treatise on Sufiism,* Reynold A. Nicholson (tr.). London: Luzar and Co.

Hussaini, Syed Shah Khusro. 1985. "Shuhdud Vs Wujud: A Study of Gisuderaz", *Islamic Culture,* 59, (4), 323 ff.

Husserl, Edmund. 1960. *Cartesian Meditations,* Dorion Cairns (tr.), The Hague.

Izutsu, Toshihiko. 1984. *Sufism and Taoism: A Comparative Study of Key Philosophical Concepts,* London: University of California Press.

Jackson, Paul. 1987. *The Way of a Sufi: Sarafuddin Maneri,* Delhi: Idarah-i Adabiyat-i Delli.

Jeffery, Patricia. 1981. "Creating a Scene: The Disruption of Ceremonial in a Sufi Shrine", in Imtiaz Ahmed (ed.), *Ritual and Religion among Muslims in India,* New Delhi: Manohar.

al-Jili, Abd al-Karim. 1983. *Universal Man,* Titus Burkhardt and Angela Culme-Seymour (tr.), Paris: Beshara Publications.

Khan, Khan Sahib Khaja. 1976. *The Secret of Ana'l-Haqq,* Lahore: Sh. Muhammed Ashraf.

Khan, Khaja. 1972. "A Leaf from Sheyk-i-Akbar", *Islamic Culture,* 1 (April edition). London: John Reprint Company, p. 238

Khan, M. A. Murid. 1956. "Kitabu Ta`bir-ir-Ruya of Abu Ali Ibn Sina", in *Indo-Iranica,* 9, (4), 43.

Khomeini, Ayatollah Sayyed Ruhollah Mousavi. 1984. *A Clarification of Questions: An Abridged Translation of Resaleh Tawzih al-Masael,* J. Borujerdi (tr.), Boulder: Westview Press.

Khosla, K. 1987. *The Sufism of Rumi,* Dorset: Element Books.

Kidder, Louis H. and Judd, Charles M. 1986. *Research Methods in Social Relations,* CBS Publishing Japan.

Kingston, Jeremy. 1975. *Healing without Medicine,* London: The Danbury Press.

Kothari, C. R. 1985. *Research Methodology: Methods and Techniques,* New Delhi: Wiley Eastern Limited.

Lawrence, Bruce. 1986. "The Earliest Chistiya and Shiakh Nizamuddin Awliya (d.

1325)", in R. E. Frykenberg (ed.), *Delhi through the Ages: Essays in Urban History, Culture and Society*, Delhi: Oxford University Press.

Levy, Marion J., Jr. 1968. "Functional Analysis: Structural- Functional Analysis", in David L. Sills (ed.), *International Encyclopedia of Social Sciences*, Vol. 6, New York: The Macmillan Company and the Free Press.

Lewis, I. M. 1975. Ecstatic Religion: *An Anthropological Study of Spirit Possession and Shamanism*, Harmondsworth: Penguin.

Loeffler, Reinhold. 1988. *Islam in Practice: Religious Beliefs in a Persian Village*, Albany: State University of New York Press.

Lofland, John. 1971. *Analysing Social Settings: A Guide to Qualitative Observation and Analysis*, Belmont, California: Wadworth.

Malinowiski, Bronislaw. 1954. *Magic, Science, and Religion, and Other Essays*, Glencoe III: Free Press.

Mannheim, Karl. 1936. *Ideology and Utopia: An Introduction to the Sociology of Knowledge*, Louis Wirth and Edward Shils (tr.), New York: Harcourt Brace Jovanovich.

Merton, Robert K. 1975. *Social Theory and Social Structure*. New Delhi: Amerind.

Metcalf, Barbara Daly (ed.). 1984. *Moral Conduct and Authority: The Place of Adab in South Asian Islam*, London: University of California Press.

Moinuddin, Sheykh Hakim Abu Abdullahal Gulam. 1985.*The Book of Sufi Healing: Kitab al-Tibb-Rauhi as-Sufi*, New York: Inner Traditions International Ltd.

Mohammed, Afzalur Rahman. 1981. *Encyclopaedia of Seerah*, London: The Muslim Schools Trust.

Morris, Bryan. 1987. *Anthropological Studies of Religion: An Introductory Text*, London: Cambridge University Press.

Mottahedeh, Roy P. 1980. *Loyalty and Leadership in Early Islamic Society*, Princeton, N.J.: Princeton University Press.

Muda, Dayang. 1933. "The Path of God", in *Islamic Culture*, vol. 7, pp. 607 ff.

Mujeeb, M. 1967. *The Indian Muslims*, (London: George Allen and Unwin.

Nabi, Mohammed Noor. 1965. "The Conception of God as Understood by Early Muslim Mystics of India" in *Islamic Culture*, 39, (4), (Kraus Reprint, 1979, Nendeln), pp. 285-95.

Nanda, Bikram N. and Mohammed Talib. 1989. "Soul of the Soulless: An Analysis of Pir-Murid Relationship in Sufi Discourse", in Christian Troll (ed.), *Muslim Shrines in India: Their Character, History and Significance*, Oxford University Press.

Nath, R. 1979. *Monuments of Delhi: Historical Study*, New Delhi: Indian Institute of Islamic Studies.

Oldenberg, Herman. 1988. *The Religion of the Vedas*, Shridas B. Shrotri (tr.). Delhi: Motilal Banarsidass, pp. 251-70.

Otto, Rudolf. 1959. *The Idea of the Holy*, John W. Harvey (tr.), Harmondsworth: Penguin.

Parsons, Talcott. 1974. *The Structure of Social Action: A Study in Social Theory with Special Reference to a Group of Recent European Writers*, New Delhi: Amerind.

———————. 1975. *Essays in Sociological Theory*, New Delhi: Light and Life

Publications.

—————; D. Edward Shils; Naegele kaspar; Jesse R. Pitts. 1961. *Theories of Society: Foundations of Modern Sociological Theory*, Vols. I and II, New York: Free Press of Glencoe.

Phillips, D. Z. (ed.). 1967. *Religion and Understanding*, Oxford: Basil Blackwell.

Pritchard, E. E. Evans. 1956. *Nuer Religion*, Oxford: Clarendon Press.

Rahman, Mutazid Waliur. 1967. "Al-Farabi and His Theory of Dreams", in *Islamic Culture*, vol. X. 1936, New York: Johnson Reprint Corporation, pp. 137-52.

Richter, Hans. 1986. *The Struggle for the Film: Towards a Socially Responsible Cinema*, Jurgen Pomhild (ed.), Ben Brewster (tr.), Aldershot: Scholar Press.

Rizvi, Sayyid Samad Husain. 1982. "Amir Khusraw and Astrology", in *Hamdard Islamicus*, vol. V. (1), 83-92.

Sabbah, Fatna A. 1984. *Women in the Muslim Unconscious*, Mary Jo Lakeland (tr.), Oxford: Pergamon Press.

Sawanson, G. B. 1960. *The Birth of the Gods*, University of Michigan Press.

Schimmel, Annemarie. 1978. *The Triumphal Sun: A Study of the Works of Jalaloddin Rumi*, London: East West Publications.

—————. 1975. *Mystical Dimensions of Islam*, chapel Hill: University of North Carolina Press.

—————. 1985. *And Mohammed is His Messenger: The Veneration of the Prophet in Islamic Piety*, Chapel Hill: The University of North Carolina Press.

Schleiermacher, F. 1958. *On Religion*, New York: Harper and Row.

Schmitt, Richard. 1967. "Phenomenology", in Paul Edwards (ed.), *The Encyclopedia of Philosophy*, New York: Macmillan and Free Press, pp. 135-51.

Shahid, Shah Ismail. 1974. *Support of the Faith (Taqwiyat-ul-Iman)*, Mir Shahamet Ali (tr.), Lahore: Sh. Muhammed Ashraf Press.

Sharif, Jafar. 1921. *Islam in India: Qanun-i-Islam*, G. A. Herklot (ed. and tr.), London: Oxford University Press.

Sharma, V. D. 1974. *Delhi and Its Neighbourhood*, New Delhi: Archaeological Survey of India.

Sharp, Henry. 1928. *Delhi: Its Story and Buildings*, Bombay: Humphrey Milford Oxford University Press.

Sharub, Dr. Zahurul Hassan. 1959. *The Mystical Philosophy of Khwaja Moinuddin Hassan Chisti*, Ajmer: Khwaja Publishers.

Singh, Darshan. "The Nature and Meaning of Tawakkul in Sufism", *Islamic Culture*, 56 (4) pp. 265-74.

Stack, C. B. 1975. *All Our Kin: Strategies for Survival in a Black Community*, New York: Harper Colophon Books.

Stark, R. and C.Y. Glock. 1968. *American Piety: The Nature of Religious Commitment*, London: University of California Press.

Subhan, John A. c. 1938. *Sufism, Its Saints and Shrines*, Lucknow: Lucknow Publishing House.

al-Sulami, Ibn Al-Husayn. 1986. *The Book of Sufi Chivalry: Lessons to a Son of the Moment: Futuwwah*, London: East West.

al-Suhrawardi, Abu-al-Najib. 1975. *A Sufi Rule for Novices: Kitab Adab al- Muridin*, Menahem Milson (tr.), Cambridge: Harvard University Press.

Syed, Dr. M. Hafiz. 1971. "Hazrat Nizamuddin Aulia", in *Islamic Culture*, vol. 34, 1960, London: Johnson Reprint Corporation, pp. 264- 69

Thurston, Herbert. 1953. *Ghosts and Poltergeists*, J. H. Crehan (ed.), London: Burns and Oats.

Turner, Bryan S. 1974. *Weber and Islam: A Critical Study*, London: Routledge and Kegan Paul.

Tweedie, Irina. 1986. *Daughter of Fire: A Diary of Spiritual Training with a Sufi Master*, Nevada City: Blue Dolphin Publishing.

Tweedie, Irina. 1979. *The Chasm of Fire: A Woman's Experience of Liberation through the Teaching of a Sufi Master*, Dorset: Element Books.

Ulla, Shah Wali. 1971. *Al-Qawl al-Jamil fi Bayan Sawa' al-Sabil.*

Valiuddin, Mir. 1971. "The Perfect Man", *Islam and the Modern Age*, 2 (1), 51.

Valiuddin, Mir. 1972. "Virtue is Knowledge: The Sufi Approach", *Islam and the Modern Age*, 3 (3), 65.

——————. 1974. "The Problem of the One and the Many: The Sufi Approach", *Islam and the Modern Age*, 5 (4).

Wasti, Sayyid Zahid Ali. 1987. "Medicine and Knowledge of God" in *Hamdard Islamicus*, 1 (3), 79.

Weber, Max. 1964. *The Theory of Social and Economic Organization*, A. M. Henderson and Talcott Parsons (tr.), New York: Free Press.

——————. 1978. *The Protestant Ethic and the Spirit of Capitalism*, Talcott Parsons (tr.), London: George and Unwin.

——————. 1963. *The Sociology of Religion*, Ephraim Rischoff (tr.), Boston : Beacon Press.

Whyte, W. F. 1943. *Street Corner Society*, Chicago: University of Chicago Press.

Wilson, Bryan R. 1973. *Magic and the Millennium: A Sociological Study of Religious Movements of Protest among Tribals and the Third-World Peoples*, New York: Harper and Row.

Worsely, P. 1986. *The Trumpet Shall Sound*, McGibbon Kee.

Zeitlin, Irving M. 1969. *Ideology and the Development of Sociological Theory*, New Delhi: Prentice-Hall of India.

INDEX